THE FUTURE OF PEACE AND JUSTICE IN THE GLOBAL VILLAGE

The Role of the World Religions in the Twenty-first Century

Thomas R. McFaul

PRAEGER

Westport, Connecticut
London

Library of Congress Cataloging-in-Publication Data

McFaul, Thomas R.
  The future of peace and justice in the global village : the role of the world religions in the
  Twenty-first century / Thomas R. McFaul.
     p. cm.
  Includes bibliographical references and index.
  ISBN 0–275–99313–2 (alk. paper)
  1. Peace—Religious aspects.   2. Religion and justice.   3. Religions.
   4. Globalization—Religious aspects.   I. Title.
  BL65.P4M34   2006
  201′.7—dc22   2006021027

British Library Cataloguing in Publication Data is available

Library of Congress Catalog Card Number: 2006021027
ISBN: 0–275–99313–2

First published in 2006

Praeger Publishers, 88 Post Road West, Westport, CT 06881
An imprint of Greenwood Publishing Group, Inc.
www.praeger.com

Printed in the United States of America

(∞)™

The paper used in this book complies with the
Permanent Paper Standard issued by the National
Information Standards Organization (Z39.48–1984).

10 9 8 7 6 5 4 3 2 1

This book is dedicated to Sally and our children and grandchildren, who deserve living in a global village filled with peace and justice.

CONTENTS

Contents

ACKNOWLEDGMENTS

I owe a debt of gratitude to several persons for their many helpful suggestions. Together their comments have added depth and insight into many of the book's central ideas. In alphabetical order they are Wendell Bell, Peter Bishop, Edward Cornish, Robert Edgar, Jay Gary, Thomas Hoffman, Michel Laurent, Tad Lehe, and Allen McKiel. Suzanne I. Staszak-Silva, Senior Editor, Praeger Publishers, deserves special mention for her guidance and steady hand.

I also wish to express appreciation to the many diverse students who, over the past years, offered far-reaching foresights into the potential impact that the world religions might have in shaping the global village of the twenty-first century. Their shared experiences and keen observations helped uncover core issues and stimulate new and imaginative ways to think about the future.

Finally, my family deserves special mention. Their encouragement has been a bedrock foundation of constant support. Any shortcomings of this book rest entirely on my shoulders.

Thomas R. McFaul

INTRODUCTION

"The world is shrinking." This phrase is repeated so often that it is rapidly becoming one of the twenty-first century's main mantras. Of course, the word "shrinking" does not imply that specific geological changes are altering the size or circumference of the earth. Rather it refers to overcoming the geographic isolation that for centuries kept societies separated from each other. This is no longer possible because the dynamic changes that are spreading into every nook and cranny of the planet are creating an increasingly integrated global village. The world is experiencing the interpenetration of cultures on a scale never before witnessed in human history.

This book focuses on what life in the emerging global village of the twenty-first century will be like. It addresses one specific question. Will the global village be a place where the inhabitants experience an increase in peace and justice or hatred and hostility? Several factors will contribute to which of these two possible futures becomes the actual future. Many writers and commentators have already given careful consideration to the potential impact of technology and of economic and political factors. Far fewer authors have addressed the role that the world religions will have in shaping the twenty-first century global village. This book is intended to fill this vacuum.

In order to accomplish this goal, the book is divided into four main sections that include a total of twelve chapters. Section I contains the first two chapters. It lays out the foundation of the emerging global village. Chapter 1 defines the meaning of peace and justice and examines in detail the major social change forces that are forming the global village. Special attention is given to the role of religion. Chapter 2 describes the nature of human religiosity and explains why the quest for spiritual truth and fulfillment appears in every society from ancient to modern. These first two chapters identify the issues that the remainder of the book examines in detail.

Section II includes the next three chapters that examine the *worldviews* of various world religions. Chapter 3 compares and contrasts the views of Ultimate Reality that exist among the major religions that arose in Asia. Chapter 4 does the same for religions that emerged in the Middle East. The main purpose of these two chapters is to prepare for Chapter 5, which examines both the challenges and possibilities for finding common worldview ground for cooperation among the followers of the world's diverse religions.

Section III contains the next three chapters that discuss the *ethics* of the world religions. The book assumes that all religions incorporate both a worldview and a code of morality. Each complements the other as two sides of the same coin, and neither can exist without the other. The three chapters in Section III parallel the three found in Section II. Chapter 6 describes the ethics of Asian religions, and Chapter 7 of Middle Eastern religions. These two chapters set the stage for Chapter 8, which examines the challenges and possibilities for finding common ground among the moral standards of the diverse religions of the world.

After reading Sections II and III, the reader will have a twofold understanding. The first entails an awareness of the areas of overlap—both worldviews and ethics—that offer opportunities for constructive cooperation among the followers of the world's diverse religions. The second involves knowledge of the limitations that differences in the worldviews and ethics impose on the possibility of finding common ground. The first may serve as a stimulus for bringing greater peace and justice into the emerging global village of the twenty-first century. The second may fuel more hatred and hostility.

Section IV (the last four chapters) involves applying the ideas developed in Sections I, II, and III to three of the world's most urgent issues. Chapter 9 deals with violence and the world religions; Chapter 10 examines diverse religious views of sex, sexuality, and gender; and Chapter 11 examines how proponents of various religions relate to the modern world's separation of the sacred from the secular. The assumption behind the selection of these practical areas is that while other important topics exist, these three are among the planet's mega-issues and involve dilemmas that have worldwide implications. In a nutshell, how adherents of the world religions deal with them will determine to a very large extent whether religious pluralism will lead to bringing more peace and justice, or hatred and hostility into the twenty-first century.

The final chapter, Chapter 12, develops three possible scenarios of the potential impact that the world religions might have on bringing greater good or ill to the expanding global village. The chapter does not presuppose that all three scenarios are equally probable. To conclude the book, the author will project which of these scenarios is the most preferred as well as which one, or possible combination, is the most probable. By the end of the book, the reader will have a clear understanding of the alternatives that await all of us as the possible futures that are described in this chapter evolve in the direction of becoming the actual future.

Not all of the world religions are covered in this book. The reason is simple. Given the hundreds of religions that exist around the planet, it is not possible to deal with all of them in such limited space. This does not mean that the ones that are excluded are not important. Since one of religion's main purposes is to bring meaning to life, any religion that serves this purpose is significant for the believers that adhere to it. The religions that have been selected for discussion in this book are the ones that will exert the greatest influence on the future. These include religions that originated in Asia and the Middle East. In combination they encompass about 76 percent of the world's population.

Membership size alone is not the main criterion for including or excluding any given religion. Global impact is. For example, Judaism is included in this book as among the world's most significant religions. While small in number—20 million worldwide adherents or less, depending on which count one follows—Judaism has and will continue to exert international influence far beyond its numbers. However, three of the great historic religions of Confucianism, Taoism, and Shintoism are not included. Since the rise of Communism in China, the impact of Confucianism and Taoism has receded, although some scholars maintain that these two religions continue to influence modern China in indirect ways.

Likewise, Shintoism, which provides Japan with a sense of historic continuity and identity, is omitted. Since the end of World War II in 1945, Shintoism has ceased being a state religion that motivates the Emperor and the Japanese nation to military conquest. While Shintoism and Buddhism continue as Japan's two dominate religions, unlike Buddhism that claims millions of followers beyond Japan, Shintoism has few adherents beyond the Japanese Islands. In addition, Shintoism is now mainly centered on personal devotion and worship of the thousands of Shinto nature spirits and other deities called *kami*.

Also excluded are the hundreds of indigenous religions of native populations around the world. While large in number, the scope of their influence is limited to the small number of people who adhere to them. In addition, many of the images and ideas that are found in these religions have become absorbed into the world religions that will exert the greatest influence in the twenty-first century. Also, many newer religions that have emerged in the past 100–200 years are not included. While some of them are growing in influence, such as Baha'i and The Church of Jesus Christ of the Latter-Day Saints (Mormons), in many ways they embrace worldview concepts and ethical norms of the religions out of which they evolved. They are unique by virtue of what they added to the core concepts of the parent religions, which will be the focus of this book.

The book will not include so-called secular religions that are based on Western materialist, atheist, or agnostic worldviews. These include Marxism and various forms of secular humanism or nature-based belief systems. While the followers of these combined perspectives comprise about 14 percent of the world's population, their focus is primarily on ethics. They often express antagonism toward traditional religious points of view. Moreover, they lack a sense of humanity's deeper needs that include the desire for spiritual fulfillment in life as well as in life after death. Buddhism and Jainism have atheist worldviews and rigorous ethical standards, but their principal focus is on fulfilling spiritual or mystical goals. Thus, Asian atheism and Western atheism differ from each other in very significant ways. Atheism and spirituality are closely coupled in the Asian worldviews, whereas in the Western worldviews, they are not.

In short, this book is not a comprehensive Comparative Religions text in the traditional sense. It is not meant to be a nonevaluative, descriptive comparison of the vast variety of the world's religions. Rather, it is both descriptive *and* normative, especially the latter. One overarching question lies at the heart of this book. Will seven of the world's major religions that provide the ideas by which 76 percent of the earth's inhabitants perceive the world be a force for bringing greater peace and justice, or hatred and hostility, into the emerging global village of the twenty-first century?

SECTION I

Foundations—The Emerging Global Village and Human Religiosity

CHAPTER 1

Globalization and World Transformation in the New Millennium

In 1964, Marshall McLuhan created the image of the emerging "global village"[1] to describe the dynamic transformations that are occurring throughout the world. Since then, a growing number of writers have analyzed the powerful forces of social change that are progressively propelling our planet toward greater global interconnectivity as McLuhan envisioned it. They have labeled this process "globalization." It would not be an exaggeration to say that the globalization phenomenon is one of the world's major transformative trends of the new millennium. For our purposes, globalization will be defined as the *means* by which the earth is moving steadily toward the *end* of becoming an integrated global village.

The globalization phenomenon is characterized by extraordinary complexity and uncertainty with regard to its future direction. In addition, it is surrounded by considerable controversy. Some writers perceive that globalization will bring steady social and economic improvements for everyone. They liken it to a "rising tide that lifts all boats." Others see a different future—one in which the conditions of rich countries will improve while those of poor nations will worsen. For others, globalization is little more than the spread of degenerate Western values around the world with the corresponding destruction of indigenous religions and cultures.

Several complex driving forces are shaping globalization. Technological, economic, and political factors both push and pull the process forward. In addition, the world religions play a major role in determining the pathway that globalization will follow. Although some exceptions exist, most globalization writers give scant attention to religion as one of the major driving forces of the future. But it is important to examine the effect that the world's major religions have on globalization and whether or not they will contribute to the goal of increasing peace and justice as the earth evolves toward greater interconnectivity. Issues of peace and justice are paramount to understanding the globalization phenomenon and the major driving forces behind it.

PEACE AND JUSTICE

Long-term harmony within the global village rests on peace and justice. The concept of peace refers to the elimination of violence as a method for resolving conflict. This definition does not imply that conflict will disappear. It would be naïve to assume that disagreements over any number of issues that range from personal to international will eventually fade away. Simply stated, peace refers to (1) the elimination of torture and killing as ways to settle disputes, and (2) the development of nonviolent procedures for resolving conflicts wherever they appear. No doubt, disagreements and the conflicts that result from them are an inherent and permanent part of the human condition. Therefore, the issue is not the elimination of conflict but how to resolve it. A peaceful global village is one in which no one resorts to violence through torture or taking the life of another person in order to resolve arguments, quarrels, or hostile clashes of any kind.

The word justice means fairness.[2] While this definition sounds simple, the idea of justice is not. Justice can be divided into different types: compensatory, retributive, or distributive.[3] This book focuses mainly on distributive justice because it has broader application to society as a whole than the other two types. Distributive justice refers to the fair sharing of the burdens and benefits of human life. It implies fairness in terms of both social equalities and inequalities. Being fair in the distribution of the burdens and benefits of society does not require the elimination of inequalities. Both equalities and inequalities might or might not be just depending on circumstances.

For example, just inequalities might involve different pay for different levels of achievement in the occupational structure of a society. Or unjust equalities could involve a forced equal distribution of outcomes where circumstances do not warrant it. In Track and Field sports, winners get the gold medal. No one considers giving the silver medal to the second place winner to be unfair. Giving gold medals to both the first and second place runners would be considered an unjust equality. The inequality of giving gold and silver medals to the first and second place winners respectively is accepted universally as a just inequality.

Another way to say this is that justice involves giving everyone what they deserve, that is, what is due to them. There is no simple formula for determining the fair distribution of all of society's burdens and benefits. Every society will interpret the concept of distributive justice in terms of its religion or philosophy of life, values, and collective sense of right and wrong. No society can function without a concept of fairness by which it determines who gets what and why. The definition of justice that exists in a society at any given point in time is the standard that citizens use to measure whether the distribution of burdens and benefits is fair, that is, whether or not everyone is getting his or her due.

For our purposes, we can assume that the degree of peace that exists in the emerging global village is proportional to the perception that the burdens and benefits are distributed fairly. Peace and justice go together in the sense that they can be viewed as opposite sides of the same coin. The more that justice exists, the more likely it is that peace will prevail, and vice versa. In short, in order for peace to spread, justice must increase. If a perception of injustice becomes widespread, the greater is the potential for conflict. How might the world's religions contribute to increasing to total amount of justice, and thus peace, in the emerging global village? I hope to try to answer these questions in these pages.

GLOBALIZATION

In truth, no single definition of globalization exists. Rather, different authors define globalization in various ways depending on their backgrounds and interests. For some writers, the word globalization is little more than "'globaloney' because it is too exaggerated and imprecise."[4] Nonetheless, many authors share a common understanding of the globalization, which refers to the growth of multiple global linkages that transform both community life and individual consciousness. As early as 1955, one writer defined globalization as a "social process in which the constraints of geography on social and cultural arrangements recede and in which people become increasingly aware that they are receding."[5] Since then, interest in the globalization phenomenon has grown steadily as these constraints have continued to diminish.

Globalization is a multidimensional, interconnected process that operates simultaneously at many levels—from the formation of global networks and regional organizations to the influence that they exert on local communities. These processes intersect and overlap in complex ways. Globalization is the coalescence and interpenetration of various transnational processes and domestic structures.[6] It is the worldwide integration of markets, nations, and technologies on a scale never witnessed before in human history.[7]

Much of the discussion centers on the duration and speed of the globalization phenomenon. Disagreements exist over whether this process stretches back as far as 5,000 years or is only a few decades old. For some, globalization has gone on for centuries. For others, it is of recent origin. In actuality both positions are correct. From a historical perspective, it is accurate to say that the current globalization phenomenon signals the accelerated continuation of dynamic forces that date back hundreds of years—even before the start of Western global expansion in the 1500s. The formation of the former League of Nations after World War I and the current United Nations after World War II demonstrates that international linkages grew steadily throughout the twentieth century.[8]

The well-known economist James H. Mittelman subdivides the process of globalization into three distinct time periods that define both the duration and rate of change. In his view, economic forces, especially capitalism, drive global transformations more than any other.[9] He calls the first period "incipient globalization," which occurred prior to the sixteenth century. He describes the second period as, "bridging globalization," which extended from the start of Western capitalism in the sixteenth century until the early 1970s. He labels the third and final period, "accelerated globalization," which has existed for only about 30 years—since the early 1970s until now.[10] During each of these three time periods, especially the last two, the pace of global transformation accelerated as market place competition spread around the world. For the past three decades in particular the rate of change has quickened very rapidly.

Mittelman's three-stage classification of the globalization phenomenon is insightful because it encompasses both the historical origins and current dynamics of the process. This three-stage time line allows us to include the technological, economic, political, and religious driving forces of the globalization process that is creating the global village. All four of these forces push the world in the direction of increasing the total number of global linkages. At the same time, they affect the diverse cultures of the world in different ways, sometime radically so.

Each of these four driving forces impacts the dynamics of globalization at different levels, and no one force by itself triggers the totality of the transformation. Only when we combine them do we see the larger picture. Technological change affects globalization differently than economic expansion even though they interact with each other through reciprocal dependence. The formation of global or regional political organizations and the role of the nation state proceed down different pathways from cultural or religious diffusion, although each influences the other.

TECHNOLOGY AND GLOBALIZATION

The galloping speed at which globalization has spread around the earth in the past three decades coincides with the development of late twentieth century transportation and communications technologies. The airplane and especially jet engine have eliminated the historic obstacles to international contact, such as wide oceans, high mountains, and other impassable terrains. These natural barriers are no longer impediments to establishing cross-cultural linkages. Crossing the ocean by ship from the west coast of the United States to an Asian destination used to take weeks, and in some cases months. Now traveling from cities like San Francisco to Tokyo, London, or Cairo takes only a few hours.

In addition to improvements in air travel, enhancements in three communications technologies have contributed even more dramatically to increasing the rate of globalization since the 1970s. They are the telephone, the television, and the networked computer. Together, these three forms of electronic communication have produced the "death of distance."[11] Although the telephone was invented in 1876, television in 1926, and the electronic computer in the mid-1940s, it was not until very recently that they began to realize their full potential during the past 30 years of accelerated globalization.

During the 1970s and 1980s, innovations in the field of fiber optics and satellites increased the capacity for instantaneous telephone communication around the world. Cellular phones made possible instant communications anytime and anywhere on the face of the earth. The statistics on the spread of television parallel those of the telephone. At the end of World War II, only 8,000 households possessed a television set. By 1996, two-thirds of the world's households, or 840 million, owned one.

Most recently, as a result of cable, satellite, and digital transmission and expanded channel capacity, viewers have gained access to a seemingly endless range of expanding broadcast options. Television has dramatically altered the way in which politicians pursue public office and businesses search for new consumers. Its fast-moving images bring to viewers everywhere on the earth news events as they are occurring.

The third communications technology is the networked computer, especially the Internet, which signaled the future of global communications in the twenty-first century. It renders distance irrelevant and makes instantly available any content in any amount to anyone who is "plugged in" anywhere. Space and time no longer impose natural limitation on global connectivity, as Marshall McLuhan anticipated during the 1960s. Virtual communities of all types and size coalesce around the use of the Internet and take their place alongside those that exist in real time and space.

While the telephone, television, and Internet, along with the jet airplane, are not sufficient in themselves to produce a global village, they are a necessary condition for its emergence. Most observers of the globalization trend agree that we have transcended the natural constraints of time and space and that instant worldwide communication has lead to the expansion of global linkages and deeper cross-national penetration. This is especially noticeable in the area of economics.

ECONOMICS AND GLOBALIZATION

Once in place, the telecommunication and cyberspace linkages rapidly facilitated worldwide corporate expansion. "All economic systems—our local communities, the stores we shop in, the companies we work for, even our personal finances—are changing their boundaries, making new linkages within the increasingly interconnected global economy."[12] While economic activity is not new, the manner in which it is conducted is. In today's global information, postindustrial society, a business opportunity anywhere in the world attracts people from everywhere.

This has not always been the case. As recently as the 1960s, the world economy consisted mostly of separate national economies. Very little direct foreign investment existed. Countries like the United States, Japan, and Germany manufactured products within their borders and sent them to other parts of the world. For receiving nations, an excessive reliance on foreign imports resulted in protectionist policies on the one hand and a foreign exchange drain on the other. This system also failed to generate benefits to local labor markets in nations that only received but did not produce their own goods and send them to other countries.

In the 1970s, this system began to change. At the beginning of the twenty-first century, the world economy is moving swiftly toward becoming an integrated system of transnational production.[13] Over the past 30 years, many corporations expanded to other countries, which resulted in the creation of an emerging integrated international system. We now live in a world in which every phase of production—money, technology, and goods—moves across national borders to the point where it is meaningless to talk about a U.S. car, a Japanese computer, or a German camera. Unless some unexpected future event derails this trend, globalization as facilitated by the instant electronic communication will continue in the direction of increasing worldwide economic integration.

However, the benefits of globalization are not universal and are far from being distributed evenly to all the nations of the world. In truth, economic globalization has been a mixed blessing. Some areas of the world have been excluded altogether while others remain marginalized despite their participation in the globalization process. For example, globalization has brought no gain at all to sub-Saharan Africa, where from 1987–1998, the percentage of the population that lives on less than $1.00 per day has remained constant at 46 percent. In parts of Latin America and the Caribbean, the poverty rate has remained constant at 16 percent.[14] Russia, parts of the Middle East, and large areas of Asia have yet to benefit substantially from globalization.

From a worldwide perspective, most of the benefits accrue to postindustrial societies such as the United States, Canada, Germany, Japan, the United Kingdom, and so on. The vast majority of direct foreign investment flows to and from northern latitude countries. As a result, economic inequality between the rich and poor nations, especially those in the southern latitudes, is growing. Globalization's twin dynamics of disproportionate participation in the linking process and uneven distribution of the benefits among nations that participate in it are the cause of this inequality.

This explains why there is emerging in some areas of the world a significant resistance movement against globalization. Starting with the Seattle demonstrations in 1999, protest entered onto the international stage of globalization with disruptive actions designed to draw attention to the downside of transnational economic activity. Global concentrations of economic power are remote and difficult to control.[15]

As the globalization trend gains momentum around the world, a countermovement has emerged to oppose the perceived harmful effects that it creates. The protestors who gathered at Seattle, Milan, and elsewhere accuse corporations and organizations like The World Bank and the International Monetary Fund of neocolonialism, labor exploitation, and environmental destruction. They further claim that globalization is little more than a mask for Westernizing or Americanizing the rest of the world, which endangers non-Western cultures.

Thus, while some celebrate the beneficial aspects of growing worldwide economic integration,[16] not everyone embraces globalization with the same degree of enthusiasm. A substantial number of protestors do not view it as either desirable or inevitable. Instead, they mightily oppose it and vigorously struggle to stop it. Their vociferous critique centers the allegation that transnational corporations manipulate at-risk countries into providing access to cheap labor and weak or nonenforced environmental laws.

Globalization critics view multinational corporations as predators who use their extraordinary power to cajole concessions from the leaders of poorer nations that desperately need foreign investment but that are susceptible to abuse. In a world where telecommunication and cyberspace technologies foster multinational corporate expansion, the role of political leaders in steering globalization in a favorable rather than detrimental direction becomes critical.

GOVERNMENT AND GLOBALIZATION

As international economic integration accelerates around the globe, it imposes new demands on the nation state. When the world economy consisted almost exclusively of national economies, regulation remained largely under the control of the governments in whose territories corporations resided. The globalization of the economy has changed this pattern by forcing government officials to rethink their role as guardians of their nation's welfare. In a very real sense, their ability to exert direct control over the future of their societies has been altered because transnational corporations increasingly hold the power over their country's fortunes.

In the new world economy, business decisions to locate a company's operations in multiple countries influence national destinies and affect local cultures in profound ways. Government leaders have to walk a fine line to accomplish twin goals. They must stimulate internal economic growth by attracting multinational corporate capital as well as protect the well being of their citizens, the environment, and their sacred traditions, such as building factories along the Rio Grande River in northern Mexico demonstrates.[17]

No doubt much of the motivation that drives the emerging globalization protest movement stems from the perception that economic arrangements between transnational corporations, national governments, and agencies like the World Bank and IMF benefit mostly the corporations that are headquartered in high technology, postindustrial nations. In seeking the economic benefits that globalization promises, national leaders in the developing regions run the risk of exposing local labor, the environment, and cultural or religious practices to maltreatment. As the integrated economy emerges around the world, politicians must find ways to not only develop their societies but also to protect them. This is especially true of poorer nations where vulnerability to exploitation is high.

In short, globalization grows when corporations stretch beyond state boundaries through regional arrangements that involve multinational investment and trade. The growing inequality gap between northern and southern latitude countries arises in part from successful northern regional arrangements that bring greater benefits to member states. As a general rule, countries that remain disconnected or isolated do not enjoy similar advantages. At the same time, through collective agreements, national public officials in poorer nations can attract foreign investment, enhance employment opportunities, safeguard the environment, and protect local customs.

Thus, skilled political leadership plays an important role in helping countries improve their economic well being in a world that is rapidly becoming more economically integrated. How far globalization will go in transforming the entire planet is the subject of much speculation. Proponents view it as humanity's best hope for ending global poverty. Opponents condemn it as a tool for the rich to get richer at the expense of the poor. Which view is correct? Is globalization a force for good or ill? The answer to these questions will become clearer as the future unfolds during the next several decades.

RELIGION AND GLOBALIZATION

The world religions were already well established throughout the incipient, bridging, and accelerated stages of the globalization process. Like technology, economics, and politics, the world religions are directly affecting the future of the global village because they have deep roots in the regions that are being transformed by globalization. Religion provides both the proponents and opponents of globalization with worldview and moral filters for assessing whether globalization is a force for good or ill.

Strategic Studies author Samuel P. Huntington notes in his recently popular book, *The Clash of Civilizations,* that human history is the history of civilizations.[18] Civilization is closely linked to the development of culture, which refers to an overall way of life. Civilization represents the broadest and deepest levels of cultural and personal identity. Civilization is defined by common elements, such as language, history, religion, customs, institutions, and by the self-identification of people. During the era of bridging globalization, European colonialism transformed the world, which created the preconditions for accelerated globalization in the 1970s.

More than any other factor, religion molds the inner core of social and personal identity and the emotional sentiments that stem from it. Religion provides a culture, and thus a civilization, with a perception of reality in the broadest sense of the term by offering explanations for the origins and destiny of the universe. It gives meaning to life and describes humanity's place in it; religion defines the nature of good and evil and creates reward and punishment images of life after death. Religion provides the foundation on which great civilizations rest both now as well as in the past. "Since the beginning of civilization religion has been at its very heart. A creative religion promotes a creative civilization; a fragmented religion results in a fragmented civilization. This is just as true now at the edge of the third millennium as it was six thousand years ago at the dawn of the first civilization."[19]

Half way through the first decade of the twenty-first century, nearly 6½ billion people inhabit the earth. No single religion dominates all regions of the planet or has a membership that exceeds 50 percent of the world's population. At the onset of the third millennium, Christianity stands as the world's largest religion—over 2 billion or about one-third of the world's population. Islam ranks second behind Christianity with 22 percent or 1.3 billion devout followers. Hinduism is third with 15 percent or 900 million followers. Supporters of secular, nonreligious, agnostic, or atheist views hold the fourth position with 14 percent or 850 million. The followers of Buddhism stand in fifth place with 360 million members or 6 percent. The remaining religious groups vary from Chinese traditional religions (225 million) to Zoroastrianism (150,000). Despite its ancient origin and small size, the core ideas of Zoroastrianism continue to provide humankind with many of the most powerful religious images of reality.

Currently, the earth is partitioned into an array of cultures or civilizations that arose from multiple religious roots. As the global village grows throughout the twenty-first century, religious pluralism will remain one of its predominant characteristics. It follows then that globalization will spread from region to region through this pluralism. Christianity and Islam incorporate more nations and geographical territory than all other religions combined. Apart from some intermixing with Indigenous religions, the geographical distribution of the largest world religions is as follows:

> Christianity (2 billion) dominates most of North and South America, Europe, Russian and western Asia, South Saharan Africa, and Australia and New Zealand.
>
> Islam (1.3 billion) prevails over the whole of the Middle East (except Jewish Israel), Northern Africa, Indonesia, and Malaysia.
>
> Hinduism (900 million) is confined mainly to one country, India.
>
> Buddhism (360 million) is spread across East and Southeast Asia.

The present global distribution of religious pluralism emerged during the incipient and bridging stages of globalization. During the current stage of accelerated globalization, the major religions of the world continue to remain deeply embedded in the cultures or civilizations they helped create; and they reflect the unique historical circumstances from which they arose.

For example, the emergence of Christianity and Islam as the world's two largest religions is tied to the political and historical fortunes of the counties where they currently predominate. After Jesus' death around 33 CE, his movement spread gradually throughout the Roman Empire. King Constantine's conversion and support of Christianity in 313 CE rapidly accelerated the growth of Church membership. By the beginning of the fifth century, two-thirds of Europe had become Christian.[20]

Two centuries later in Arabia, Muhammad (570–632 CE) started his Islamic movement, which inspired his loyal followers to spread the revelations of Allah as far and wide as possible. While Europe languished in a weakened state of fragmented fiefdoms following the fall of Rome in 410, Islam expanded through aggressive conquest and conversion. From the seventh through the twelfth centuries, Islam grew to encompass all of Northern Africa, most of the East Coast of Africa, Southwestern Asia, and most of Spain.

In the fifteenth and sixteenth centuries, the Ottoman Muslims pushed westward into Europe as far as Austria. By the start of the eighteenth century, the Islamic Mogul Empire spread eastward and blanketed most of India where it exerted its greatest impact in the North. Islamic forces eventually stretched as far as the Malay Peninsula, Indonesia, and the many islands of Southeast Asia.[21]

Christianity's growth as the world's largest religion flows directly from European colonial expansion during the sixteenth through the nineteenth centuries. At the height of Islamic advancement, most of Europe remained under the influence of Medieval Catholicism. In 1492 Spain's Catholic Monarchs King Ferdinand and Queen Isabella commissioned the Atlantic voyage of Christopher Columbus, which opened the New World to

European exploration and eventual conquest. In the same year, they expelled the Moors from Southern Spain, thereby eliminating the last vestiges of Muslim influence in Western Europe. In 1517, less than three decades later, Martin Luther launched the Reformation in Germany, which split Europe into competing camps of Protestants and Catholics.

For the next four centuries, Islamic influence declined as European power spread to every continent. Several factors contributed to this world transformation. They include Europe's exploration of the world that followed after Columbus' overseas ventures, the ascent of European nationalism fueled by religious disagreements between Catholics and Protestants or various Protestant groups, the growth of mercantilism and competition among European nations for more natural resources and new overseas markets, the rise of the Renaissance and Enlightenment, the steady spread of industrialization and urbanization, the gradual expansion of modern science and technology, and an increase in Europe's military superiority relative to the rest of the world. By the end of the nineteenth century, European countries of Spain, England, France, Portugal, Germany, and Holland had conquered all of North and South America and subjugated much of Africa, Asia, and the Middle East. By 1914, European colonial control covered about 85 percent of the planet.[22]

As the strong arm of Europe stretched around the globe, Christianity followed. Through aggressive missionary activity, the Christian Faith took root as the world's largest religion. At the same time, in regions of the world that possessed long-standing and deep-seated spiritual traditions, like the Middle East (Islam), India (Hinduism), and East and Southeast Asia (Buddhism), attempts by Christian missionaries to convert the masses met strong resistance and frequently left a legacy of hostility.

At the start of the twentieth century, much of the global religious map had crystallized into its current pattern. Despite the collapse of colonial empires throughout the twentieth century, the rise and fall of Fascism and Communism, two World Wars, and the Cold War, this map has remained remarkably stable with one noticeable exception. Apart from religious membership increases that resulted from natural population growth, during the twentieth century the largest number of religious conversions occurred throughout the colonized nations of sub-Saharan Africa. Between the years 1900 and 2000 the number of African Christian converts grew from 10 million to 360 million.[23]

By the middle of the twenty-first century the world population is expected to expand to around 8 billion. Regardless of rapid population growth throughout the planet over the next several decades, demographers project that the membership percentages of the world's religions will most likely remain consistent with the distribution that existed in the year 2000.[24] It is one of the ironies of the twentieth century that the preoccupation with conflicts related to secular ideologies and the Cold War masked this underlying, persistent religious pluralism. As the Cold War peaked during its time of greatest tension during the 1950s and the 1960s, the world appeared to be divided into only three political spheres: the free world, the Communist bloc, and the unaligned nations.[25]

As superpower hostilities began to dissipate with the fall of the Berlin Wall in 1989 and dissolution of the Soviet Union in the 1990s, many of the old antagonisms associated with religious differences, which the Cold War held in check for over 50 years, reappeared. Nowhere is this better illustrated than in Yugoslavia where Communist leader Marshall Tito kept potential hostilities between diverse cultural and religious groups from erupting into bloodshed.

As the Cold War wound down, the once united Yugoslavia splintered into heated war zones. In Bosnia alone, from 1992–1995 more than 200,000 persons lost their lives as Muslims, Orthodox Serbs, and Catholic Croatians confronted each other's hatreds over the barrel of a gun. The terrorist destruction of New York's World Trade Towers in 2001 and the Madrid and London train bombings in 2005 epitomize the fanatical side of an emergent religious diversity in the early twenty-first century.

These and similar events make it appear that increasing peace and justice in the emerging global village remains a far distant ideal. The recent emergence of an International Antiglobalization Movement has divided the world into acrimonious camps. The ongoing hostilities between Hindus and Muslims in India and Pakistan, between Jews and Arabs in Israel and Palestine, and other global conflicts illustrate that human religiosity carries a destructive side. If there is to be any long-term social harmony within the emerging global village, the world's religions must transcend the deep fissures that all too often divide them. This means that by themselves, changes in technology, economics, and politics will not bring forth a permanently peaceful and just global village. The world religions will have a central role to play in this process.

CHAPTER 2

Religious Pluralism in a Global Context

The pathway into a global future of greater peace and justice, or hatred and hostility, depends on whether the world religions emphasize their similarities or differences. The global network of electronic systems that blankets the earth makes it nearly impossible for once separate societies to continue to exist in isolation. Humanity has entered a new stage of evolution. While the long-term outcome remains uncertain, little doubt exists that the choices we make in the present will determine the directions we will take in the future.

This does not imply that throughout the long stretch of human history divergent societies never encountered each other. Rather, it means that because of recent and spectacular innovations in modern communication and transportation technologies the speed and scope of cross-cultural interpenetration have increased dramatically. In the global village, adherents of the various world religions encounter each other constantly on a daily basis. Short of dismantling the global electronic communication web, an awareness of religious and cultural differences is rapidly becoming a major part of our "global consciousness" for the foreseeable future. The only real question is how we will respond to it.

HUMAN RELIGIOSITY

While many definitions of religion exist,[1] one of the most useful comes from the well-known twentieth century theologian Paul Tillich, who defined religion as one's "ultimate concern."

The dynamics of faith are the dynamics of man's ultimate concern. Man, like every living being, is concerned about many things, above all about those which condition his very existence, such as food and shelter. But man, in contrast to other living beings, has spiritual concerns—cognitive, aesthetic, social, political. Some of them are urgent, often extremely urgent, and each of them as well as the vital concerns can claim ultimacy for a human life or the life of a social group. If it claims ultimacy it demands the total surrender of him who accepts this claim, and it promises total fulfillment even if all other claims have to be subjected to it or rejected in its name.[2]

In other words, the religions of the world address concerns that emanate from the deepest levels of human existence. Every world religion provides its followers with a sense of ultimate meaning that is grounded in a sacred view of the origins and destiny of the universe and of their place within it. In the midst of the cycle of birth and death, religion satisfies the need to believe that life has purpose at its innermost core and that it can bring fulfillment to any human being or group that embraces it.

This fulfillment applies both to history and eternity. It combines the totality of tangible historical experiences with intangible visions of humankind's destiny after death. The diverse world's religions must compete against each other in the global village at life's deepest level. In order not only to survive, but also to thrive, they must satisfy humanity's profound yearning, indeed, craving, for spiritual meaning. In the final analysis, every religion stands or falls on its power to produce emotions of intense joy and gratitude that flow from the conviction that human existence is anchored now and forever in the most fundamental force of the universe.

The insatiable and universal search for meaning can be satisfied only when an individual's ultimate concern addresses two overarching issues. The first is an awareness of finitude, and the second involves the mystery of life after death. Awareness of finitude refers to the fact that all of the plants and animals of the earth, including human beings, are mortal. Sooner or later, every person on the planet realizes that as a biological life form he or she will die. As finite human and historical beings, we cannot exist apart from our bodies, which are programmed genetically for transitory life that terminates in death. All humans are born, live for a limited time period, and die.

Only the modern science of genetics with its recent mapping of the human genome possesses the potential to alter this fundamental fact of life. While the vision of a "deathless society" inspires the imaginations of futurist-oriented thinkers[3] and science fiction writers, at this stage of human evolution the most basic truth is that to live is to die. This means that no matter how deeply we desire to keep going forever as biological beings, we cannot do so.

Nor can we remove ourselves from our bodies or "take them off" as we would an overcoat in order to put on another biological body. While in history, no individual can survive as a disembodied spirit. Even for those who believe in reincarnation, the biological body must perish before the soul can transmigrate into another life form. To be human means to be a bodied, biological being. Biological existence is an absolute barrier that no person can transcend. No way exists to get to the other side of the barrier, whether over, under, around, or through it, and still remain human. We are locked unalterably into the biological laws and ligaments of finite physical life. In the most basic sense of the term, we *are* our bodies. Without a body, there is no human self. Without bodies, we cease to be real historical beings.

While exceptions might exist, as a general norm most people do not react to the discovery of their finality with inner calm. Furthermore, sooner or later every person must face the fact that his or her biological life will end. Staring into the eyes of this inevitability is one of the most profound self-encounters that any individual will ever have. This realization can lead to temporary denial or suppression, but confronting the reality of human finitude cannot be put off forever. It is only a matter of time before each person must meet head-on the reality of his or her personal death. In that profound existential moment the only real issue is how to deal with it.

From that point forward, every person's spiritual journey through life shifts to the next stage where the awareness of finality gives way to the mystery of life after death. Suddenly, these are not just abstract philosophical issues. They become profoundly personal: What will happen to *me* after I die? What will life after death be like? Does death lead to the complete cessation of *my* self—to permanent annihilation? Or will I continue to exist in a transformed state? If so, what will it be? When my physical life is over, will my destiny after death be determined by what I think, say, or do before I die? And so on. The pathway through life ends at the doorstep of death where one final question awaits everyone: "What's next?"

In truth, nobody knows for sure what life after death holds. At the same time, not knowing does not lead to not wanting to know or to not speculating about what will happen. Because the cessation of physical life is no trivial matter, anticipating some type of postdeath transformation, whether in the form of extinction or some altered spiritual state, is central to the experience of being human. Death is the biological *terminus* of all that one is or every will be. It is the end of historical being as we know it. It disrupts human bonds by ripping at the fabric of social relationships.

For loved ones left behind, death creates deep sorrow. It produces trauma and often an emotional void that even time cannot eliminate. The reality of death forces humankind to question both the meaning *of* life as well as destiny *after* life. It drives the quest for an ultimate concern. In a word, the search for meaning in life and death is the essence of human spirituality.

From the perspective of pluralism, the world's religions overflow with multiple images of life after death. Like no other area of knowledge or skill, be it economic, political, or other, religion summons forth from the depth dimensions of the human consciousness a plethora of possible ways to achieve spiritual fulfillment beyond earthly life. In a very real sense, envisaging, projecting, and describing the nature of life after death is a "specialty," an "area of expertise," so to speak, that the religions of the world possess in abundance.

In addition, all religions view life as a testing ground for what happens after life. They tie an individual's future fate to specific beliefs and behaviors that he or she is expected to exhibit while alive. In this way, life and death are inseparably linked. The spiritual search to find meaning in an ultimate concern embraces the totality of human experience, both now and in the future. At the deepest level, life is preparation for what takes place after life. The pathways of preparation for postdeath destiny are as diverse as the images of that destiny itself.

As globalization increases cross-cultural linkages in the global village, the followers of the world religions can relate to each other across the horizons of their diverse views of life and death in mainly three ways. They are inclusivism, exclusivism,[4] and pluralism.

INCLUSIVISM

Inclusivism is the most optimistic of the three because it embodies a vision of worldwide commitment to a shared set of religious or philosophical beliefs. It holds that humanity will evolve, or is already evolving, in the direction of a common consciousness of shared perceptions that in due time will unite the planet. Inclusivism assumes that religious antagonisms will weaken as cross-cultural contacts increase.

Social isolation is the enemy of an emerging global consciousness, whereas social interaction is its friend. For the inclusivist, humanity is on a long march toward global solidarity, where peace and justice will spread with the gradual disappearance of cross-cultural differences and the antagonisms they create. Global consciousness will lead to the creation of a global culture or civilization that will congeal around a common core of convictions.

There are three possible pathways into this inclusivist future. First, despite the high degree of spiritual diversity that exists around the globe, one of the current world religions will expand and replace the others. Although possible, this is a low probability scenario at this point in time given both the diversity of global religious beliefs and the tenacity with which devotees maintain allegiance to their perceived spiritual truths. When aggressive proponents of one religion endeavor to universalize their convictions by converting or coercing believers of other faiths, they drift in the direction of exclusivism.

The second way that inclusivism might emerge in the future is through the development of an entirely new perspective that will differ from the myriad belief systems that currently envelope the world. The well-known futurist author Marilyn Ferguson writes of the immense changes that are currently transforming the world—the appearance of a new paradigm that promotes the "autonomous individual in a decentralized society"[5] and leads to constructive humanistic action that affects personal and cultural factors at every level. The potential long-term global success of this or any other alternative rests on its ability to draw followers from existing faith communities or recruit members who do not currently belong to any of them.

This is no small task for two reasons. First, the ability of any new vision to carve out its own terrain on the already overcrowded global "spiritual landscape" is formidable because the vast majority of the world's people already ground their lives in deeply held beliefs. Second, more likely than not, any new spirituality will become yet another viewpoint among the many rather than replace the many. Thereby, it will add to worldwide diversity rather than diminish it. With rare exception, worldview shifts develop very slowly. The world's major spiritual communities took centuries to achieve their current global status. While the possibility exists that a completely novel perspective might appear and expand rapidly to a position of worldwide dominance, the probability that this will occur is very low.

A third alternative for the future emergence of an inclusivist belief system involves combining the deepest spiritual insights of the world's religions into a new synthesis that transcends the limited belief boundaries of any one of them. For some advocates of this position, the spiritual wisdom of India as expressed in the sacred writings of Hinduism could serve as the main source for such a synthesis.[6] Many of the recent New Age religions parallel this approach by fusing existing Eastern and Western beliefs with modern science in an effort to create a more encompassing spiritual outlook.

Advocates of the "new synthesis" positions share an underlying supposition about the nature of Truth and the human capacity to ascertain it. They assume that no single perception of Truth is all encompassing. While all religions possess truths about the nature of ultimate reality, they are only partial truths (small "t") and not the whole Truth (capital "T"). At the same time, it is precisely because of the capacity to comprehend at least some portion of the Truth that all of the world's major religions can lay claim to authentic spiritual insights.

This does not mean that all religious truths are equal in the measure of Truth they contain. No doubt, some come closer to the Truth than others. However, despite the degree to which any community's truth approximates the actual Truth, all religious truths fall short of completely comprehending the totality of Truth. This is so because all religions filter their limited truths through finite historical and cultural conditions. All human communities look at the world and try to make sense of it through finite lenses. They see only in part and not in full.

At the same time, for the inclusivist the answer to the question of why humans will accept some views of truth more than others lies in the nature of human evolution. As the global village continues to expand in the third millennium, the corresponding consciousness, which is already emerging out of a synthesis of the most truth-filled spiritual insights of the world's religions, will grow with it. In the give and take of global religious interaction and debate, the most comprehensive (although not total) truth "will out." A new and inclusive spiritual worldview, planetary in scope, will come forth and shape the future of human consciousness. No doubt, inclusivism represents the most optimistic end of the "future of global consciousness" continuum.

EXCLUSIVISM

At the opposite end of the continuum are critics who reject as naïve and unachievable the inclusivists' optimistic vision of the future. Under the banner of "realism," they assert that such idealists lack any sense of the harsh realities that fragment humanity into hostile, hate-filled factions whose future reconciliation seems only a remote possibility at best. For the hardcore realist, the most obvious fact of human existence is that the world is split into hugely dissimilar groups that proclaim that they and only they possess the Truth. While not holding a monopoly over this tendency, three millennia of human history shows that religious groups are especially prone to it. Despite periods of tolerance and cooperation, history is filled with cycles of bloody conflict among religious groups of all kinds. In matters of faith, true believers from across the spiritual spectrum would rather embrace martyrdom than betray their highest ideals. Once convinced that they are the recipients of an ultimate truth and charged with the duty to disseminate it, they are driven to convert humankind, by the sword if necessary.

When the fervent followers of any religion insist that their truth is the Truth, by self-declaration they become exclusivists.[7] By definition, exclusivists view all other perspectives as inferior or false. Because of their intense dedication to a single-minded vision, they are incapable of envisioning that an inclusivist point of view might emerge in the future by combining the best spiritual insights of existing religions, which they have already concluded are either untrue or contain lesser truths. Nor can they accept that a newer and truer view of Truth might surface because they are convinced that they already possess it in full measure.

Many exclusivists combine their powerful religious passions with apocalyptic visions. Some resort to violence to spread their views. Others do not. Apocalyptic exclusivists often anticipate the coming of a Savior figure or Messiah who will radically transform the planet. In the meantime, they must endure quietly amidst the seeming "confusion of tongues" that epitomizes the religious pluralism of the global village. Their task is to persevere and prepare themselves for the impending transformation when the world as we know it will be changed forever. On that coming Day of Judgment, the Messiah either will come for the first time or return again to cast out all falsehood in the name of their perceived truth. On that great Day, only they will be rewarded for their dedication while nonbelievers will be punished.

For centuries, Christianity and Islam set the standard for expansive global transformation. Both derive their passion from deep-rooted convictions about God's purposes. Christianity grounds its drive for worldwide development in Biblical references like those found the Gospel of Matthew (see chapter 28:16–20), which depicts Jesus as proclaiming that all authority on heaven and earth has been given to him. In this passage, Jesus commissions his loyal followers to make disciples of all nations.

From the seventh century CE onward, Islam demonstrated its commitment to aggressive expansion. On numerous occasions, Mohammad took his devoted loyalists into battle to spread his new Islamic faith across Arabia. After his death, his followers sustained the momentum. To this day the image of *dar al-Islam*, or house of Islam, motivates many Muslims in their quest to unite humanity under Allah's revelations as conveyed in the *Qur'an*. As a result of centuries of advancement through missionary fervor coupled with military conquest, Christianity and Islam currently claim as adherents over half of the world's population.

As the new millennium unfolds, Christianity and Islam continue to maintain their presence at the forefront of global expansion. At the same time, the pattern of interreligious competition grows in complexity. Within the emerging global village, all religions find themselves challenged by the truth claims of other religions. Propelled by mass communication and rapid transportation, spiritual devotees of all persuasions have fanned out around the globe to spread their truths. The result of this growing pattern of worldwide religious diversity is that today "every religion, like every culture, is an existential possibility offered to every person. Alien religions have become a part of everyday life."[8]

The last hundred years stand as an exception to this pattern. As conflicts among secular ideologies such as Fascism and Communism arose during most of the twentieth century, age-old religious rivalries moved into the background. In their era of dominance, both fascists and communists proclaimed their "truths" based either on belief in Aryan racial superiority or the inevitable victory of Karl Marx's version of socialism over capitalism. Despite the defeat of fascism during World War II and dissolution of the Soviet Union and world communism at the end of the Cold War, during their peak of power the true believers of these now defunct or declining systems sought to transform the planet according to their exclusivist secular truth claims. In the process they plunged the planet into one of its most hellish nightmares ever. Tragically, millions of innocent people lost their lives.[9]

With the end of the Cold War, the centuries-old religious antagonisms that super-power competition had held in check during the last half of the twentieth century reemerged. Accompanying this post-Cold War transformation, a renewed spirit of interreligious competition has arisen fueled by aggressive global missionary outreach. Modern communication and transportation systems have enabled followers of all the world's great religions to establish a growing international presence beyond their native borders—except in those nations where the guardians of exclusivist views prohibit other religions from taking root.[10]

Despite the differences that exist among exclusivists over the means of achieving universal recognition, one conclusion seems clear: inclusivists and exclusivists stand at opposite ends of the religious continuum. As the global village emerges in the twenty-first century, inclusivists anticipate the broadening of a new religious consensus capable of unifying humankind. Exclusivists anticipate an eventual victory for their viewpoint. For inclusivists, global conflict will gradually dissipate as a one-world community appears. For exclusivists, worldwide struggle will escalate as their truth marches toward the day of universal triumph.

PLURALISM

The third position is pluralism, which assumes that the array of religions that populated the world at the end of the twentieth century will persist well into the twenty-first century and beyond. Pluralists hold that none of the existing religions, or even an entirely new one, will prevail over all the others. For good or ill, the many faces of human religiosity in the growing global village of the new millennium will remain persistently plural. The only real question is how humanity will deal with it.

Pluralists approach the issue of religious diversity from a different starting point than either inclusivists or exclusivists. For pluralists, all of the world's major religions are internally self-sustaining because they offer their adherents an all-encompassing worldview capable of answering humanity's most basic philosophical questions and of satisfying the deepest spiritual needs.

At their best, all religions confer personal meaning and create cultural coherence. They are total structures of beliefs and behavior through which communities define their existence in space and time. They also incorporate images of eternal life or some form of spiritual fulfillment in life or beyond death. Religious pluralism in the global village is best described as a mixture of comprehensive, self-sustaining belief systems that compete for the allegiance of humanity.

The primary strength of the world's religions is that they provide the societies that they helped to create and sustain with a conceptual foundation for intergenerational continuity. They produce their own distinct spiritual and cultural images for ordering all aspects of communal existence from birth to death as well as life after death. All societies construct their own sacred canopies,[11] and without them they would lose their sense of historical continuity and long-term viability. This is their common strength.

At the same time, this strength is also their weakness. Many of the virulent hostilities that erupt in the global village emanate from interreligious diversity. In a word, the downside of religious pluralism is its capacity to generate extraordinarily intense hatred and bloody conflict. The dissimilar worldviews that developed in relative isolation and remained geographically separated for centuries have been drawn together into the global commons. The adherents of all the world's religions increasingly encounter each other across the boundaries of their own sacred traditions. In a word, growing worldwide religious competition is the name of the game.

Assuming that pluralism is here to stay for the foreseeable future, the major challenge confronting religious leaders everywhere is to move beyond the impasse created by their differences and to discover ways to bring greater peace and justice to the global village. The alternative is bleak: continuing discord, social chaos, warring, and deadly violence. The real issue, then, is how religious pluralism might be viewed positively as the basis for bringing forth the "better angels of our nature," as Abraham Lincoln called them.

SECTION II

World Religions—Worldviews

CHAPTER 3

Asian Religions

COMMON THEMES

Five common themes cut across Hinduism, Buddhism, and Jainism, three of Asia's major religions. They are enlightenment, reincarnation, karma, detachment from desire, and duty. The first three apply exclusively to their worldviews. The fourth overlaps with worldviews and ethics. The fifth and last involves ethics.

The three religions of Asia assume that the ultimate goal of life is the achievement of enlightenment, which also goes by the word liberation. In order to attain this goal, all living creatures must go through an unspecified number of reincarnations on the Chain of Being, which are also called transmigrations or rebirths. Through reincarnation, each person progresses toward the goal of enlightenment, moves away from it, or remains in the same place. The number of reincarnations that it takes to get to enlightenment varies for each person depending on his or her karma.

Karma is the law of moral conservation, a kind of impersonal "cosmic accounting system" that keeps track of everyone's beliefs and behavior—both good and bad. Like any other law of nature, karma is structured into the universe as a system of cause and effect relationships that govern each individual's destiny. After death occurs, the next stage of rebirth depends on the karmic balance of good and bad accomplishments that a person accumulates during the just-ended lifetime. An individual can reincarnate either up or down in successive rebirths depending on his or her karmic outcome with no guarantee of automatic or uninterrupted progress toward enlightenment. One can always move downward to a lower level of rebirth by accumulating more bad than good karma.

The purpose of life is to continue achieving rebirth at a higher spiritual level in each successive cycle of reincarnation, which in turn strengthens the capacity to reach enlightenment more quickly. The number of rebirths that any individual undergoes before achieving enlightenment depends solely on his or her choices during each life cycle. The better the choices, that is, the more good karma one accrues, the fewer the rebirths. Amassing bad karma over a series of reincarnated lifetimes slows down progress toward enlightenment. Each individual is responsible for the pace at which he or she progresses toward enlightenment.

Despite variances in the amount of time and number of reincarnations that it takes each individual to bring his or her transmigration cycle to an end, all of the Asian religions presume that sooner or later everyone will achieve enlightenment. The point where they differ is how to get there. In other words, the end is the same, that is, release from the cycle of rebirth, but perceptions of the means and the pace vary. Thus, while all the Asian religions include the same three themes of enlightenment, reincarnation, and karma, their devoted followers differ in how they interpret them in terms of the specific beliefs and behaviors that lead to liberation.

HINDUISM

Hinduism is the oldest of the three traditions and the parent religion of both Buddhism and Jainism. Hinduism begins with a simple yet very profound question that leads to answers involving enlightenment, reincarnation, and karma. The Hindu answer to the question of whether any spiritual force lies within, behind, or beyond the empirical world as it is experienced through the five senses takes the form of a spiritual pantheism that defines God and the world as one and the same. For Hinduism the universe is the body of God, although God's presence remains hidden within it. The goal of each Hindu believer is to discover the sacred essence that permeates every aspect of existence, including oneself, and to become unified with it in a moment of mystical exhilaration called enlightenment that results in ending the cycle of reincarnation.

Then upon death, one fuses with God forever in the same way that a drop of water loses its distinctiveness when it falls into and dissipates in the ocean. In other words, in the Hindu worldview a pervasive spiritual reality lies at the heart of the universe. It is everywhere and in everything, and it unites all the separate objects of existence into an integrated whole. The Hindu word for the Ultimate Reality that infuses all creation is *Brahman*. Brahman is God.

The assumption that the universe is the wholly integrated body of Brahman would appear to conflict with the everyday human perception that the world is comprised of separate and disconnected objects. The empirical world outside consciousness is known only through an individual's subjective awareness of it; and the diverse images that appear in the mind are assumed to have an objective status that is independent of an awareness of them. Ordinary human experience is one of diversity and subjective-objective dualism sustained by the belief that subjective impressions correspond to external reality.

Hinduism transcends the subject-object dualism through which the outside world is experienced by asserting that at the level of Ultimate Reality, dualism does not exist. The universe is an integrated whole fused together by Brahman. The subjective perception that the world is objectively comprised of an inexhaustible number of distinctive objects is a false view of the Ultimate. While humans experience the world as "the many," in reality it is only "One." How is this possible?

Hinduism resolves the dilemmas of the One and the many by positing the existence of two levels of reality. One is Ultimate, the highest or last level; and the other is penultimate, or next to last. Both levels are real. The Ultimate level is Brahman and the penultimate is the physical universe, which is the body of Brahman. Humans err when they confuse the penultimate with the Ultimate. To perceive the material world of diverse objects as the Ultimate is to make the mistake of *maya* or illusion.

This does not mean that the physical universe is an illusion in the sense that it does not really exist. The physical universe does exist. It is real but only penultimately real. Maya means that an individual lives with the illusion that the penultimate material world is the Ultimate Reality rather than the spiritual presence of Brahman that lies hidden within it. In simple terms, only Brahman is Ultimate (last) while the universe is penultimate (next to last). Brahman is the "One" that integrates the "many." To believe otherwise is to live in a state of maya (illusion caused by confusion or lack of truthful understanding).

Hinduism connects the Ultimate One or Brahman to the penultimate many through the concept of the *atman* or "soul." The atman *is* Brahman, writ small, so to speak. It is a smaller spiritual piece of the larger Brahman; it is a soul (small "s") that is part of the larger Soul (big "S") and it is embedded in every person and object in the universe. The atman has one goal: to return to Brahman through the process of reincarnation as determined by the law of karma. Every atman is reborn into many forms of physical life as it makes its transmigration journey back to the source from whence it came: Brahman.

The Hindu spiritual journey to attain enlightenment begins by recognizing that all life forms are merely temporary, physical, and perishable containers for the atman as it transmigrates back to Brahman though successive reincarnations. Hinduism summarizes the relationship between Brahman and atman with the saying, "That (Brahman) you (that is, the atman within you) are."[1] The Ultimate Reality of the universe lies within one's penultimate physical body. Life's spiritual journey starts with this most basic of all beliefs, which every true Hindu accepts as the first step on the karma-driven transmigration journey that ends in freeing the atman.

Whether the atman moves toward or away from this goal, or merely stays at the same reincarnation level, depends on the balance of good and bad deeds that are accumulated during an individual's lifetime. With a preponderance of good deeds, one's atman transmigrates upward, or vice versa. Bad deeds send one's atman downward. Briefly stated, transmigration of the atman to the next life form is determined by karma, the law of moral conservation, which regulates the speed at which every person progresses toward enlightenment. After the devout Hindu starts his or her spiritual journey by believing that the inner atman is Brahman, the next step involves accumulating good karma, which will lead to a higher rebirth.

BUDDHISM—THERAVADA OR HINAYANA

Although Buddhism shares the same common worldview assumptions as Hinduism, Buddhists interpret them so differently that we can treat the two religions separately. There are two distinct branches of Buddhism. Some scholars identify three branches, but it will be assumed that there exist only two main branches and that the third can be subsumed under the second.[2] The two major divisions of Buddhism are Theravada, which also goes by the name Hinayana, and Mahayana. Hinayana means "small boat or vehicle" and Mahayana is called the "large boat or vehicle." First, the Hinayana form will be discussed and then contrasted with the second branch Mahayana. The word Theravada that is also synonymous with Hinayana refers to the "way of the elders," because it is the original form of Buddhism. Currently Hinayana is practiced throughout Southeast Asia, whereas Mahayana appears in Northern and Eastern Asia. The number of offshoot variations is far greater in Mahayana than Hinayana.

Unlike Hinduism, which emerged through the combined efforts of numerous unknown sages and spiritual leaders, Buddhism had its origins in the unique experiences of one person, Siddartha Gautama (born ca. 563 BCE). He was born into the nobility caste of ancient India and grew up in palatial luxury, which was surrounded by widespread poverty. Siddartha's father sought to protect him from the harsh realities of the outside world by confining him within the walls of his comfortable estate. When he was a young married man and also a father in his early twenties, he ventured beyond this secure enclave for the first time.

As he explored the world beyond his walls of confinement, he made four specific observations, known as the four sights, which made an indelible impression on his mind. He saw persons plagued by disease, ravaged by old age, and the corpses of dead bodies. These three encounters with disease, old age, and death changed him forever. He saw life as it really was for the first time. He recognized that every living creature travels through life toward death and that nothing lasts forever. He anguished over the realization that all the joys and jubilations that he and others experience must sooner or later fade away. Suddenly and dramatically, the protected Siddartha grasped for the first time how atypical were the privileges that his father had bestowed upon him. He saw suffering beyond belief; and this invoked within him deep and powerful feelings of compassion.

In addition to these three negative sights, Siddartha witnessed a fourth sight. He saw an elderly Hindu monk who was seeking his liberation from the karmic cycle of rebirth. This fourth sight gave him hope that one day he, too, might be released from the physical deterioration and inevitable afflictions that result from being repeatedly reborn. With his own eyes he had observed both the bondage that human suffering produces among the human masses as well as a way to overcome it. Together the four sights left the young and impressionable Siddartha with a new view of reality. They stirred his nascent imagination and compelled him to embark on a spiritual journey that led him to found a new religion.

He became convinced that his life of luxury was a trap that locked him into endless cycles of transmigration from which there was no escape. He left the security of his sheltered estate, including his wife and young child, and set out in pursuit of his own liberation. He joined a band of wandering aged Hindu sages who were also seeking their release from reincarnation. He embraced their spiritual discipline and practiced the rigors of self-denial by eating only one grain of rice per day to the point of almost dying from starvation. Even though he labored to perfect the art of meditation, in the end he was no closer to enlightenment than when he started. After years of struggling unsuccessfully to attain his spiritual goal, Siddartha was ready to seek a new direction—a middle way between the extremes of his childhood life of luxury and the adult self-denial that nearly killed him.

Determined once and for all to achieve his goal of liberation, he sat down to meditate in the shade of a welcoming tree that his disciples later labeled the *bodhi* tree, the tree of enlightenment. He vowed not to rise until he satisfied his quest for spiritual release. In the midst of deep meditation, the temptation to return to earlier childhood comforts swelled within him. As that inner impulse grew, Siddartha realized that he had not yet totally detached himself from the desires that once motivated him. At that precise moment, he let go of the last vestiges that bound him to all earthly attachments. At long last, he had emptied himself of any and all remaining internal cravings.

Suddenly and dramatically in the midst of his feelings of total detachment, an overwhelming sensation of spiritual serenity swept over him. In that moment, he became enlightened. The liberation that had eluded him for so long had finally arrived. In his own words, he gave testimony to his mystical release from reincarnation, his own personal *nirvana*. From that day onward, Siddartha Gautama became known as the enlightened one, the

Buddha. Out of compassion for the world's suffering, he arose from beneath the branches of the bodhi tree and set out to teach others how they, too, could attain their nirvana and thereby end the cycle of rebirth, suffering, and death.

After his enlightenment, Siddartha began to develop his own doctrines. He combined the lessons that he garnered from the four sights with his own liberation. This resulted in Theravada Buddhism's core beliefs: the Four Noble Truths and the Eightfold Path. Buddha's observations of disease, old age, and death led him to formulate the First Noble Truth that all life is suffering. The Second Noble Truth presumes that suffering is caused by attachment to desires, which causes rebirth, more suffering, and death. His Third Noble Truth states that there is a way to end suffering. This leads to the Fourth Noble Truth: the way to end suffering is to follow the Eightfold Path that culminates in the mystical experience of nirvana, which stops the cycle of reincarnation.

Through the Four Noble Truths and the Eightfold Path, Buddha created a new philosophical framework for making sense out of suffering in life and a way to end it. He democratized the search for enlightenment and detached it from the hierarchical social system of ancient South Asia. For Buddha, any individual, whatever his or her station in life and at any time, could embrace the Four Noble Truths and undergo the rigorous ethical demands of the Eightfold Path, which we will examine in depth in Chapter 6.

Buddha's new approach for attaining enlightenment redirected his followers' attention away from the layered complexities of the Hindu caste system. In its place he proposed a pragmatic program of progressive steps that ended with meditation—the final step on the pathway to nirvana. Above all, he disavowed the usefulness of Hindu or any other kind of philosophy as a way to achieve enlightenment. For Buddha, there was but one truth (suffering) and one goal (ending it). He developed the Eightfold path as a practical means of getting there. All the rest was merely a distraction.

Buddha retained the worldview concepts of reincarnation, karma, and enlightenment and also held fast to the notion that attachment to desire perpetuates reincarnation, while enlightenment stops it. At the same time, he offered fundamentally different interpretations of these doctrines. Buddha's most radical reinterpretation of the Hindu worldview involved his redefinition of the nature of selfhood. Unlike the Hindu sages who espoused the existence of an inner soul or atman, Buddha asserted that the soul does not exist.

This no-atman (no-soul) perspective, or *anatta*, became Buddhism's most controversial, as well as esoteric, doctrine. Only emptiness lies at the heart of everything, not atmans working their way back to the cosmic Brahman through progressive cycles of life, death, and rebirth. Buddha's contemporaries found his doctrine of anatta troubling. If no soul exists in anything because emptiness lies at the heart of everything, what is it that transmigrates from one life form to another?

They questioned whether Buddha's view of anatta ultimately undermines the credibility of reincarnation itself. When asked, Buddha responded with a resounding "No." The reality that reincarnates is not an atman or soul of any kind but merely a bundle of karmic energy. Buddha called this energy bundle a *skandha*. Through reincarnation, each bundle assumes a new biological form that combines a physical body with consciousness, perceptions, feelings, and volition or will. It is karma that holds these elements of energy together and gives them their unique outward appearance.

In short, for Buddha, every person's earthly form is nothing more than a reincarnated cluster of energy or skandha. The law of karma causes the transmigration of each independent energy bundle from one skandha to the next until nirvana dissipates the energy altogether, that is, causes it to cease to be, just as the flame of a candle disappears when it is blown out. In other words, the spiritual goal of Buddhism is for each distinct life form to extinguish itself through nirvana and thus end the cycle of human suffering.

As long as an individual remains attached to worldly desires, then his or her existence as a self-contained energy field will continue to transmigrate through a series of skandhas. It is only through enlightenment that this cyclic process can be stopped. Then upon death, the self that is only a bundle of energy that karma causes to reincarnate into a series of transitory and perishable life forms disappears forever.

This means that all skandhas or forms of biological life exist in a state of constant change. Permanency is an illusion. Everything deteriorates as it moves through time. Material life forms are but temporary channels through which separate and distinct bundles of energy reincarnate themselves. Impermanency, or *anicca* as Buddha called it, is one of the most fundamental facts of the universe. Just as there are no souls at the center of anything, every life form is in a state of nonstop ebb and flow. Everything exists in a state of perpetual transition as it moves inevitably toward dissolution and extinction.

Buddha understood well the universal need to believe in the existence of a permanent soul that transcends physical deterioration and that continues to exist beyond death. However, in the course of his own spiritual journey, he rejected this idea and departed from the dominant Hindu beliefs of this upbringing. His emerging convictions took him in an altogether different direction. In his quest to stop the suffering that he witnessed in the world all around him, he reinterpreted the core worldview concept of Hinduism. In the process he created new images of both the universe and the self: Emptiness and impermanency. Through the Four Noble Truths and the Eightfold Path, he articulated an innovative method for achieving the spiritual bliss of nirvana and thereby ending the dreaded cycle of disease, old age, and death.

In his original formulation, Buddha rejected another aspect of his up-bringing. He discarded belief in the existence of the millions of deities that Hindus believed could help them along the road to enlightenment. As Buddha began spreading his new message, he attracted a growing number of converts who were seeking their release from reincarnation. As a result, he organized a religious order of monks, called the *sangha*, which provided these devoted followers with a disciplined setting for learning and practicing his new teachings.

Even though they met as a group, each monk knew that traveling the road to spiritual liberation was no easy matter. Buddha's doctrine was de-manding and his discipline difficult. It called for hard work and rigorous self-denial. Each monk knew that attaining enlightenment Buddha's way required sustained commitment and initiative. At the same time, he inspired them through his personal example. Buddha's followers knew that he could have luxuriated his life away as a member of the nobility caste, but he gave it up voluntarily in order to pursue a higher spiritual goal. They recognized that Buddha did not ask them to do anything that he had not already done himself. In the final analysis, this was the source of his charisma and cred-ibility. As a result, during the centuries after his life, Buddha's movement grew into one of the world's great religions.

BUDDHISM—MAHAYANA

As Buddhism expanded into Northern and Eastern Asia, it underwent significant transformation to the point of evolving into distinct branches that differ according to the ways in which they understand the nature of Ultimate Reality as well as the spiritual discipline that leads to nirvana. Both branches retain the traditional worldview elements of karma, rein-carnation, and enlightenment, but they interpret them differently. As indi-cated in the preceding section, the original branch that Buddha began is called either Hinayana (small boat or vehicle) or Theravada (the way of the elders) that thrives throughout Thailand, Sri Lanka, and Myanmar (for-merly Burma). The newer Mahayana branch (large boat or vehicle) emerged in China, Korea, and Japan where its many manifestations exert major influence.

The metaphor of the two types of Buddhism as either "small" and "large" boats or vehicles grasps well their dissimilarities. During his lifetime, Buddha frequently used the image of life as a raging river to depict the challenges associated with attaining enlightenment. Every person starts life's spiritual journey on the shore of reincarnation with the goal of crossing the raging river in a small boat to the opposite shore of nirvana.

In Buddha's original understanding, each individual must undergo this passage single-handedly. In keeping with the metaphor, everyone sits alone in a separate "small boat" with only the Four Noble Truths and Eightfold

Path to serve as a guide for navigating through the turbulent waters. With each transmigration cycle, every person's bundle of karmic energy returns to the shore of reincarnation and acquires a new boat, that is, a new life form (skandha) to begin all over again the journey across the raging river. After innumerable restarts everyone eventually arrives safely on the shore of nirvana.

Like Hinayana Buddhism, the followers of Mahayana view their spiritual journey in the same manner. To get to nirvana, everyone must go through the turbulent water. However, in Mahayana Buddhism, the passage from reincarnation to enlightenment is not a solo voyage. One does not sit alone in a small boat. Instead, one sits in a large boat and is joined by others who are there to keep the boat from capsizing and to help steer it to the shore of liberation. Thus, in the process of retaining and transforming the core worldview concepts of reincarnation, karma, and enlightenment, the newer branch of Buddhism stretched the small boat of Hinayana into the large boat of Mahayana.

Who sits in the large boat and helps guide each believer to the safe shore of nirvana? They are called *bodhisattvas* whom Mahayanists believe are reincarnated savior figures. In the original form, Buddha taught that each person walks alone in traveling the spiritual pathway that leads to enlightenment. The community of monks, the sangha, could provide monastic support, but in the final analysis each convert has to commit to following Buddha's guidelines that culminate in meditation and blissful entrance into the vibrant void.

As Buddhism spread beyond South Asia to the Northern and Northeastern areas, it fused with local religions and absorbed many of their beliefs in the existence of deities. Over time, new Buddhist converts created two innovative doctrines that led to the development of the Mahayana branch. The first is that Buddha possesses three distinct bodies. The second and closely related belief is that there exist enlightened spiritual guides called bodhisattvas who voluntarily choose to transmigrate back to earth for one purpose only—to help others achieve their personal liberation.

In much the same way that Christianity uses Trinitarian language to describe the Father, the Son, and the Holy Spirit, and Hinduism identifies Brahman, Shiva, and Vishnu as its three main deities, Mahayana Buddhism transforms Buddha into a deity with three bodies. Buddha's first body permeates all of creation and is embedded in all the creatures and objects of the universe. According to the Mahayana worldview, each person has hidden within his or her body a Buddha nature in much the same way that Hindus perceive that the atman lies concealed within each individual's reincarnated physical shape. Buddha's second body takes the form of Siddartha Gautama, the historical Buddha who came to earth to show humankind the way to nirvana. The third body consists of a cosmic Buddha who inhabits a heavenly place called the Pure Land or Western Paradise.

In the original Hinayana doctrine of Buddha, after a person attains nirvana his or her bundle of energy known as the skandha dissipates upon death and transmigration stops. The Mahayana doctrine of the three bodies of Buddha introduces new possibilities. When an enlightened person dies, the inner Buddha nature is released from the physical body and journeys to the Western Paradise or Pure Land where it encounters the cosmic Buddha. At this point, dissipation into the blissful void of emptiness is not the only option. Rebirth is also available for those who desire to return to earth as a reborn spiritual guide, called a bodhisattva, who can help liberate others. Thus, one main difference between the two branches of Buddhism is that Mahayanists believe in reincarnated saviors who can sit in the big boat and help escort each person across the raging river of life to the safe shore of nirvana.

As the Mahayana school spread throughout Northern and Eastern Asia, it divided into many distinctive types, such as the Zen meditation and Pure Land chant groups of Japan, and the Tibetan tantric form popularized in the West by the Dalai Lama. All the Mahayana offshoots integrate the belief in earthly bodhisattvas who postpone their own blissful extinction in order to transmigrate back to earth to help others achieve theirs. They take the bodhisattva vow of compassion (which we will describe in detail in Chapter 6 on the ethics of South Asian religions), and they commit themselves to countless reincarnations in order to help end the world's suffering.

In addition to the doctrine of reincarnated earthly bodhisattvas, many Mahayanists believe that the Buddha who inhabits the Pure Land is a cosmic bodhisattva who goes by various names. Three of the most popular are *Amida*, *Amitaba*, and *Avalokita*. Tibetan Buddhists view the current Dalai Lama as the fourteenth earthly reincarnation of the heavenly bodhisattva Avalokita, who transmigrates into a new body each time a previous Dalai Lama dies. The unbroken chain of reincarnated Dalai Lamas insures that the Buddhist ideal of compassion will continue from generation to generation.

Thus, as Buddhism evolved from the Hinayana (small boat) to the Mahayana forms (large boat), the original earthly teacher who instructed his followers in the Four Noble Truths and the Eightfold Path became a cosmic savior who inhabits the heavenly Pure Land and repeatedly reincarnates along with lesser bodhisattvas to guide humanity toward spiritual fulfillment. For millions of Hinayanists, Buddha's original teachings guide believers across life's raging river to nirvana. For millions of Mahayanists, compassionate bodhisattvas lead the way.

JAINISM

In addition to Hinduism and Buddhism, a third great world religion to emerge from the ancient spiritual heritage of South Asia is Jainism. Although substantially smaller than the other two in its number of adherents

(14 million Jains worldwide compared to 900 million Hindus and 360 million Buddhists), nonetheless, Jainism deserves special consideration. Just as Gautama became the Buddha or enlightened one who reinterpreted in his own unique way the Hindu doctrines of karma, reincarnation, the negative consequences of attachment to desire, and enlightenment, so also did the founder of Jainism, Nataputta. In the same way that the followers of Gautama labeled him the Buddha or the Enlightened One, Nataputta's devotees called him Mahavira, the Great Man or Hero.

Like Gautama, Nataputta was born into the nobility (warrior caste) and grew up in palatial luxury. Also like the Buddha, he left home at age 30 to engage in the spiritual disciplines that would culminate in his enlightenment. He imitated the example of the Hindu sages of his day and adopted an extreme ascetic style, which Buddha also followed but eventually rejected in favor of the middle way. However, unlike Buddha, Nataputta stayed the course of excessive self-denial. After 13 years of disciplined detachment from all worldly desires, he achieved his goal of enlightenment. Thereafter until this death, like Buddha, he developed his own alternative spiritual worldview and method for achieving liberation from transmigration, which he taught to others.

Mahavira died by intentional starvation, which his followers interpreted as the greatest spiritual act of detachment from desire that any human being could achieve. As a result, he became a Jain. The word Jain (from the Sanskrit *jina*) means "conqueror." Nataputta became Mahavira, or the Great Man or Hero, because he epitomized the conqueror ideal. However, unlike Buddha's followers, who call themselves Buddhists, the disciples of Mahavira do not think of themselves as Mahavirans or Great Heroes. Instead, they identify themselves as Jains or conquerors in the tradition of their Great Hero Mahavira.

Mahavira's ideas of selfhood differed considerably from those of Hinduism and Buddhism, although he included some aspects of both. He accepted the Hindu belief that a spiritual essence lies hidden within all objects of the world, including humans, plants, and nonhuman species. However, he disagreed with the Hindu assumption that this inner soul, which he called the *jiva*, was but a smaller part of a larger cosmic Soul. Each jiva is autonomous and eternal. It is without beginning or end. It was not created by God, because God does not exist, which means that there is no supreme spiritual reality anywhere in the universe (like the Brahman of Hinduism) to which the jiva will one day return. Each jiva stands alone as a separate and independent spiritual essence within every animate or inanimate object in the universe. Thus, Jainism like Buddhism is atheistic because it denies the existence of God. At the same time, Jainism rejects the Buddhist belief that only emptiness lies at the heart of everything.

Jainism also shares with both Hinduism and Buddhism the basic belief that the primary purpose of life is to end the cycle of reincarnation that is driven by the law of karma based on attachment to worldly desires. However, unlike the moderate "middle way" of Buddhism, Jainism is a religion of extreme self-denial. It is based on the life of Mahavira, the Great Man or conquering Hero. By starving himself to death, he set the highest example of detachment to all worldly desires, including the most basic food and water cravings necessary for biological survival.

It was because of worldview perceptions that Mahavira concluded that dying by starvation is life's greatest spiritual accomplishment. No other religion in the world carries the concept of self-discipline to this extreme. Mahavira taught that the universe is arranged hierarchically with matter at the bottom and spirit at the top. Matter is evil and spirit is good. The universe is populated by an infinite number of jivas or souls whose unspoiled form consists of pure and self-contained all-knowing consciousness. The goal of each jiva is to transmigrate to the spiritual top of the universe, called loka, where it will coexist eternally in blissful harmony with all the other jivas that preceded it.

In order to get to loka, each jiva must reincarnate progressively up the ladder of existence, spiritual rung by rung, so to speak, until it is liberated through enlightenment. The jiva is prevented from moving upward toward loka if evil matter, which is called *ajiva* and is heavy, pulls it down. In Jain cosmology, the spiritual jiva can arrives at loka only when it frees itself from the heavier crust of ajiva that surrounds it. Mahavira viewed karma as a form of sticky matter that literally weighs down the jiva and prohibits it from rising to the top of the universe. Karma is ajiva. Each person must burn off his or her ajiva, that is, the bad sticky karma that encrusts the inner jiva, so that the jiva can transmigrate upward toward the highest spiritual point in the universe, that is, loka.

For Mahavira this can occur only through detachment from all worldly desires. In the final analysis, becoming the ultimate Conqueror requires detaching from the basic biological necessities of nutrition and hydration. It is only through total deprivation through starvation that all the heavy, sticky karma (ajiva) finally can be burned off, which in turn enables the soul (jiva) to float to the top of the spiritual universe (loka) where it can join all the other liberated jivas in eternal bliss.

Jainism has had a profound influence way beyond its numbers as a result of the ethical standards that stem from its worldview. Mahatma Gandhi integrated Jain morality into his nonviolent political philosophy as he spearheaded India's drive for independence from the British in the 1930s and 1940s. In turn, Gandhi later inspired Martin Luther King, Jr., who initiated Civil Rights activities in the United States during the 1950s and 1960s to end racism. Thus, there is a direct line of influence between the ancient Asian religion of Jainism and successful movements for social change in the twentieth century.

CONCLUSION

Several conclusions emerge from the above comparison. First, all three, Hinduism, Buddhism, and Jainism, presume that humanity's highest goal is spiritual liberation through enlightenment. From this common point of departure, they quickly divide over their visions of what actually occurs when this blissful end stage is finally achieved. For Hinduism, the atman or human soul loses its distinct identity by blending into the Brahman or Universal Soul. Ultimately, all souls return to Brahman.

Buddhism and Jainism offer alternative images. Unlike the Brahman-oriented pantheism of Hinduism, Buddhism and Jainism define themselves as spiritual atheisms even though they differ in significant ways. The traditional form of Hinayana Buddhism rejects belief in the existence of an individual soul and a Universal Soul, which by definition negates any possible future blending of the two. The self is merely a bundle of karmic energy that takes on a physical form called a skandha. Upon the death of an enlightened person, the bundle of karmic energy disappears forever. All life is transitory. No permanent or unchanging spiritual source out of which everything comes and to which it eventually returns exists. To this traditional Hinayana Buddhist form of spiritual atheism, the Mahayana Buddhist branch adds the doctrine of Buddha's three bodies, a Buddhist heavenly paradise, and belief in savior figures called bodhisattvas.

As a form of spiritual atheism, Jainism shares with Hinayana Buddhism the belief that no Universal Soul exists. However, unlike Hinayana, Jainism accepts the existence of eternal individual souls or jivas that have no beginning or end. While there is no Ultimate Creator of the universe to which they return, as Hindus believe, nonetheless, in the cosmology of Jainism, all souls eventually rise to the spiritual peak of the universe called loka, they join together in eternal bliss and perfect knowledge.

Second, all three of the South Asian religions incorporate concepts of karma and reincarnation. Hindus, Buddhists, and Jains share the belief that everyone transmigrates through an indeterminate number of rebirths that culminate in spiritual enlightenment that ends the transmigration cycle. Accumulating good or bad karma drives the reincarnation cycle either toward or away from the soul's final destiny of liberation. While they hold this presumption in common, they also differ in their perceptions of the prerequisites that lead to the accrual of either good or bad karma.

Jainism provides the most extreme interpretation of the soul's journey to liberation by attaching it to starvation as the ultimate spiritual act. Both Hinduism and Buddhism also include the doctrine of detachment, but only Mahavira connects it to self-denial unto physical death. Buddha's experience of nearly starving to death led him to the middle way. Hinduism requires withdrawal from worldly attachments, but starvation is not the goal. For

Hinduism and Buddhism, the road to mystical bliss requires keeping the body alive in order to experience it. The body's existence is not an impediment to achieving enlightenment. Disciplining the mind to detach from worldly desires is.

Finally, although differently conceived, Hinduism, Buddhism, and Jainism share the belief that no action, good or bad, is wasted. The impersonal, universal law of moral conservation called karma records every thought, word, and deed. In the final analysis, the accumulated balance of good and bad determines the pace of each person's spiritual progress toward his or her ultimate destiny. While they differ in their conceptions of selfhood and perceptions of the pathways that believers must follow, all three envision that the ultimate goal of life is liberation from karma-driven reincarnation. In sum, the three South Asian religions share common themes with variations that mark them as distinct spiritual traditions for nearly one-fifth of the world's population.

CHAPTER 4

Middle Eastern Religions

COMMON THEMES

Zoroastrianism, Judaism, Christianity, and Islam share common themes. They are all monotheistic and presume that there exists an Ultimate Power that created the universe. At the same time, the Creator God remains separate from the creation. As a result of this conceptual distinction, one of the major challenges for all the monotheistic religions is to determine how the Creator connects to the creation while remaining autonomous.

In the language of theology, this is the issue of the relationship between God's transcendence and immanence. Each of the Middle Eastern religions addresses this topic in different ways. The more they emphasize God's immanence, the more they move toward monism or a form of pantheism, like Hinduism, where God and the universe are one and the same. The more they stress God's transcendence, the more they employ revelation images to explain how God bridges the gap.

All four monotheisms of the Middle East presume that God selects specific persons as prophets or mediators to disclose the divine plan of the universe. Christianity is the only Middle Eastern religion to equate its founder with God and make the claim that Jesus is the world's Savior. Next, all of the Middle Eastern religions possess their own unique sacred history that includes the special circumstances in which God sent forth the prophets or mediators. From this point forward, the similarities among the four Middle Eastern religions end as each one branches off into different interpretations of the common themes.

Three of the traditions, Judaism, Christianity, and Islam, share a common heritage through Abraham. Although Zoroastrianism relates thematically to this Abrahamic threesome, it emerged out of an entirely different set of circumstances. The chronological ordering of Judaism, Christianity, and Islam plays a significant role in how each understands its relationship to the other two Abrahamic offshoots. All three possess distinctive sacred stories that tie together interrelated revelations. Starting with Judaism, both Christianity and Islam assert the progressive nature of God's revelation. Many of their disagreements flow from different perceptions of God's unfolding revelations.

All of the four Middle Eastern monotheistic religions reinforce their separate identities through sacred scriptures that record the unique revelations of their spiritual legacies. The elevated status that all four of the Middle Eastern religions confer on their scriptures, especially in the Abrahamic tradition, cannot be overstated. Sacred scriptures enable the monotheistic communities to define the belief boundaries that separate them from one another. Many of the hostilities that have scarred Jewish-Christian-Muslim relationships for centuries arose out of each community's uncompromising commitment to the revelations recorded in its sacred scripture.

The Middle Eastern religions also possess a similar view of the nature of the self's destiny after death. On this issue, two main perceptions exist: immortality of the soul and resurrection of the dead. All four monotheisms incorporate both of these images in their views of afterlife. All of them presume a final Judgment Day—a time of reckoning when God will determine who merits eternal blessedness or damnation. Each of them envisions an interim status for the soul between the moment of each person's death and the final Day of Judgment when God will bring history, as we know it, to an end.

The monotheistic religions share a common view of the nature and origin of evil. The perception that evil exists is not an illusion. Evil is real, and it stands in opposition to goodness. At the same time, followers of the Middle Eastern faiths do not hold God responsible for the existence of evil because by definition God is the perfectly good Creator of the universe. This means that evil must originate from some other independent source like the Devil who goes by many names such as Satan, Mephistopheles, Lucifer, Beelzebub, Iblis, Angra Mainyu, and so on.

In its simplest terms, life is a cosmic conflict between God and the Devil to win the hearts and minds of human beings. When people side with God, they make good choices. When they surrender to the Devil, they make bad choices. On the Day of Judgment, God (good) will triumph over the Devil (evil). Those who keep God's commandments will receive their heavenly reward, and those who follow the Devil will be cast into hell.

Each of the monotheistic religions of the Middle East uses its own language to describe the nature of the cosmic battle between God and the Devil. Each tradition also specifies in its sacred scripture and traditions the kinds of moral choices each person must make in order to be on God's side and not the Devil's. The spiritual struggle that goes on inside each person's soul is merely a microcosm of the macrocosmic battle that rages throughout the universe between God's forces for good and the Devil's legions of evil. In the end, everyone's eternal destiny in heaven or hell rests entirely on willful choices.

ZOROASTRIANISM

Zoroastrianism is based on the writings of the prophet Zoroaster, who also goes by the name Zarathustra, and his followers. His core teachings are found in the *Avesta*, the Zoroastrian sacred scripture.

Like the seers of many religions, Zoroaster was able to enter into rapturous trances during which he believed that divine forces appeared to him. At age 30, during one of his many ecstatic moments, he encountered the angel Vohu Mana (called good thought), who transported him to the heavenly throne room where he found himself standing in the presence of none other than the Creator of the universe whom Zoroastrians call Ahura Mazda or Wise Lord. It was during that brief meeting that Ahura Mazda commissioned Zoroaster to become a special prophet and appointed him to reveal to humankind the Wise Lord's will for ethical conduct in this world. During the remainder of his life, Zoroaster received additional revelations regarding the high moral standards that Ahura Mazda required of all persons and by which they would be judged in the afterlife.

In the worldview that the Wise Lord revealed to Zoroaster, the universe is embroiled in a cosmic conflict between a good spirit (Spenta Mainyu) and an evil one (Angra Mainyu). This macrocosmic struggle has a microcosmic counterpart that rages like a whirlwind within the mind of every person. Like the universe itself, each individual's conscience is a battleground between the forces of good and evil. Those who follow Spenta Mainyu will take the moral high ground of good thoughts, words, and deeds. Ahura Mazda will reward them in the afterlife. Those who follow Angra Mainyu will descend into the depths of bad thoughts, words, and deeds. Ahura Mazda will punish them. The formula is straightforward. Choose the good and go to paradise or heaven. Choose evil and go to hell.

This aspect of the Zoroastrianism worldview is identical to the position that adherents of the three Abrahamic religions hold about the nature of Ultimate Reality. At the center of all four Middle Eastern monotheistic faiths lies the belief that God, who goes by many names, Ahura Mazda, Yahweh, Jehovah, Lord, or Allah, is perfectly just. Good people will be rewarded and bad people will be punished, if not in this life then in the one to come. God is not fooled at any moment in time—now or ever.

When death occurs, Zoroastrian faith invokes an image of the soul's passage into eternal life. The soul of the deceased person rests in the body for 3 days before journeying to the point of entry into either heaven or hell. Zoroastrians refer to this as the Chinvat Bridge that the believer must cross successfully in order to enter into heaven. This process is not automatic because the Bridge spans the abyss of hell. Some cross the bridge successfully and others do not.

In Zoroastrian afterlife imagery, for anyone who accumulates in life more good thoughts, words, and deeds than bad ones, the Bridge becomes wide, and the passage into paradise is easy. Multiple pleasures await the faithful believer. A different fate awaits those who during life walked the road of wicked thoughts, words, and deeds. As they step onto the Bridge, it starts rotating until it becomes as thin and sharp as a razor's edge. As the soul goes forward, it tumbles into the filthy depths of hell where it enters into a wretched afterlife of pain and suffering.

Whether they cross the Chinvat Bridge safely into heaven or fall into hell, all souls must then await the Day of Judgment when Ahura Mazda will bring history to an end and the forces of good will triumph over evil. From that moment forward, the Wise Lord will determine each soul's final destiny. At the same time, no soul will remain in hell forever. On Judgment Day, Ahura Mazda will assign all souls their due place according to the severity of their sinfulness. The souls that are already in heaven will remain there. Others may ascend into heaven if their time in hell is over. Still others will continue to stay there until they have completed their allotted punishment.

In the final analysis, according to the Zoroastrian worldview, Ahura Mazda's mercy is greater than justice. Evil souls receive their proportionate punishment in hell according to their bad thoughts, words, and deeds. In the afterlife, rewards and punishments follow a strict formula of measure for measure. Then, in due course, out of compassion the Wise (and just) Lord of the universe will bring all souls to paradise.

JUDAISM

Zoroastrianism stands as the thematic archetype for all the monotheistic religions of the Middle East. The remaining three traditions of Judaism, Christianity, and Islam share with Zoroastrianism a deep reverence for their special prophets and divine mediators, possess sacred stories, and perceive that God's will is revealed to humankind through their sacred scriptures. However, unlike Zoroastrianism, these three claim a common heritage through Abraham whose life and unique mission is recorded in *Genesis*, chapters 12 through 25:11, of the Hebrew Scripture. All three religions view God's charge to Abraham as the starting point of their faith.

God's call to Abraham to build a great nation is set against the background of humanity's spiritual and moral deterioration that is described in the first eleven chapters of *Genesis*, which begins with an account of creation and ends with the construction of the Tower of Babel. In the well-known story of the Garden of Eden, Adam and Eve enjoy the pristine pleasures of life in paradise. They dwell in perfect harmony with the God Yahweh who created them. Yahweh's only requirement is faithful adherence to the divine will. They have complete freedom to do as they choose with one stipulation: They must not eat of the fruit (the famous apple) of the tree of the knowledge of good and evil. As the story goes, they fail; and as a result Yahweh punishes them for the sin of disobedience by expelling them from the Garden. Now they must wander the earth, survive by their wits, and come face-to-face with the twin sorrows of suffering and death.

The Adam and Eve story of the origins of human sin sets up the theological problem for which the three Abrahamic traditions provide alternative solutions. The remainder of the first eleven chapters of *Genesis* describes Yahweh's growing disenchantment with the post-Adam and Eve generation that follows the path of murderous corruption and further disobedience. In anger, Yahweh floods the earth for 40 days and destroys all the earth's creatures except for the righteous Noah, his family, and the hoard of animals he loaded onto the ark.

After the famous flood, Yahweh covenants with Noah never to annihilate the human race again. Then, like the descendents of Adam and Eve, Noah's offspring follow the same downward path into spiritual and moral deterioration. Rebelling against their creaturely status, they erect the Tower of Babel in order to climb to heaven to be like the Creator. Their defiance is total. With the vivid imagery of the Tower, the first eleven chapters of *Genesis* come to an end. Only one question remains. Can humankind ever be restored back to the Creator?

The Jewish, Christian, and Muslim answers to this question begin with Yahweh's call to Abraham. All three Abrahamic religions mark this moment as the starting point of their shared spiritual heritage. In *Genesis*, Chapter 12, Yahweh commissions Abraham to begin a world-transforming journey of faith with the promise that a great nation will be created in his name. This nation will become a light unto the world. It will shine so brightly with God-filled righteousness that nations everywhere will want to imitate it. All the peoples of the earth eventually will find their way back to Yahweh by imitating the obedient behavior that the inhabitants of the great nation will exhibit in Yahweh's name.

From this starting point forward, the Hebrew scripture tells the Jewish sacred story of the "chosen people." It chronicles the patriarchal and matriarchal travels that end with Egyptian enslavement. In a time of dire need, Yahweh sends Moses, the greatest Jewish prophet and liberator of any era, to free the Jews from their bondage in Egypt and to lead them to the promised land of Canaan. In the course of wandering for 40 years in the desert, Moses delivers the Law of the Covenant that sets forth the theological, moral, and cultic framework for their future development.

A formula of blessings and curses stands at the center of the Jewish sacred story with an explicit projection of two alternative futures. According to the

Torah (the first five books of the Hebrew Scripture), if the Israelites obey the divine commandments that Yahweh revealed to Moses on Mount Sinai, then they will enjoy a future filled with "milk and honey." They will become the great and holy nation that Yahweh promised Abraham. If they refuse to follow the commandments, then Yahweh will cast them into the wilderness. Like the Zoroastrianism imagery of the cosmic conflict between good and evil, the Mosaic Covenant spells out the moral prescriptions that the Jews must follow and the proscriptions that they must avoid.

Following the *Torah*, from the sixth book Joshua through Two Kings, the Hebrew Scripture tells the story of ancient Israel's rise and fall as an autonomous nation. This story includes the accounts of Joshua's conquest of the promised land of Canaan, how David and Solomon led the nation to its height of glory, the hostilities that splintered the nation into two kingdoms, the Assyrian destruction of the northern kingdom in 721 BCE, and finally the Babylonian capture of the southern kingdom in 586 BCE. In the end, the foreign conquerors destroyed the beloved Jerusalem Temple that Solomon built and forced the Jews into Babylonian exile hundreds of miles from the promised land.

For half a century, the Jews anguished through their Babylonian captivity and pondered how the once powerful Israelite nation that spanned more than 400 years could collapse so catastrophically. In the end, the Hebrew writers of the ancient sacred story blamed the Jews themselves. Yahweh had fulfilled the promise to Abraham. When the people and their kings obeyed the stipulations of their Covenant, Yahweh gave them the promised land and made a great nation. Then, as they became progressively disobedient, Yahweh punished them with national destruction and expulsion from the promised land.

After almost 50 years of Babylonian confinement, Cyrus, the new Persian King and tolerant Zoroastrian who conquered the Babylonians, permitted the Jews to return to their homeland. He allowed them to recreate their community and rebuild the Jerusalem Temple with one provision—that they would disavow any desire to reestablish political independence.

For the next two-and-a-half centuries, even as they resettled in and around Jerusalem, the Jews never lost sight of the basic lesson that the Babylonia captivity taught them. They learned how to endure as a distinct religious community away from their original homeland and apart from the Temple-centered worship of Yahweh in Jerusalem.

Exile forced the Jews to find new ways to preserve their identity through religious innovations. In addition to the Temple traditions, while in a foreign land they created new synagogue-based forms of gathering under the leadership of rabbis.

In addition, to their Mosaic framework of rewards and punishments, Jewish leaders added a "remnant theology" based on the belief that Yahweh would never abandon them. Whatever future fate might befall them,

Yahweh's Covenantal love would continue without end. The experience of exile demonstrated that even though Yahweh punished them for their sins, Yahweh preserved a remnant to start the journey of righteousness all over again. The postexilic Jews returned to Jerusalem with a renewed dedication to follow the commandments of the *Torah*. They believed beyond doubt that in rekindling obedience to their Covenant Yahweh would bless them. If not, then Yahweh would curse them all over again. Either way, Yahweh promised through Abraham that they would be the chosen people—forever.

One final issue remains to be discussed in our overview of the Jewish tradition: the role of the leader-liberator. Egyptian enslavement nearly extinguished the early Israelites; but it was in the midst of oppression under Pharaoh's lash that Yahweh brought forth Moses as the first and greatest of all Jewish leader-liberators. He not only led them out of bondage and gave them the Law of the Covenant, but he also became the archetype in whose footsteps all future leader-liberators walked. This early experience of oppression followed by freedom foreshadowed a pattern that repeated itself during later centuries of Hebrew history.

The Hebrew Scripture writers even concluded that the Persian King Cyrus, who was a Zoroastrian, was one of Yahweh's chosen liberators when he consented to let the Israelites return to Jerusalem in 538 BCE, thus ending the Babylonian exile. In the tradition of Moses, Cyrus freed the Jews from captivity even though he was not Jewish. When Alexander the Great captured Palestine in 321, he placed numerous deities in the Jerusalem Temple in an aggressive effort to spread Greek polytheism throughout the region and to eradicate Hebrew monotheism. This infuriated the Jews. In 165, Judas Maccabee and his band of fanatical followers drove the Greeks from Palestine and cleansed the Jerusalem Temple of all foreign influences. Like Moses, Judas liberated the Israelites from the oppressive hand of their enemies.

This newfound freedom did not last. Barely 100 years later in 63 BCE, the Romans marched into Jerusalem and imposed their authority over the entire region. Once again, the Jews found themselves ruled by outside forces. Like the Greek occupation that preceded it, Roman domination was no less tolerable. As time passed, many radical Israelites became convinced that Yahweh would bring forth another leader-liberator—a Messiah—who would drive the Romans from the Jewish homeland. These militant zealots spearheaded active resistance against Roman rule.

Following the example of Moses, Cyrus, and Judas Maccabee, in 66 CE Jewish extremists launched an all-out rebellion against the Romans with the confidence that Yahweh once again would liberate them from foreign domination. They were wrong. Their revolt ended in disaster. In 70 CE, Roman legions crushed the rebellion, destroyed the rebuilt Temple, and scattered the entire Jewish population outside of the Palestinian region. During the centuries that followed, the Jews lived away from the promised land and under circumstances that seldom afforded them long-term protection or security.

Despite forced dispersal, the Jewish sacred story does not end here. Just as they learned how to survive in Babylon, they adapted to 2000 years of life in the Diaspora. Then after suffering through centuries of endless discrimination, late nineteenth and twentieth century Zionists began migrating back to Palestine in search of a homeland where they would be free of all future persecution. Under the leadership of Theodore Herzl, they either bought land or forced Palestinians from theirs, thereby creating Jewish enclaves in the Palestinian area.

Conflicts with the Palestinian population grew steadily as the Jewish migration expanded. By 1920, 50,000 Jewish immigrants had resettled into the region. Then, during World War II, 6 million European Jews were exterminated in the Holocaust. After the War, the world watched in horror when open exposure to the once secret Nazi death camps revealed the enormity of Jewish suffering during Hitler's Third Reich. As worldwide sympathy for the persecuted Jews grew, support for the creation of a separate Jewish state gained momentum. In 1948, the United Nations created the modern nation of Israel, which in turn intensified the Jewish-Palestinian discord that had been building for decades during the first half of the twentieth century.

In the last half of the twentieth century, regional hostilities spilled into wars and bloodshed as anger over the UN action deepened throughout Palestine and the Arab world. As of this writing, the future fate of the Palestinians and the relationship between Israel and its neighbors still hangs in the balance. In the meantime, despite the challenges of surviving as a separate Jewish state surrounded by Muslims who believe that the Palestinians are the region's rightful heirs, many Jews perceive that Yahweh, the God of Abraham, kept the promise. After centuries of life in the Diaspora that ended with the Holocaust, Yahweh brought them back to their native soil, even as the struggle to preserve it as a permanent Jewish homeland is a daily reality.

CHRISTIANITY

Christianity is the second of the three Abrahamic religions and shares with both Zoroastrianism and Judaism the same monotheistic themes. At the same time, the early followers of Jesus, all of whom were Jewish, reinterpreted the Jewish sacred story and the Hebrew Scripture so radically that they created a new religion. Jesus began his religious movement during one of the most tumultuous periods of ancient Jewish history—the Roman occupation of Palestine. As discussed in the previous section, zealot Jews anticipated that a new leader, a Messiah (like Moses or Judas Maccabee) would arise amidst their oppression and liberate them from foreign domination. The Roman rulers lived with the constant fear that radicals would stir up violent resistance against their domination.

In order to control the region, Rome assigned Pontius Pilot to the position of local magistrate and charged him with the task of keeping the peace. His reputation for quelling potential uprisings by preemptively eliminating outspoken critics of Rome was well known. His temperament melded easily with tensions and intrigue that entangled Jerusalem's politics. When push came to shove, Pilot had few qualms about sending would-be liberators to their deaths through crucifixion. Not only did this eliminate any threat of an uprising, but it also terrified the local population.

It is within this volatile setting that Jesus began to call Israel to repentance in preparation for the pending arrival of God's Reign. After joining the movement started by John, whom Herod later beheaded, and being baptized by John in the Jordan River, Jesus branched out on his own. Starting beside the Sea of Galilee, Jesus gathered together several disciples and started preaching among the poor peasants of the region. They flocked to his message that God favored them over the wealthy landowners and spiritually proud leaders of Jerusalem.

As with John the Baptist before him, Jesus' message fell on the suspicious ears of the Roman rulers and the Jewish Council in Jerusalem, the Sanhedrin, which joined forces with the Romans to quell any potential uprising. In all likelihood, Jesus' vision of the imminent arriving of a new Kingdom threatened both the official, political, and religious establishments. With the support of the Sanhedrin, Roman soldiers arrested Jesus, and Pilot sentenced him to death. Jesus' crucifixion scattered his disciples and left his embryonic movement in disarray. However, soon thereafter, the disciples regrouped and began the collaborative process that led to the emergence and development of the Christian Church.

The conversion of the Apostle Paul provided the impetus for spreading the emerging Faith of Jesus as the long-awaited Messiah who died for the sins of the world beyond the confines of Palestine and into Asia Minor. During the next three centuries, Christianity established a permanent presence within the Roman Empire although it remained a peripheral, and at times persecuted, movement within a predominantly polytheistic society.

After King Constantine's conversion to Christianity in 312 CE, Christianity enjoyed the political support it needed to shift from its perimeter status outside of the mainstream culture to the center where it became the empire's dominant religion. Under the umbrella of political protection that the monarchy provided, the Church convened a series of Councils to clarify the core beliefs of the Faith and to resolve ongoing debates regarding Jesus' true nature and purpose. During the fourth and fifth centuries, Christianity created a sacred Scripture (the *Bible*), standardized liturgical practices throughout the Church, and established the Apostles and other Creeds that gave voice to the principal affirmations of the Faith.

As a direct outcome of five centuries of struggle over issues of self-definition, Christianity reinterpreted the common themes of the Middle

Eastern religions around the meaning and purpose of the Christ event. Leaders of the Church translated these themes through their core conviction that Jesus was the risen Christ. The strict monotheism of Zoroastrianism and Judaism gave way to a three-in-one Trinitarian formula that Church leaders insisted was not a new doctrine of three gods but rather a reaffirmation of the One True God who takes three distinct forms: the Father, the Son, and the Holy Ghost. When confronted with questions to explain what appeared to others as a form of polytheism, they maintained that in the final analysis the doctrine of the Trinity was a mystery that had to be accepted on faith.

They also defined Jesus' nature as being both fully human and divine. He is equal to God in all respects. Jesus is God's only begotten Son who gave his life to redeem the world. In effect, God chose to become a perfect human being who was crucified as a final blood offering and resurrected in order to restore humankind back to God. As a result of Jesus' sacrifice, personal salvation occurs at the moment one accepts in faith this atoning gift as the ultimate expression of God's grace and love. It is at this point that Christianity's divergence from Judaism reaches its highest point. The outcome is a paradigm shift that flows from a comprehensive reinterpretation by Christians of the Jewish sacred story.

According to the Hebrew Scripture, Yahweh promises Abraham to build a great Jewish nation that will serve as a supreme example of righteousness in the midst of an estranged humanity. Being chosen for this special privilege comes at a cost. If the chosen people follow the commandments of the Mosaic Covenant, Yahweh will bless them. If they do not, Yahweh will curse them. According to the ancient Hebrew writers, they fell short of their Covenant ideals time and again and were punished for their errant ways. However, Yahweh did not abandon them. Yahweh always preserved a remnant to start anew the journey of righteousness. If other nations modeled themselves after the holiness standards of the beloved chosen people, they would find their way back to the Creator. In essence, the Jews viewed the *Torah* as a sacred story of restoration back to Yahweh first for themselves and then for the whole of humanity.

Christianity reinterprets this sacred story through a completely different theological lens—one that sees the entire sweep of Jewish history as preparation for the arrival of Jesus as the resurrected Christ who saves humanity through faith and not works, righteousness based on obedience to the *Torah's* Covenant Law. For the early Jews who became Christ's followers, the Old Covenant was but preparation for God's New and final Covenant built on the cornerstone of Christ's Cross. When the Apostle Paul, the *Gospel* writers, and other *New Testament* authors gave an accounting of Jesus' life and mission, they often quoted the Hebrew Scripture or *Old Testament* to footnote their convictions.

Given the *New Testament* writers' radical reinterpretation of the Jewish sacred story in light of their devotion to Christ, the split between Christianity and Judaism was inevitable. Though they share the same themes as the other Middle Eastern religions, they separate over their application of them to specific persons and events as windows into the will of God. Despite these differences, the early Church did not discard the Jewish Scripture. The early Jewish converts to Christianity continued to view it as part of their sacred story even as they created their own.

Thus, the *Bible* that Christians canonized at the end of the fourth century CE contains both the *Old* and *New Testaments*—and for clear historic reasons. The Christian sacred story cannot be told from the perspective of the New Covenant alone. It presupposes the existence of an Old Covenant from which it emerged. For *New Testament* writers, God's plan for the coming of Jesus as the world's savior is found in the *Old Testament*. The account of the Messiah's life on earth, his death and resurrection, and the early years of the Church are contained in the *New Testament*. From the standpoint of the Christian sacred story, the two *Testaments* are inseparable.

By the end of the fifth century, Christianity stood as a fully institutionalized religion at the heart of a civilization that it was helping to shape. Over the next several centuries, the once embryonic Jesus movement grew steadily until it became the dominant power in Europe. As the Roman Empire disintegrated into separate fiefdoms after waves of barbarian invasions took their toll in the fourth and fifth centuries, Christianity stood alone as the foremost influence capable of creating a common worldview among very divergent groups. Even with the ebb and flow of political conflicts that often pitted the Church against regional powers, Christianity's influence never waned.

In 1044 CE, the first major fracture within Christianity occurred because of disagreements between Eastern and Western leaders over issues of administrative structure and geographical location. Despite this split, the Western Church's sphere of authority continued to expand until it reached its zenith in the thirteenth and fourteenth centuries. During this period, the Church's sway penetrated virtually every area of personal and social life. This dominance, however, did not last. Slowly, Europe began to change. The shifting tide of public perception affected the Church's future at a profound level. Three emerging social movements in particular chipped away at its hegemony.

The first was the Renaissance that started in Italy in the twelfth century and gradually spread throughout Europe. With fervent dedication, philosophers of this new image of humanity extolled the virtue of individualism. The central issue that challenged the Church turned on the question of authority in determining truth. For ecclesiastical leaders, the Church was Christ's Kingdom on earth until he should come again on Judgment Day. Christ created the Church as the repository of the revealed truths recorded in the *Bible* and the Church's accumulated theological and moral traditions. The clergy saw themselves as both the guardians and interpreters of the sacred truths.

The Renaissance offered an alternative view: the individual, and not the Church, became the source of authority for determining the nature of truth. For many writers, embracing the new individualism did not result in rejecting Christianity. They merely maintained that any view of the truth, including the Church's, had to be inherently persuasive to human reason and not imposed by some external authority that possessed the power to do so. The impact of this conflict over legitimizing truth cannot be overestimated. In time, it evolved into a full-blown philosophy of individualism that undermined the Church's central claim that it alone was God's earthly receptacle for preserving revealed truths.

The second major movement to erode the hegemony of Medieval Christianity was the Reformation, which applied the expanding Renaissance philosophy of individualism to the realm of religion. When Luther nailed his ninety-five theses on grievances and disagreements to the door of the Wittenberg castle in 1517, he knew little of the firestorm that he was about to ignite. In the course of debates that followed, Luther and his generation of reformers redefined many of the core worldview beliefs that the Church had held for centuries. As a result of Luther's protest, Reformation provided Europe with a new image of the Church, the *Bible*, the role of revelation, and of Christ's relationship to believers. The Medieval Church's top-down collectivism gave way to a new vision of Christianity that more closed paralleled the Renaissance's bottom-up image of individualism.

The Renaissance emphasis on individualism parallels many of Luther's modified doctrines, the most important of which is the priesthood of all believers. For the Catholic Church, the ordained clergy serve as Christ's surrogates on earth and bestow salvation on believers through the forgiveness of sins. Church membership is a prerequisite for priest-mediated salvation, and the sacraments serve as the means of grace. Luther changed all this: Salvation comes directly to individuals through faith given in grace for believers who turn directly to God for spiritual guidance. The *Bible* is the sole source (*sola scriptura*) of knowledge necessary for the gift of salvation, which the Holy Spirit mediates between Christ and the believer.

The comparison with past experience is striking. Just as the Jesus movement led to an irreparable split between Christians and Jews in the first century, Luther's revisions of basic Christian doctrines created a permanent fracture between Catholics and Protestants in the sixteenth century. Even though Luther remained conservative in many of his social, political, and economic views and very distrustful of human nature in general, he reinforced the growing spirit of individualism that the Renaissance spawned.

Together the Renaissance and the Reformation set the stage for the third and final movement that undermined the Medieval Church's dominance of Western civilization: the Enlightenment, which added another layer to the spirit of individualism. The Renaissance made the individual, not some external group, the source of authority. The Reformation made the individual, not the institutionalized Church, the center of faith. The enlightenment made rational empiricism, not revelation, the means of determining truth. In combination, these three social change forces, the Renaissance, the Reformation, and the Enlightenment, changed the world forever.

Through the application of rational-empirical methods to the study of nature, modern science developed—fueled by a Renaissance-like passion among scientists to uncover the physical laws of the universe. Once discovered, these laws became the basis for the advancement of technology and its application to society. The combination of science and technology, as we know it today, transformed the world like nothing that preceded it.

This does not mean that other societies knew nothing of science and technology before the rise of modern Western science. The contrary is true. All societies have developed techniques for studying nature and applying its lessons to communal life. However, there is a difference. The Enlightenment's unswerving emphasis on a strict rational-empirical approach to truth led scientists to penetrate the veil of nature at a level that existing procedures did not permit.[1]

Those nations that embraced the Enlightenment approach to the development of science and technology gained an edge over those that did not. In time, they would conquer the world through the application of superior technologies to virtually every area of society, from weaponry to ship building. It is one of the great ironies of history that an Enlightenment-oriented Christian culture emerged from a moribund Medieval Europe whose relative achievements in most fields of endeavor languished well behind those of other civilizations, most notably Muslim, which will be discussed shortly. Once the Enlightenment came to Europe, it was only a matter of time before Western influence spread outward in every direction and engulfed the globe.

By the end of the nineteenth century, European nations had colonized 84 percent of the world's population and carved up the planet according to their political desires. As the European nations blanketed the earth with their colonial empires, Christianity followed in their wake. Despite earlier discord between Church leaders and proponents of the Enlightenment over alternative methods for determining truth (i.e., revelation versus rational-empiricism), the political fruits of the Enlightenment, along with the Renaissance and the Reformation, became the means by which both Catholics and Protestants spread to every continent. As a direct result of European colonial expansion between the sixteenth and the middle of the twentieth centuries, Christianity became the world's largest religion.[2]

ISLAM

The third and last of the three Abrahamic religions is Islam. The start of the Islamic sacred story is expressed through two main sources. The first is the *Qur'an* and the second the accounts of Mohammad's life found in the Hadith and Sunna or life of the prophet. The staunchly monotheistic *Qur'an* includes references to many of the same prophets who appear in the Jewish and Christian Scriptures, including Noah, Moses, and Jesus. Even though Islam did not descend directly from Christianity in the way that Christianity grew out of Judaism all three are tied together through Abraham.

In addition, Islam holds that the three Abrahamic traditions are religions of the book, which means that they all possess sacred scriptures that reveal the will of Allah. At the same time, Islam affirms that the *Qur'an* is Allah's ultimate revelation for humanity. It builds on and incorporates insights from both the Hebrew and Christian Scriptures and at the same time supersedes them. Muslims believe that the earthly *Qur'an* is a carbon copy of the heavenly *Qur'an* that is engraved on a tablet in paradise.

For the Islamic faithful, Allah did not reveal all the divine commandments at once but rather in stages starting with the Hebrew Scripture and concluding with the *Qur'an*. This is called the doctrine of progressive revelation, and it consists of three stages. First, Allah gave the Jews the Law and the Covenant. Next came the New Covenant that Allah granted to Christians based on the teachings of Jesus. Then in the third and final stage, at a time that only Allah knew, Allah instructed Muhammad the last or seal of the prophets to recite the revelations that became the *Qur'an*.

The Muslim ranking of the Hebrew Scripture, the Christian Scripture, and *Qur'an* into a kind of "good, better, and best" progressive revelation sequence coincides with the chronological evolution of the three Abrahamic religions. In a very real sense, Islam benefits by being last. Muslims defend the authority for the *Qur'an* over the other two sacred books by appealing to the notion of progressive revelation: the revelations of subsequent Scriptures surpass the divine insights that appear in earlier Scriptures. The actual historical time line through which the three Abrahamic religions developed gives Islam the edge over Judaism and Christianity in making the case for the gradual unfolding of Allah's will. Muslims believe that the *Qur'an*, which is the third and final book in a sequence of three sacred texts, is perfect in every way.

The doctrine of progressive revelation helps resolve the issue of why Allah found it necessary to make separate revelations that resulted in three distinct sacred books. One of Islam's most basic beliefs is that Muhammad did not create a new religion. He merely reinstated the original religion that started with Abraham but that later evolved in a direction Allah did not intend. For example, when the ancient Israelites considered themselves "the chosen people," they misconstrued Allah's will. According to Islam, all human beings are Allah's chosen people.

As a result of the Jewish misinterpretation of Abraham's call to build a great nation that would include all humankind, Allah called forth the prophet Jesus who delivered the message that Allah's mercy and compassion apply universally to everyone. Then, when Christians began equating Jesus with God and created the doctrine of the Trinity, they committed the error of blasphemy. For Muslims, no human being, including Muhammad himself, is equal to God.

As a consequence of this Christian deviation, Allah found it necessary to intervene again. Only this time, it would be different. Allah called forth the prophet Muhammad to restore the original Abrahamic religion and to reveal additional commandments that became compiled into Islam's sacred scripture. Because Muslims consider Muhammad the last of Allah's prophets in a line of great prophets, they believe that Allah has no further need to send other voices to communicate new or improved messages. Through Muhammad, the seal of the prophets, Allah's perfect will has been made known in the *Qur'an* that not only contains the best spiritual insights of the Jewish and Christian sacred books but that also includes other and final revelations that go beyond them.

No discussion of the role of Islam in the emerging global village would be complete without describing its historical growth and interaction with Judaism and Christianity. The story of Muhammad's life is well known. During his lifetime from 570 to 632 CE, Jews remained in the Diaspora away from their Palestinian homeland and Christianity struggled through the European disintegration of the Roman Empire. According to the Muslim sacred story, Islam began on the Night of Power during the month of Ramadan in 610 CE. The angel Gabriel visited Muhammad as he meditated in the hills surrounding Mecca and instructed him to recite the revelations of Allah. For the next 22 years, until his death, he continued to receive ongoing messages that eventually became written down and organized under the *Qur'an's* current subheadings.

Like many prophets with a new message, Muhammad met stiff opposition from the local tribes around Mecca where he grew up, married, and raised a family. Mecca also served as the home base and major crossroad for caravans that traveled and traded throughout Arabia and surrounding regions. Because of Mecca's strategic location, area tribes placed their many deities at various city shrines, including the Kaaba that later became the location of Islam's Grand Mosque. After receiving his revelations, Muhammad returned from the hills to Mecca where he preached his message of radical monotheism at different locations throughout the city.

Believing themselves threatened by this new prophetic voice, the opponents of Muhammad tried to kill him. In 622 CE, he escaped to the northern city of Yathrib, later called Medina (the city of the prophet), where he was warmly welcomed as the town's new chief administrator. Building on his reputation for honesty, he helped settle disputes among local tribes and manage community affairs. Slowly his message attracted a growing group of devoted followers who proclaimed that he was a prophet of God.

As Muhammad's Medina community (also called the *umma*) of converts doubled in size, the residents of Mecca began to fear for their safety. Conflicts between the two towns grew as Muhammad began expanding his new community of the faithful beyond Medina toward Mecca. After a series of deadlocked battles that produced no clear victor, in 630 CE Muhammad led a final assault on Mecca with 10,000 of his followers. The leaders of Mecca recognized that their small force was no match for Muhammad's military might and conceded without a fight. In a gesture of generosity, Muhammad forgave the townspeople of their past hostilities against him.

Soon after he conquered Mecca, Muhammad destroyed the 360 or so polytheistic deities that other religious leaders had placed at the Kaaba, except for a black meteorite stone that Muhammad believed Abraham placed there centuries earlier as a dedication to Allah. In one grand mass conversion, the citizens of Mecca announced their allegiance to Allah and to Muhammad as Allah's prophet. With the elimination of all religious, political, and military opposition in both Medina and Mecca, Muhammad launched an aggressive campaign in order to expand his new Faith to the entire world.

He wasted no time. For the next 2 years until his unexpected death in 632 CE, Muhammad spread his religion and the community or umma that he created throughout the entire Arabian Peninsula. For 22 years, from the time he received his first revelation in 610 until 632 CE, he single-handedly started a new spiritual tradition and an innovative form of communal organization based on his revelations. It would not be an overstatement to say that for centuries the story of Muhammad's life has remained a constant source of inspiration for Muslims all over the world. He infused his followers with his energy and gave them a divine plan for managing every aspect of their existence, including the Five Pillars that constitute the core of Islam's spiritual life.

The first Pillar consists of the Muslim Creed that there is no God but Allah and Muhammad is Allah's messenger. Second, he counseled his followers to pray five times a day in the direction of Mecca and, third, to be generous in sharing wealth with the needy. Fourth, he called for fasting from sunup to sundown during the month of Ramadan as a spiritual exercise that would help his adherents remember the month when the angel Gabriel first instructed him to recite. Fifth and last, he encouraged his able followers to culminate their Faith by making a pilgrimage to Mecca at least once before their earthly lives ended. By the time of his unexpected death, Muhammad had created a dynamic revelation-based community that was well on its way to becoming one of the major religious, political, and social forces in the world.

After his death, two issues in particular determined Islam's future direction. First, Muhammad did not appoint a new leader to succeed him. Second, Muhammad's goal of spreading the new Faith inspired his followers to continue his plans for political expansion. As these two matters intertwined, they gave rise to major disagreements that (1) resulted in the creation of the two major branches of Islam, Sunni and Shi'ite, and (2) generated intense conflict among political contenders for control of the growing Muslim empire.

The first issue involved disputes over who could legitimately replace Muhammad as head of the Muslim community. Among his closest companions, four in particular are important because they became Islam's first four political and spiritual leaders. Muslims call them the rightly guided caliphs. All four were devout followers of Muhammad. However, only one of the four, Muhammad's cousin Ali, was a blood relative. The other three, Abu Bakr, Umar, and Uthman, had no blood connection at all to Muhammad. Shortly after Muhammad's death, major disagreements arose over the criterion for determining leadership succession. Should it follow the bloodline only or be based on other factors such as group consensus?

As a result of these disagreements, open warfare soon erupted among Muhammad's devout followers. As a result, Muhammad's dream of a unified Muslim community that would convert the world according to Allah's revelations was short-lived. Soon after Muhammad died, Muslims began attacking each other over leadership issues related to political control. The devout followers of Ali pushed for a policy of bloodline replacement, while others advocated the alternative route of succession by group consensus, especially among those who comprised Muhammad's inner leadership circle.

The first three caliphs were chosen by consensus. When the fourth, Ali and his allies, tried to gain political control through military conquest, they were killed fighting. Later, Ali's son, Husayn, followed his father's footsteps but to no avail. He too died in battle. The Shi'ite branch of Islam traces its origins to Muhammad's blood relatives Ali and Husayn, whereas the Sunni line begins with Abu Bakr, Umar, and Uthman, whose selection as Islam's first three rightly guided caliphs occurred by group choice.

Today, Sunnis comprise about 85–90 percent of all Muslims and Shi'ites most of the remaining 10–15 percent. The Sufi branch of Islam, which developed centuries after the Sunni-Shi'ite split, currently constitutes less than 1 percent of all Muslims. Unlike the other two groups of Muslims, Sufis emphasize that internal mystical union with Allah is more important than mere conformity to the written commandments of the *Qur'an*.

During his 12 years reign from 644–656 CE, the third rightly guided caliph Uthman, authorized the creation of an official *Qur'an* in order to end the arguments that began to surface among Muslims over the authenticity of Muhammad's many sayings. Because Muhammad could neither read nor write, it was necessary for others to remember his revelations as he spoke them over the course of 22 years. This group became known as the Reciters who preserved Muhammad's revelations in oral form even though they did not always agree on the issue of authenticity.

In addition, different factions used Muhammad's words to justify their political maneuvering. Uthman was keenly aware that Jews and Christians had separated over scriptural disagreements, and he acted to prevent this from occurring among Muslims. When the final edition of the *Qur'an* was written down and organized into a format that started with the longest sections and ended with the shortest, Uthman destroyed all other versions. As a result, Uthman gave Muslims their Scripture before the advent of Ali, the fourth rightly guided caliph who precipitated the Sunni-Shi'ite split over the issue of bloodline leadership. Even though the early separation of Islam into two main branches persists to the present day, Muslims everywhere in the world accept Uthman's version of the *Qur'an* as their sacred text.

Despite the initial clashes that split Muslims into competing factions, Islam continued to expand—with the sacred *Qur'an* in hand. Good fortune favored the Muslims as they carried the message of Muhammad to the larger world. The Islamic Empire blossomed precisely at the time Byzantine and Persian power faded due to exhaustion and depletion of resources caused by decades of fighting. During the 100 years that followed Mohammad's death in 632 CE, Islam broadened its boundaries without interruption until the Prophet's revelations blanketed all of northern Africa and into most of Spain. In 732 CE the Muslim march into Europe came to an end with a defeat at Tours, France.

Between 661 CE, the year Ali lost his life in battle, until 750 CE the Umayyad tribe held control over the mushrooming Muslim domain and moved the political center from the birthplace of Islam in Mecca and Medina to Damascus. In less than 120 years after Muhammad, the Muslim Empire stretched for miles beyond Arabia in all directions. In 750, the Abbasids replaced the Umayyads and moved the capital east to Baghdad from where they continued to extend Islam's controlling arm until it reached from the Atlantic Ocean to India. The Abbasids governed a united Muslim Empire for more than 500 years from 750 to 1258 CE, when the Mongolian army swept out of Central Asia and destroyed Baghdad. The single Islamic state that began with Abu Bakr, Islam's first caliph, came to an end.

For almost six centuries after Muhammad's death in 632 CE, Muslims enjoyed a Golden Age despite the early Sunni-Shi'ite split. In the absence of any significant opposition to Islamic hegemony, Muslim culture flourished. Islamic scholars added new discoveries to the fields of science and mathematics. Legalists expanded the Law. Authors developed new literary traditions that included both poetic and narrative forms. Architects created unique Muslim designs that integrated engraved sayings from the *Qur'an* within interior spaces that fostered peaceful harmony and balance. At the height of their Golden Age, Muslims no doubt exuded high confidence that Allah was bestowing blessings beyond belief.

Only the Crusades, which lasted from 1098 to 1291 CE, threatened Islamic domination. At the end of the eleventh century, the Pope sent crusaders from Europe to Palestine to recapture Jerusalem and create a Christian state at Jesus' birthplace. In 1099 the crusaders took control of the holy city and held it for about 90 years. Then in 1187, the Muslim leader Saladin drove the Christians from Palestine, which remained under Muslim control until the United Nations created the modern state of Israel in 1948. No doubt, after centuries of exclusive control of Palestine, Muslims were deeply offended by the UN action even as Jews welcomed it as a gift from Yahweh who led them back to their historic homeland.

When the Mongols sacked Baghdad in 1258, Islamic domination did not immediately come to an end. Instead, the invasion set in motion a process of fragmentation. Over the next few centuries, three new Muslim Empires arose, the Turkish Ottoman Empire, the Iranian Safavid Empire, and the South Asian Mogull Empire. At the start of the sixteenth century, although politically divided, Islamic influence stood at its highest peak then slowly began to decline. By 1702 Safavid unity disintegrated into several tribal centers. In 1848 the British took control away from the Mogull rulers in India. Finally, in 1922 at the end of World War I, Kemal Ataturk dissolved the Ottoman caliphate and created the modern state of Turkey.

Once again the wheel of history seemed to be rolling but this time against rather than in favor of Islam. Just as Muslims had risen to power as the Persian and Byzantine Empires waned, Europe's colonial expansion increased as the Muslim Empires lost strength. No doubt, the demise of the Islamic control eroded the once abundant sense of Muslim self-confidence. The loss of global power to the West under colonial expansion created an enormous crisis of confidence in the minds of clerics and political leaders throughout the Muslim world. Like the Jews of old, whom the Babylonians drove into exile in 587 BCE or Catholics during the Reformation, Muslims everywhere must have asked themselves: Why is this happening to us? Have we fallen out of Allah's favor? If so, what must we do to get it back?

The modern Islamic journey back to the center stage of world politics has been a slow and arduous process involving multiple strategies. During the past 200 years, Muslims followed alternative political and religious routes in their attempts to regain lost ground. As they struggled to reverse their sliding fortunes, Muslims everywhere confronted the issue of how to deal with modernity and the changes that the Renaissance, Reformation, and Enlightenment produced throughout the world without losing grip of their most cherished beliefs.

Many Muslim conservatives began to connect the decline of Islam with an accommodation to modern and Western ideals. Adjusting to modernity had distracted Muslims from focusing on the Faith that once made them the world's most powerful people as Allah had provided. For conservative Muslims, the only way to regain Islam's bygone glory was to return to the purity of the past. Consequently, modern states like Saudi Arabia followed the path of orthodoxy advocated by the late eighteenth century Muslim scholar Muhammad ibn Abd al-Wahhab who died in 1791. In its modern manifestation Wahhabism advocates strict adherence to the *Qur'an* and to imitating the way of life that existed during Muhammad's lifetime. Wahabists like Osama bin Laden and his extremist Al-Qaeda movement represent the total rejection of any and all values associated with Westernization.

On the other end of the spectrum, Turkey, where over 90 percent of the population remains Muslim, exists as a modern secular nation. When Ataturk created the current state of Turkey after the World War I, he intentionally broke with many past Muslim practices. Unlike the conservative wing of Islam, for modernist Muslims, it is not only impossible to return to the glory days of old, it is undesirable as well. If Muslims want a front-row seat into the future of world politics, they must accept and adapt to the positive changes that have occurred during the past several centuries. The alternative scenario is bleak: The Islamic world will continue to spin forever in the stagnant backwaters of nostalgia. For millions of liberal Muslims, modernity is here to stay. It cannot be abolished either through wishful thinking or violence. The only question is how to adapt without losing the best ideals from the past.

CONCLUSION

This chapter began with an overview of the common themes that permeate the family of Middle Eastern monotheistic religions. All four (Zoroastrianism, Judaism, Christianity, and Islam) possess their special interpretation of the historical events through which God (variously called Ahura Mazda, Yahweh, the Lord, or Allah) acted and the prophets who revealed God's purposes to humankind. All of them include a linear view of history that has its beginning in God's creation of the universe and that will end on a final Day of Judgment when God will determine everyone's eternal destiny based on earthly accomplishments.

They all have different written Scriptures and sacred stories through which they interpret God's goals and purposes for the human family. Each seeks to restore humankind back to God through its own spiritual pathway. Judaism, Christianity, and Islam look to Abraham as the founder of their Faiths even though all three spin off in different directions in identifying important persons, places, and experiences that give them their unique identities. While Zoroastrianism does not tie directly to the three Abrahamic religions, nonetheless all four of them share the perception that the universe is a battlefield between the forces of good and evil. All believe that in the end God (good) will triumph over the Devil (evil).

CHAPTER 5

Worldview Comparisons: Search for Common Ground

Both challenges and possibilities exist for finding common ground between the Asian and Middle Eastern religions. If the core ideas about the Ultimate are similar across the boundaries of the religions, then similarities in other areas can also be expected. To the extent that the main ideas about Ultimate Reality differ, wide variations in other perceptions will exist as well.

CHALLENGES TO FINDING COMMON GROUND

At first glance, it appears that more initial agreement on the nature of Ultimate Reality exists among the Middle Eastern religions than among those traditions that emerged in Asia. However, the Middle Eastern monotheistic traditions tend toward greater exclusivism than the Asia pantheistic or atheistic spiritualities. In addition, it is clear that very little direct worldview overlap between the two families of religion exists. At the same time, there are significant areas of convergence that permit constructive dialogue. Thus, the quest to find the common ground that would enable the creation of a genuine meeting of the minds on core worldview ideas between the seven religions of Hinduism, Hinayana and Mahayana Buddhism, Jainism, Zoroastrianism, Judaism, Christianity, and Islam is a challenge of the highest order.

WORLDVIEW DISSIMILARITIES

Asian Religions

Within the South Asian traditions, the pantheism of Hinduism and the atheism of both Hinayana Buddhism and Jainism are incompatible perspectives on the nature of Ultimate Reality. Only Hinduism posits the existence of God, or Brahman. The universe is the body of Brahman. Every object or person in the universe possesses a soul called the atman that is a part of Brahman. The original Hinayana form of Buddhism rejects the existence of both Brahman and atman. For the Buddha, Ultimate Reality is emptiness or a vibrant void of nothingness. There is no God; there is no soul. The self is only a transitory bundle of dissipating energy called the skanda.

At the level of cognitive understanding, that is, the way in which humans use reason and logic to construct concepts for rational discourse, these ideas are contradictory. Ultimate Reality cannot exist as Brahman and emptiness at the same time. Humans and physical objects either have some kind of permanent soul that persists in some form after enlightenment or they do not, by whatever name it is called. Jainism falls somewhere between these two ends of the conceptual continuum. It accepts the existence of a permanent soul called the jiva but rejects the notion that there exists an Ultimate Reality or God of which it is a part. Each jiva is eternal, without beginning or end, and is separate from all other jivas. Like the original form of Buddhism, Jainism's disbelief in the existence of God qualifies it as a form of atheism. Thus, at the level of defining the nature of Ultimate Reality, the dissimilarities that exist between the South Asian religions pose a significant challenge to the task of finding common conceptual ground.

Middle Eastern Religions

At the level of Ultimate Reality, the Middle Eastern religions begin with a monotheistic assumption, which might lead to the conclusion that they share more common ground than do the South Asian religions of pantheistic Hinduism and of atheistic Buddhism and Jainism. In fact, this is so—initially. In addition, all Middle Eastern monotheisms share the supposition that God communicates to an estranged humanity through God's chosen prophets who convey God's revelations. Each of the four religions possesses a sacred history that appears in its sacred scripture. Each of the scriptures contains the core worldview convictions and moral mandates by which the four monotheistic religions organize their communities.

While numerous examples of constructive interaction between monotheists exist, much of the hostility that is present in the world flows from the dissimilar interpretations related to diverse revelations, prophets, and sacred scriptures. At the level of understanding of God's specific purposes, the

Middle Eastern religions part company despite their shared monotheistic beginning, as the following three areas of disagreement illustrate.

Exclusivism and Progressive Revelation

First, the dissimilarities that exist between the Middle Eastern religions derive from an exclusivist approach to Truth based on revelation. All of them believe that the God who created the universe has revealed exclusively to them the true road of restoration. By definition, their core convictions block out the possibility of envisioning in broader terms that God might have created multiple and equally legitimate spiritual pathways that lead to God. Each of the Middle Eastern traditions claims the priority of its interpretations.

Zoroastrian monotheism builds on the image that the entire universe is embroiled in a battle between Spenta and Angra Mainyu, the forces of good and evil, which plays out in the moral conscience of each individual. On the Day of Judgment, each soul's eternal destiny will be determined according to the balance of good thoughts, words, and deeds. If all four of the Middle Eastern religions believe anything about Ultimate Reality at all, it is that the Creator God is inherently just. If perfect justice cannot be achieved in this life, then it will be in the afterlife to come. God will make it so.

Despite this shared belief, all the Middle Eastern religions, especially in the Abrahamic tradition, possess an exclusivist view of the criteria God will use to determine each person's ultimate fate. Judaism, Christianity, and Islam anchor their exclusivist claims in the doctrine of progressive revelation and employ it to assert their superiority over the others. Judaism started with Yahweh's call to Abraham to build a great nation that would serve as a beacon of righteousness in the midst of human sinfulness and disobedience. Yahweh's will became known through progressive revelations that appear in the Hebrew Scripture, especially the *Torah*.

Christianity began as a Jewish sect that centered on Jesus and that radically reinterpreted the Hebrew Scripture. Early Jewish converts to Christianity saw their new faith as the religious end point in a series of progressive revelations that started with Abraham, continued through Moses and the prophets, and culminated in Christ the Redeemer. Islam extended the Abrahamic time line to Muhammad and viewed both the Jewish and Christian sacred books as spiritual stepping stones to Allah's final revelation as conveyed in the *Qur'an*, which contains numerous references to both *Old* and *New Testament* prophets, including Jesus.

Thus, the followers of each of the Abrahamic Faiths perceive that their revelations embody the perfect will of God and that later revelations are enhancements over earlier ones. Jews perceive that no need exists for further revelations beyond those that Yahweh gave to successive prophets during the long history of ancient Israel. Christianity views the *Old Testament* revelations as preparation for the life and mission of Christ as recorded in the *New Testament*, which improves on the *Old Testament*. For Muslims, the revelations of the *Qur'an* are superior to those that appear in both the *Old* and *New Testaments*.

Relative Superiority

Second, an alternative to exclusivism that is reinforced by the doctrine of progressive revelation is belief in the relative superiority of one set of revelations over others. This eliminates the claim that any particular religion possesses Truth in full measure. This alternative views the process by which God reveals truths as incomplete and ongoing. Later revelations do not replace previous ones, and earlier ones do not become obsolete. All revelations, including earlier ones, contain truths about God, even though the ones that appear later in chronological sequence rank higher than the others. In this case, the issue is not the finality of Truth only the relative superiority of it.

While this alternative appears to have advantages over exclusivism because it makes room for the revelations of all religions, in the final analysis it does not. The same mindset associated with any religion's claim that it possesses a greater measure God's Truth reappears in a different form. For one who favors the doctrine of relative superiority over exclusivism, the thought process goes something like this: "Just as God has sent updated revelations in the past, God will continue to do so in the future. God will commission new prophets with more profound revelations than those that currently exist. In the meantime, 'ours' is 'the best.'" When the followers of any single religion claim the spiritual high ground over the devotees of other religions, they perpetuate the same hierarchical mentality that pervades the exclusivist position. Such a stance radiates a subtle condescension, although possibly unintended, that can easily inhibit constructive interreligious cooperation.

Anonymous Believers

Third, another way whereby the believers of the Middle Eastern traditions may view the adherents of other faiths is through the notion of the "anonymous believer." In a very real sense, this idea represents a linguistic outer limit, so to speak, beyond which the committed followers of any particular religion would need to develop a new and more universal theological language for expressing not only their basic beliefs but also those of others. The image of the anonymous believer is a theological "bottom line" for those who genuinely desire to engage in interfaith dialogue but do so from the perspective of their own faith language. This concept represents a compromise position between commitment and openness. At the same time, this good intention may mask a patronizing attitude.

The following example illustrates this point. A renowned Catholic theologian[1] defines the followers of other faiths as anonymous Christians who can experience salvation through their own non-Christian doctrines because their beliefs incorporate the divine mystery that is perfectly revealed in Christ. Christ is the ultimate spiritual standard for understanding the religious experiences of non-Christians. In other words, the language of Christianity is used to interpret the deep spiritualities of other faiths. In the final analysis, it is doubtful that this approach will do little more than perpetuate paternalism.

What is to keep Mahayanists from contending that devout Christians are really hidden followers of Buddha or that Christ is merely one of many bodhisattvas? What is to prevent Hindus from asserting that Muhammad is actually an anonymous avatar of Vishnu or that the revelations that appear in the *Qur'an* are already hidden in the sacred books of the Vedas or Upanishads? However spoken or written, the claim that the divine mysteries of one's own faith are anonymously veiled in the deepest spiritual insights the other world religions is in the final analysis a not-so-subtle form of condescension. Non-believers will see through it right away.

Despite a shared monotheistic starting point, all three types of hierarchical thinking based on the doctrine of progressive revelation represent challenges to the search for common ground. Blatant exclusivism occupies one end of the continuum and takes the form of "Only we possess God's Truth." Subtle paternalism exists at the other end: "The followers of other religions are really anonymous believers of our religion." The third type stands somewhere in the middle of these two. It is neither overtly exclusivist nor subtly paternalistic. Instead it is expressed as: "No religion is perfect, but until God reveals a higher truth, ours is the best."

LIFE AFTER DEATH: ASIAN AND MIDDLE EASTERN RELIGIONS

On the issue of life after death, the dissimilarities between these two families of religion could not be greater. The South Asian spiritualities can be described as "many chances" religions, whereas the Middle Eastern traditions are "one chance only" religions.

A person whose religious beliefs include reincarnation perceives that the inner self, whether defined as atman, skanda, or jiva, can transmigrate through an indefinite number of rebirths on the journey toward spiritual liberation. Hinduism, Buddhism, and Jainism are "many times around" religions. Like the main character in the movie *Groundhog Day*, one keeps recycling until one "gets it right." Prior to the moment of enlightenment, the law of karma determines the physical forms of every person's transmigration cycle. After enlightenment, rebirth stops.

For a believer who stands in the Middle Eastern traditions, multiple opportunities over more than one lifetime do not exist. Each person has only one lifetime to do what is necessary to go to heaven or paradise after death and to avoid going to hell. All four of the Middle Eastern religions of Zoroastrianism, Judaism, Christianity, and Islam presume the existence of a human soul that exists in some form beyond the grave. Through their separate sacred texts and stories, each tradition delineates the prerequisite beliefs and practices that God uses to judge every person's earthly accomplishments, which in turn determine his or her destiny after death.

Thus, for the Middle Eastern religions, there is only one *Groundhog Day*. Each person has only "one time around" to get it right. For the South Asian religions, there is reassurance that if one does not achieve enlightenment in this lifetime then one can try again in the next, and in the next, and in the next, and so on. For Middle Eastern religions, there is no such spiritual comfort zone. It is either now or never.

In sum, while the South Asian and Middle Eastern families of religion share the general viewpoint that some kind of spiritual destiny awaits everyone after death, they do not occupy common ground in their specific visions of what this involves or in their understanding of the beliefs and behaviors that determine the outcome.

MYSTICISM AS AN ALTERNATIVE ROUTE TO FINDING COMMON GROUND

Given the significant differences that exist between and among the worldviews of the Asian and Middle Eastern families of religion, the temptation exists to abandon the quest altogether or to search for some nonconceptual alternative such as mysticism, which emphasizes the direct experience of the divine rather than rationality. This path would appear to provide an attractive alternative, but in reality it does not. Sooner or later, the mystics of different faiths must communicate what is happening "inside" the self, that is, the head, heart, or soul, during their moments of intense ecstasy. When they do, they use multiple and very dissimilar images.[2]

For example, the followers of the South Asian family of religions describe their mystical encounters in impersonal terms. For Hindus, the atman melds into the impersonal Brahman. When Theravada Buddhists encounter the vibrant void of emptiness, their bundle of karmic energy disappears. Zen Buddhists discover their internal Buddha nature "in a flash" and use nonsensical rational puzzles called *koans* to penetrate beyond ordinary rationality to the deepest spiritual levels of being. The mystics of the Abrahamic traditions understand that their nondisappearing individual souls commune with a personal God in a loving and blissful embrace that transcends external commandments and the limitations of finite existence.

While it is always a possibility that the inner ecstasies that mystics experience across the boundaries of their diverse spiritualities may be identical, their verbal descriptions of them are not. Is the Ultimate Reality that is encountered in the mystical moment personal, impersonal, or nothingness? No single answer to this question exists. As a result, trying to discover worldview common ground through mysticism presents as many challenges as searching for it through rational inquiry.

CONCLUSION ON CHALLENGES FOR FINDING COMMON GROUND

Despite their dissimilarities, both the Asian and Middle Eastern spiritual traditions share a common starting point. They all incorporate images of Ultimate Reality, ideas about the origins and destiny of the universe, and convictions about the self's existence after death. In other words, all of the seven religions are united in their quest for the Truth. However, in reality the common ground is hard to find because basic contradictions exist at the most fundamental conceptual levels: (1) God and the universe are one; (2) God and the universe are separate; and (3) there is no God.

In the final analysis, anyone who searches for a unified common ground among the world's religions will sooner or later encounter the differences in how they define Truth as well as how they relate to it. Simply stated, *a common conceptual foundation that could lead to the development of an inclusive worldview among the Asian and Middle Eastern religions of the emerging global village does not yet exist.* At this stage of the human evolution, the 76 percent of the world's population that identifies with Hinduism, Buddhism, Jainism, Zoroastrianism, Judaism, Christianity, and Islam adhere to views of Ultimate Reality that are theologically and philosophically incompatible.

Despite these differences, a word of caution is in order. Concluding that the followers of the world's diverse religions will never arrive at a common worldview consensus on fundamental issues regarding the nature of Truth should be avoided. No doubt, building such a convergence is a slow and arduous process. Thus, it should be accepted that at this point in human evolution that only a very low probability exists regarding the likelihood that an inclusive worldview will emerge among the religions of the world. At the same time, it should also be recognized that this remains a distinct possibility in the far distant future, although it may not happen for centuries.

POSSIBILITIES FOR FINDING COMMON GROUND

Several possibilities exist for finding common ground. The quest starts with an attitude of humility that lessens the tendency to self-righteous arrogance. The second extends from the first and involves openness to a genuine dialogue of differences without covertly viewing such occasions as merely opportunities to proselytize others. The third, and possibly most difficult of all, is adopting the view that the diverse religions of the world are spiritually equal.

For many steadfast followers of any religion, it is an undertaking of the highest order even to consider the possibility of spiritual equality among the world's diverse religions. Engaging in open and honest interfaith conversation requires living with the contradictory emotions of (1) powerful commitment to one's view of truth, and (2) openness to the truths of others. If the followers of the world's diverse religions grow in their acceptance of each other as spiritual equals, then an increase in both tolerance and openness to dialogue is sure to follow. How might this happen?

ASIAN RELIGIONS—SOURCES OF TOLERANCE

The Nature of Truth

It is one of the ironies of the large and diverse family of Asian spiritual traditions that they share worldview possibilities for expressing remarkable interfaith tolerance. This does not mean that ongoing competition among them to preserve and promote their traditions does not exist. It does. At the same time, they share the conviction that there are multiple paths to the same spiritual goal: to end reincarnation. In other words, the South Asian religions have developed a spiritual temperament that is capable of sustaining the tension between nurturing commitments within a tradition, while instilling tolerance toward others who hold convictions within other traditions.

This does not mean that all of the adherents of the South Asian religions are equally tolerant of the beliefs of others. It would be an error to make such a statement because all religions include exclusivists who perceive that their beliefs alone embody the Truth. Despite this tendency among the adherents of all religions, the South Asian spiritualities show a great capacity for interreligious tolerance and appreciation of pluralism. Two factors contribute to this tendency. The first consists of respect for multiple views of truth, and the second involves detachment from desire. Both emerged in Hinduism and were incorporated into Buddhism and Jainism.

The first stems from the Hindu adage that Truth is one and there are many paths to it. The millions of Hindu deities or avatars point in one direction: toward Brahman or Truth. Hinduism provides the faithful with multiple paths for expressing their spirituality. As a result, Hinduism fosters respect for the manifold practices that lead to Brahman, the Ultimate Reality that is larger than smaller realities embraced by individual worshippers.

Like Hinduism, Jainism also contributes directly to nurturing tolerance and appreciation of difference. It does so through the belief that the Truth of human existence is greater than any single person's experience of it. Jains express this belief through the parable of the elephant and the blind persons. All "touch" only a part of the elephant. Thus, at the practical level, both Hinduism and Jainism encourage tolerance even though at the conceptual level they are opposites. Jains do not believe in God, only in the eternal existence of the soul or jiva. Hindus believe in God or Brahman who encompasses the manifold ways in which believers express their devotion. For Hindus, tolerance stems from the top down. For Jains, it flows from the bottom up. Either way, the result is the same. Each religion nurtures an attitude of humility and openness and a viewpoint that accepts others as spiritual equals in the pursuit of Truth.

Detachment from Desire

Even though Hinduism is pantheistic and Jainism and Buddhism are atheistic, all three occupy common ground in their belief that humankind's spiritual destiny is release from karma-driven reincarnation. Whether they call it moksha, nirvana, or other, when that moment of overwhelming mystical exhilaration erupts at the end of a spiritual journey, the essential self is finally liberated from the dreaded cycle of rebirth. Where they disagree is on how to get there.

Both Buddhism and Jainism retained the original Hindu belief that detachment from desire is a precondition for enlightenment. In Jainism, detachment from even the most basic need for food and water is necessary for burning off bad karma or ajiva so that the soul or jiva can float upward to the spiritual peak of the universe. Among the three Asian spiritualities, the Buddhist view of liberation through detachment from desire is the most esoteric. Both Hindus and Jains perceive that they have a soul that either melds into Brahman or goes to *loka*. In other words, at least "something" (atman or jiva) goes "somewhere" (Brahman or loka). In the Theravada view of liberation, it is "nothing" that goes "nowhere." How is this possible?

Buddha's Four Noble Truths and Eightfold Path are practical guidelines that lead to enlightenment. He based the First Noble Truth that life is suffering on his early adulthood observations of disease, old age, and death or, as they are called, the three sights. According the Second Noble Truth, suffering is caused by attachment to desire. His Third Noble Truth states that there is a way to end suffering. His Fourth Noble Truth, which is also the Eightfold Path, exists to put an end to suffering by providing the spiritual discipline necessary for learning how to detach from all desires (including the craving for Truth). In Theravada Buddhism, all metaphysical doctrines have equal *non*-value because none of them leads to liberation. For Theravadists, the central purpose in life is getting on with the business of getting rid of being reborn. This can be achieved only through meditation and the experience of nirvana, which cannot occur without prior detachment from all worldly desires.

It is counterintuitive that one of the ways in which Buddhism promotes tolerance is by neutralizing, so to speak, all metaphysical views as distractions. All have equal value by virtue of being meaningless in regard to the central task of getting to enlightenment. Hinduism and Jainism take the opposite point of view. It is through the discovery of truth, or one of the many views of it, that an individual learns why detachment from desire is essential. It contributes either to the atman's transmigration to Brahman, or to the jiva's journey to loka.

However the South Asian religions interpret the doctrine of detachment from desire, in practical terms their diverse viewpoints promote tolerance by orienting believers away from imposing their views on others. In order to achieve the shared goal of enlightenment, the devout followers of all three religions, Hinduism, Buddhism, and Jainism, must focus on their own inner spiritual transformations and not on ways to convert others through external proselytizing or coercion. In this sense, they share common ground that contributes to increasing interreligious tolerance.

MIDDLE EASTERN RELIGIONS—SOURCES OF TOLERANCE

The answer to the question of whether the Middle Eastern religions contribute to increasing interreligious tolerance is both yes and no. The yes side of the answer begins with the recognition that all four Middle Eastern traditions share a common belief in monotheism. They agree on many assumptions about the nature of Ultimate Reality. All of them believe that there exists only one God who brought the universe into being. They all presume that God created humanity in perfect harmony with God but that humans separated themselves from God by choice. This separation derives from the fact that humans decided to live according to their own will rather than God's. As a result, humanity remains alienated from the Creator.

The spiritual goal of all the four Middle Eastern religions is to restore humanity back to God in both earthly life before death as well as eternal life after death. That is to say, Zoroastrianism, Judaism, Christianity, and Islam all agree that the primary purpose of life is to go to heaven or paradise after death and to create heaven or paradise on earth to the extent that this is possible given humanity's inherent selfishness and capacity for making wrong or evil choices rather than good ones. In theological terms, the issue is human sin and how to overcome it. No parallel concept exists in the South Asian religions where the basic obstruction along the road to liberation is ignorance and not sin.

Radical Monotheism and Spiritual Equality

Despite their common starting point, the exclusivism of the Middle Eastern religions keeps them from cultivating a spirit of greater openness and tolerance toward each other's differences. The erosion of common ground occurs when their followers reduce the monotheistic image to their worldviews.

There is an alternative. As a shared conviction among all four of the Middle Eastern religions, monotheism can be understood readily as more encompassing than any particular understanding of it. Just as the goal of all the Asian religions is liberation from reincarnation, monotheism itself needs to be liberated from the exclusivist interpretations that each of the Middle Eastern religions gives it.

Conceptually this is a relatively easy shift to make when the idea of monotheism is expanded beyond the boundaries that each Middle Eastern religion has erected around it. The starting point for broadening the meaning of the word monotheism is to add the adjective "radical" in front of it.[3] Radical monotheism means that the total reality of God transcends any religion's specific revelations from God. None of the Middle Eastern religions can know the whole or final truth about God. Radical monotheism frees the Middle Eastern religions from having to defend exclusivist views based on the doctrine of progressive revelation, the belief in the relative superiority of one religion over the other, or the perception that the devotees of other faiths are really anonymous believers of one's own. Most important of all, this expanded definition of monotheism throws open the door of interfaith dialogue because it leads to a new way of thinking about God's multireligion revelations as collective insights. Each can learn from the others.

Each Middle Eastern religion's sacred story and scripture reveal something about God's purposes in part but not in full. The real issue is not to use monotheism in the narrow sense so that it results in an impasse over why the revelations of one religion rank above all the rest. Rather, employing monotheism in this broader sense promotes the search for how the combined revelations of all the Middle Eastern religions result in a deeper understanding of God's will for the whole of humankind.

In theological terms, radical monotheism incorporates the concepts of transcendence and immanence. God is both above and beyond creation, that is, different from the creation or transcendent. At the same time, God is in creation, that is, immanent. In many times and places, God has communicated divine revelations to humankind through chosen mediators. Ongoing revelation is one way in which the will of God becomes increasingly known. In short, the revised view of radical monotheism fosters the view that all the religions of the Middle East can be seen as spiritual partners who are equal in revealing truths about God and whose combined revelations provide a more comprehensive understanding of God's purpose for life than the specific revelations of any single one of them.

From Progressive to Continuous Revelation

The doctrine of progressive revelation can also be redefined. This requires substituting the word "continuous" for "progressive." The idea of continuous revelation preserves many of the strengths of progressive revelation and also goes beyond them by stimulating greater openness to interfaith dialogue.

Within the Middle Eastern religions, progressive revelation has been understood historically as a stepladder to perfection. According to this tradition, as revelations appear in chronological sequence, each successive one improves on those that preceded it. Continuous revelation preserves the time sequence component but disassociates it from the notion that later revelations are necessarily superior to earlier ones. Continuous revelation combines chronology and equality in the same way that all the pearls in a necklace are lined up next to each other and contribute equally to its beauty.

The concept of continuous revelation opens the door to moving beyond exclusivism in two important ways. First, it implies that God's revelations are ongoing and second that no single past revelation contains God's final or superior revelation. If God continues to reveal truths to humankind, then we can expect that at some point in the future God will call forth other voices to deliver additional revelations.

This does not mean that the revelations of the past are necessarily obsolete. It means only that new revelations will be added to the total pool of past revelations. From the perspective of the Middle Eastern religions, the combined insights of past revelations serve as a repository of wisdom for guiding decisions in the present. The only change that occurs when the word continuous is substituted for progressive is that no single religion can claim that its revelations alone embody God's perfect will for humankind. From a theological perspective, this change allows "God to be God" in the sense that no religion arbitrarily imposes limitations on God's capacity to reveal new truths when and where God pleases. No religion possesses or uses God exclusively for its own purposes. Each religion's truths are part of a larger repository that includes the revealed truths of multiple religions through which all of humanity stand to benefit.

Thus, despite the exclusivist positions that the Middle Eastern religions espouse with regard to the nature of divine revelation, in combination they offer a rich storehouse of spiritual insights. When they interpret monotheism narrowly to promote their own views over those of others, they diminish the possibility of finding creative common ground. They perpetuate exclusivist claims and reinforce the drift toward distrust and hostility.

By embracing the concept of radical monotheism they open the door to more constructive interaction. Accepting that God's transcendence is greater than the specific revelations of any one of them can lead to the search to discover the authentic revelations that God has given to each one of them.

Each religion can preserve its special identity without claiming that it alone possesses the Ultimate Truth. In addition, the combination of continuous revelation and radical monotheism is oriented to the future as well as the past because it assumes that God's work is not done. God is still revealing truths to humankind in the midst of social change.

Another way of saying this is that the revealed truths of the past serve as stepping-stones on the path toward future revelations. The theological combination of radical monotheism and continuous revelation promotes viewing all of the Middle Eastern religions as equals in revealing spiritual truths. Through a positive acceptance of one another as faith partners who stand on the same broad monotheistic common ground, the followers of all the Middle Eastern traditions can collectively search their sacred stories and scriptures for the best insights that will unite them in building a future filled with greater peace and justice.

CONCLUSIONS ON POSSIBILITIES FOR FINDING COMMON GROUND

There exist multiple pathways for finding common ground among the religions of the world. Of greatest importance is the search for sources of tolerance. The Asian religions would appear to have the edge over those of Middle Eastern origin despite their pantheistic and atheistic assumptions. Both Hinduism and Jainism explicitly espouse multiple perceptions of truth as well as avenues to it. Buddhism contributes to tolerance, especially the Theravada branch, by rejecting altogether that the philosophical search for truth is helpful for achieving enlightenment.

While the religions of the Middle East stand on the common ground of monotheism, they quickly divide over their specific interpretations of God's revelations as recorded in their sacred stories and scriptures. The doctrines of progressive revelation, relative superiority, or anonymous believers contribute significantly to their interfaith disagreements. Emphasizing God's transcendence and elevating monotheism beyond the boundaries of exclusivist claims opens the door to greater tolerance. In addition, shifting from progressive to continuous revelation stimulates the search for the multiple and overlapping spiritual insights that God has revealed to all of them in various times and places. Increasing the possibilities for tolerance among the Middle Eastern religions enhances the chances of finding more common ground among all the world's religions.

SUMMARY OF WORLDVIEW COMPARISONS AMONG THE WORLD'S RELIGIONS

It is clear that no unifying conceptual framework currently exists either within or between the South Asian and Middle Eastern religions. At the same time, it is remarkable how much potential there is for moving in this direction, although on the surface this may not be readily visible. At a minimum, the world's religions contain theological and philosophical concepts that allow for creative adaptation in the search to find common ground that will stimulate movement toward constructive pluralism and away from destructive exclusivism. The potential exists not only within the two families of religion but also between them.

The search for universal common ground starts with the assumption that for all faiths Truth is greater than any one community's understanding of it. It is easier to draw this conclusion from the religions of South Asia than from those of the Middle East, although the shared monotheism of the latter possesses high potential for imaginative adaptation. While it appears that the atheism of Jainism and the monotheism of the Middle East religions are at opposite ends of the theological spectrum, far more convergence exists than first meets the eye.

Starting with the idea that God does not exist, Jainism ends with the belief that there are multiple views of truth, as the familiar elephant parable illustrates. Starting with the idea that God does exist and employing the broad concept of radical monotheism, the Middle Eastern religions can conclude that God has provided multiple revelations because divine transcendence surpasses any religion's capacity to contain all of Truth. Thus, while it might seem counterintuitive, both Jainism and Middle Eastern radical monotheism lead to the same conclusion that truth is many even though they start at the opposite ends of the worldview spectrum.

The parallel between Western radical monotheism and Hindu pantheism is equally striking although once again the connection between the two is not immediately self-evident. Hinduism begins with the affirmation that Truth is one and there are many paths to it. This allows for widespread diversity among Hindus regarding their choice of worship rituals and deity images. Radical monotheism presupposes that the multiple revelations of the Middle Eastern religions in combination convey insights into the nature of God to a far greater extent than those of any single tradition. When we shift the theological ground from exclusivist monotheism to radical monotheism, it is but a small step to recognize that God has provided multiple revelations. In other words, like Hinduism the Middle Eastern religions in total provide multiple paths to God.

Thus, Jainism, Hinduism, and the Middle Eastern religions viewed through the theological lens of radical monotheism intersect on one of the most important matters related to all religions, that is, search for Ultimate Reality. As we have seen, they all provide many constructive avenues of inquiry into the nature of Truth. At the same time, this does not mean that their differences are suddenly dissolved into some overarching spiritual gestalt. Many disparities, especially at the conceptual level, continue to separate them from one another.

However, in the final analysis, trying to develop the perfect theological or philosophical synthesis that will overcome all the differences that exist among the worldviews of the world religions is not the most important issue. If devotees emphasize only their differences and settle in at the level of their exclusivist claims to Truth, then at best only an uneasy accommodation based on the clash of civilizations is possible. At worst, the scourge of terrorism that has grown steadily over the past two decades will continue and possibly spread. What is at stake is whether in combination the religions of the world will be able to contribute to greater peace and justice in the global village rather than hatred and hostility.

At the end, one final issue needs to be addressed. As described earlier, the South Asian religions are either pantheistic or atheistic. The Middle Eastern religions are monotheistic. Sooner or later, the participants of even the most open and constructive interfaith dialogue will encounter these "bottom line" differences where God is believed to exist or not exist and where the universe is understood as either God's body or separate from God altogether.

It would appear that these different fundamental assumptions about the nature of God and the universe permanently block any effort to reconcile them. Can the differences that divide the world religions into conceptually irreconcilable worldviews be overcome? The only way to answer this question is to assume that Ultimate Reality, by whatever name it is called, can incorporate attributes that humans perceive as opposites. In the final analysis, it is an article of faith to believe that an existing Ultimate Reality can be personal, impersonal, and nonexistent, all at the same time. While it can be assumed that Truth exists, it would appear that humans can experience it only as many and seemingly contrary truths. In this sense, the human mind is permanently blocked in its ability to grasp, as the great German philosopher Immanuel Kant has called it, the "thing in itself."[4] Another way of saying this is that humans cannot view existence through the eyes, metaphorically speaking, of Ultimate Reality itself. If the inconsistencies that exist in human reason can be integrated into a noncontradictory and coherent concept of Ultimate Reality, then only Ultimate Reality knows how to do it.

In the final analysis, on this side of reality, human existence is comprised of varied communities and worldviews. Diversity is a fact of human life as we currently experience it. Clearly, learning to live with religious pluralism in the emerging global village of the twenty-first century is one of humanity's greatest challenges.

SECTION III

World Religions—Ethics

CHAPTER 6

Asian Religions

HINDUISM

The ethics of Hinduism, as well as Buddhism and Jainism, extend from two of its basic worldview concepts, karma and reincarnation, which lead to a shared ethical ideal call *dharma* or duty. Simply stated, good dharma stops bad karma. The road to enlightenment goes through the proper performance of duty as each religion defines it.

The Hindu view of duty balances the tension between the twin needs of freedom of choice and social stability without which society would become anarchic. In order to progress up the ladder of enlightenment, Hinduism assumes that each person is free to make decisions that will lead to the accumulation of either good or bad karma. Once decisions are freely made, then the law of karma operates in a mechanical fashion by automatically adding up and balancing the good and the bad choices and outcomes, which in turn determine the nature of each person's rebirth. Belief in the capacity for choice, that is, free will, is a necessary assumption that supports the doctrine of karma.

At the same time, the need for social stability limits the range of choices that are available to each individual. The Hindu approach to insuring that society undergoes an orderly transition from one generation to the next is twofold. The first involves the caste system and the second the stages of life, which are discussed below.

The ancient Hindu Scripture called *The Laws of Manu* divides society into four main castes. The highest caste (*Brahmin*) is comprised of priests and religious leaders who have achieved the uppermost reincarnation level and provide spiritual guidance to others. The second caste includes the nobility-warriors (*Kshatriya*) whose mission is to govern and protect society. The third caste consists of merchants, farmers, and skilled workers (*Vaisya*) who apply their skills to the maintenance of life. Unskilled workers (*Shudra*) constitute the fourth and lowest caste. They exist to serve others.

This means that Hindu ethics begins by connecting the concept of duty to each person's social status at the time of birth. For example, chapter 4.80 of *The Laws of Manu* specifies that "Among the several occupations, the most commendable are: teaching the Veda for a Brahmin, protecting (the people) for Kshatriya, and trade for a vaishya."[1] A member of the Shudra caste always remains "the servant of his betters, gentle in his speech, free from pride, and who always seeks a refuge with Brahmins, attains (in his next life) a higher caste." (8.335)

Duty has both a positive and negative side. The proper performance of caste duty leads to the accumulation of good karma and guarantees a higher rebirth. Improper performance of duties results in rebirth at a lower level. Here are some examples. "A brahmin, or a kshatriya, living by a vaishya's mode of subsistence, shall carefully avoid agriculture, (which causes) injury to many beings and depends on others." (4.83) Or "By (selling) flesh, salt, and lac a brahmin at once becomes an outcaste; by selling milk he becomes (equal to) a shudra in three days." (4:92) Finally, "By willingly selling in this world other (forbidden) commodities, a brahmin assumes after seven nights the character of vaishya." (4.93)

Over the centuries, as Hinduism took root and expanded in India, this fourfold caste system further subdivided into multiple caste levels. As a result, modern India has become a tiered society governed by a system of complex caste regulations that foster social stability as well as promise upward spiritual mobility through reincarnation as a result of performing caste duties. The freedom that each person possesses relates to decisions about whether or not to follow his or her caste duties.

The second approach to insuring social stability consists of defining specific behaviors that are appropriate for the four stages of the life cycle. The integration of spiritual and ethical beliefs applies not only to the caste system but also to human development. *The Laws of Manu* specifies the duties that are associated with the four stages of life, which are: student, householder, forest-dweller, and ascetic or world renouncer.

Here are the relevant passages. A student "who has studied in due order the three Vedas, or two, or even one only, without breaking the (rules of) studentship, shall enter the order of the householders." (3.2) "In accordance with the precepts of the Veda and of the traditional texts, the householder is declared to be superior to all of them, because he supports the other three." (6.89) "When a householder sees his (skin) wrinkled, and (his hair) white, and the sons of his sons, then he may resort to the forest." (6.2) "Having thus passed the third part of his life in the forest, he may live as an ascetic during the fourth art of this existence, after abandoning all attachment to worldly objects." (6.33) Finally, "He who after passing from order to order, after offering sacrifices and subduing the senses, becomes, tired with (giving) alms and offerings of food, an ascetic, gains bliss after death." (6.34) "An ascetic . . . shakes off sin here below and reaches the highest Brahman." (6.85)

In addition to insuring social stability, the life cycle approach to the proper performance of duty provides the Hindu faithful with a way of making the transition from material to spiritual goals and of detaching from worldly desires, which is necessary for spiritual liberation. As the above quotations indicate, certain kinds of behavior are appropriate at the earlier stages of life while other kinds are relevant to the later ones. During the first stage, students prepare for their lifelong journey by studying the sacred scriptures and preparing for future vocations that are appropriate to their caste. As they make the transition to adulthood, they become householders by marrying and providing for their family's welfare. During this stage it is acceptable to accumulate ample material possessions because this is essential to health, security, and the enjoyment of life. Householders also participate regularly in the devotional practices of their caste and family background.

When the householder's child-rearing stage of life is over, the devout Hindu enters the forest dweller stage in order to concentrate more completely on attaining emotional detachment from earthly or material desires. After pursuing the goal of nonattachment, the dutiful adherent enters the final stage of renouncing all worldly desires. Living alone and without possessions, the renunciant turns to the life of meditation in the hope of arriving at that moment of ecstatic enlightenment when the atman melds mystically back into Brahman after journeying through countless rebirths, castes, and stages of life. Then upon death, reincarnation finally comes to an end.

Thus, the Hindu hierarchical arrangement of social roles based on caste and life cycle guarantees the orderly transition of society across generations. The Laws of Manu reinforces this hierarchy through the concepts of karma and reincarnation. Getting to enlightenment is not something one does privately apart from the performance of the duties that are associated with every aspect of life. In this way, the Hindu worldview and moral standards are fully integrated.

In addition to the duties associated with caste and life cycle stages, Hindu pantheism leads to a deep and general respect for all life, which is expressed in the doctrine of ahimsa or belief in noninjury. It is one of Hinduism's core religious beliefs that humans share a spiritual affinity with the entire universe, which is infused with the presence of Brahman. To show disrespect for life is to risk harming the atman that resides in all living creatures. In turn, the virtue of respect inspires other values as well, such as compassion, kindness, gentleness, and self-restraint, which comprise the core of Hindu character development. These are traits that it is desirable for every devout believer to have. They lead to empathy for suffering and the desire to alleviate it.

At the same time, performing caste duties may conflict with the principle of ahimsa. Nowhere is this more vividly depicted than in one of the most beloved Hindu Scriptures, the *Bhagavad-Gita*. The *Gita* is part of a larger epic writing called the *Mahabarata*, which describes the lengthy conflicts that erupt between two clans, the Pandavas and the Kauravas who battled each other for control of northern India. The story centers on the Pandava warrior Arjuna who is the most revered fighter of his era. The setting of the story is the field of battle where two armies face each other prior to the moment of engagement.

Arjuna instructs his charioteer Krishna to chauffeur him to the front of the enemy so that he can see the faces of his opponents. Although Arjuna does not yet know it, his chariot driver is really an avatar of Vishnu, who is one of Hinduism's three most important deities along with Brahman and Shiva. As Arjuna approaches his foes, he begins to recognize the faces of his relatives and friends. He is both horrified and distraught over the prospect that he will have to injure or maybe even kill his loved ones when the two clans join in battle.

He turns to his charioteer and says, "When I see all my kinsmen, Krishna, who have come here on this field of battle, life goes from my limbs and they sink ... a trembling overcomes my body, and my hair shudders in horror; ... I am no longer able to stand, because my mind is whirling and wandering."[2] Overwhelmed and despondent Arjuna declares, "I cannot therefore kill my own kinsmen, ... What happiness could we ever enjoy, if we killed our own kinsmen in battle?" (2.37)

It is precisely at this point that the *Gita* presses the moral conflict between duty and noninjury to the forefront. Arjuna is a member of the warrior caste that *The Laws of Manu* charges with protecting the people. In simple terms, Arjuna must wage war when called upon to do so because it is his duty. This conflicts with his moral obligation not to inflict injury but to show deep reverence for all life. The prospect of violating the norm of ahimsa, especially by killing relatives and loved ones sends him into a state of despair that immobilizes him.

In the depth of Arjuna's despondency, Krishna intervenes. "Whence this lifeless dejection, Arjuna, in this hour, the hour of trial? Strong men know not despair, Arjuna." (2:2) From this point forward, Krishna consoles the distraught Arjuna and lays down some of Hinduism's most fundamental worldview beliefs and their moral implications. "The Spirit that is in all beings is immortal in them all: the death of what cannot die, cease thou to sorrow. Think thou also of thy duty and do not waver. There is no greater good for a warrior than to fight in righteous war ... But to forgo this fight for righteousness is to forgo thy duty and honour: is to fall into transgression." (2:30, 31, 33) As a member of the kshatriya caste, Arjuna is duty-bound. "Therefore," says Krishna, "great warrior, carry on thy fight." (2:18)

Krishna continues by assuring Arjuna that the performance of his duty will not be in vain. "The soul that moves in the world of the senses and yet keeps the senses in harmony, free from attraction and aversion, finds rest in quietness.... This is the Eternal in man, O Arjuna. Reaching him all delusion is gone. Even in the last hour of his life upon earth, man can reach the Nirvana of Brahman—man can find peace in the peace of his God." (2:64, 72) From this point forward, Krishna helps Arjuna rekindle his courage by assuring him that should he or any of his beloved kin die in battle while fulfilling their caste obligations, they will receive their spiritual rewards.

The enduring value of the *Gita* lies in subtly weaving together worldview and morality. Through its understanding of the relationship of atman to Brahman, Hinduism nurtures the development of the virtuous character based on traits such as ahimsa or noninjury to life in all of its manifold forms. At the same time, *The Laws of Manu* defines the moral obligations that are attached to both caste and stages of life. As the *Bhagavad-Gita* demonstrates, the kshatriyas or warriors who must protect the population through military service may come face to face with a clash of values between caste duty and noninjury.

This is Arjuna's dilemma. When confronted with a moral conflict at the extremes of life and death, what should he do? As an avatar of Vishnu, Krishna provides the answer. Arjuna must do his duty because in doing so, even if he must kill his kinfolk, he will accumulate the good karma that will enable his inner atman to be reborn into a higher caste or to find its ultimate dwelling in Brahman.

Despite Arjuna's decision to carry on the fight as his caste duties demand of him, the clash of values that the *Gita* portrays so vividly need not result in giving priority to caste duties that might lead to taking life. Nowhere is this more fully demonstrated than in the life of Mahatma Gandhi, leader of the twentieth century political movement that resulted in India's independence in 1947. Gandhi's extraordinary leadership abilities sprang from the strength of his character that was nurtured in the spiritual and moral traditions of Hinduism. His life embodied the major beliefs that Hinduism holds together in creative tension.

He supported the caste system, worshipped Krishna and Rama, and was deeply dedicated to the belief in ahimsa, which he converted into an effective nonviolent political "truth force" that liberated India from British colonialism. His commitment to the principle of noninjury along with his admiration for Jesus cultivated his compassion for India's poorest masses, the untouchables. He remained a lifelong advocate of democracy, which dovetails with the Hindu conviction that there are many paths to the one Truth, including multiple viewpoints related to creating political consensus within a modern state.

More than anything else, Gandhi wanted the citizens of India to be in charge of their own political destiny, and he dedicated his life to the achievement of this goal. Gandhi joined together in his personality and character both Hindu spirituality and politics, that is, worldview and public morality.[3] In 1947, under Gandhi's guidance, a politically independent India adopted a legal Constitution that created a secular state and guaranteed the freedom of expression to all religious groups. Although most Indians are Hindus, the Constitution prohibits the establishment of a state religion. Gandhi's life and achievements demonstrate that for centuries Hinduism provided India with the religious and ethical legacy for both preserving the best from the past and adapting to changes in the modern world.

BUDDHISM—THERAVADA OR HINAYANA

Buddhism contains many of the same enduring features as Hinduism even though it started as a protest against the Brahmin-dominated caste system of ancient South Asia. Both Hinduism and Buddhism inculcate the norm of ahimsa as one of the dominant virtues in the development of the human character. Hinduism balances the norm of noninjury against the demands of social duty as this connects to both caste and life cycle stages. While both religions aim for the same goal of enlightenment, the focus of Buddhism is consistently more internal.

Buddhism disavows altogether belief in the importance of an external caste system as a social framework that is integral to achieving spiritual goals. It disconnects entirely the pursuit of nirvana from the performance of specific social roles. This does not mean that Buddhism lacks a demanding code of ethics. The opposite is true. The moral mandates of Buddhism are rigorous but for reasons that differ from those of Hinduism. For Buddhism, social status is irrelevant to the achievement of liberation from reincarnation. For Hinduism, it is inseparable from it.

In addition, the potential exists for every person to reach nirvana in this lifetime even though Buddha recognized that this would not happen. Persons differ in their inner capacities to submit to the discipline necessary for the journey to life's final destiny. It may take many lifetimes to get there. With each rebirth, every person has the opportunity to strengthen his or her inner spiritual capacity to undergo the demands of the Eightfold Path all the way to the final stage of meditation.

In a very real sense, in the original Theravada form of Buddhism, each rebirth becomes a testing ground for the individual to follow or not to follow the eight stages that Buddha laid out as the stepping-stones to nirvana. Each person is free to choose what to believe and how to behave. These choices determine the pace at which one travels through the reincarnation process, that is, the number of rebirths it takes before achieving enlightenment. Morality, viewed in terms of developing the virtuous character, is an integral part of the process of achieving spiritual goals. As in the case of Hinduism, Buddhist ethics flows directly from worldview.

At the same time, the differences in the ways in which Hinduism and Hinayana Buddhism view the connection between worldview and morality are substantial. Whereas Hinduism ties many of its ethical norms to the performance of caste social duties, the original form of Buddhism integrates internal moral development into the Eightfold Path. Both view morality as a form of preparation that leads to detachment and meditation, which are the dual preconditions for experiencing moksha (Hinduism) or nirvana (Buddhism).

Even though Hinayana Buddhism disconnects spiritual growth from both caste status and life stage development, it links morality to meditation through the Eightfold Path. The first two steps involve right belief and right aspiration. The interior steps of three through five require right speech, conduct, and livelihood. These three in particular aim at enhancing the believer's moral character without which it is not possible to advance to the final three steps of right effort, mindfulness, and meditation. In short, ethics precedes meditation and nirvana.

Buddhist monasteries enabled monks to pursue the rigorous discipline necessary to follow the Eightfold Path without being disrupted by outside influences. At the same time, Buddha recognized that not everyone is ready or able to leave the everyday world of the laity for the meticulous nirvana-oriented routines of the monastery. As a result, early Buddhism developed a dual-level moral system, one for the monks and the other for the laity. In order to accommodate the differences between the monks and the laity, Buddha required that the monks commit themselves to higher standards than the laity.

Within the monasteries, Buddha created rules that molded the monks' behavior. These are called the Ten Precepts, which build on steps three through five of the Eightfold Path. Buddha required that the monks adhere to all Ten Precepts, whereas he expected that the laity would follow only the first Five. Here is the list of the Ten Precepts:

1. Do not destroy life (ahimsa).
2. Do not steal.
3. Do not engage in sexual misconduct.
4. Do not lie.
5. Do not drink alcoholic beverages.
6. Do not eat after midday.
7. Do not take part in amusements such as dancing, singing, and the theater.
8. Do not wear ornaments, use perfume, or dress extravagantly.
9. Do not sleep on comfortable beds.
10. Do not accept money.[4]

Precepts 1 through 5 are the most general, which means that they are more achievable by the largest population of laity. Precepts 6 through 10 involve specific moral mandates, including proscriptions against the enjoyment of many worldly pleasures.

This list of Ten Precepts derives directly from the first two of Buddha's Four Noble Truths: All life is suffering; and, suffering is caused by attachment to desire. Buddha's purpose in developing the Ten Precepts was to provide the monks and laity with a "how to" guide that would lead to ending the cycle of suffering caused by death and rebirth. Buddha recognized that on the ladder of rebirth, not everyone stands on the same wrung. As a result of previous reincarnations, some of the devout are better prepared spiritually than others to undergo the rigors of all Ten Precepts. Those who are not, the laity in particular, must follow the first Five in order to transmigrate to a higher level that the monks already occupy.

As Buddhism grew, the Ten Precepts expanded into 227 rules that regulated every aspect of the monks' monastic lives from sunrise to sunset. Twice each year they would recite all 227 rules to remind themselves that walking the spiritual road to liberation is no easy task. It requires extraordinary discipline and dedication. Thus, what began as Four Noble Truths and the Eightfold Path evolved into the Ten Precepts and 227 rules that provided Hinayana Buddhists with a comprehensive program for achieving enlightenment. In the process, Hinayana Buddhism also created a spiritual pathway that leads to the transformation of character. It provides Buddha's followers with a way of being in the world.

BUDDHISM—MAHAYANA

In Mahayana Buddhism, extinction is not the only option. One may choose to be reborn as a bodhisattva, a savior figure, in order to guide others successfully across the raging river of life. After everyone finally arrives safely on the shore of nirvana and all suffering ceases, then the bodhisattva will finally enter the realm of blissful emptiness. In other words, anyone who chooses to become a bodhisattva postpones his or her spiritual reward until all other past, present, or future persons achieve theirs. The bodhisattva willingly reincarnates into the world of suffering in order to show others how to end it.

The bodhisattva ideal of self-sacrifice is based on a morality of compassion that flows directly from the Four Noble Truths. The Mahayanist image of the bodhisattva is an extension of Buddha's original perception that all life is suffering. In Mahayana Buddhism, the bodhisattva ideal is disconnected from monasticism. The bodhisattva does not seek a sanctuary by withdrawing from the outside world, but through compassion for world's suffering re-enters into the mainstream of daily life to help others discover a way to end it. The Mahayanist ethic of compassion is summarized in the bodhisattva vow that conveys the depth of commitment of all those who would place this heavy load upon their shoulders.

> I take upon myself the burden of all suffering; I am resolved to do so;
> I will endure it. . . . At all costs I must bear the burdens of all beings . . .
> I have made the vow to save all beings. All beings I must set free. The
> whole world of living beings I must rescue from the terrors of birth, of
> old age, of sickness, of death and rebirth, of all kinds of moral offense,
> of all states of woe, of the cycle of birth-and-death. . . . My endeavors
> do not merely aim at my own deliverance. For with the help of the
> boat of the thought of all knowledge, I must rescue all these beings
> from the stream of Samsara (cycle of rebirth), which is so difficult to
> cross . . . I must free them from all calamities, I must ferry them across
> the stream of Samsara . . . I am resolved to abide in each single state of
> woe for numberless aeons; and so I will help all beings to freedom, in
> all states of woe that may be found in any world system whatsoever.[5]

As the above quotation makes clear, the dedicated bodhisattva is devoted to ending suffering even if it takes countless eons to accomplish. The bodhisattva does not commit to a limited number of reincarnations prior to ending the cycle of personal rebirth. Rather, the pledge of the bodhisattva is open-ended: whatever it takes.

The bodhisattva vow incorporates a commitment to ahimsa or noninjury. As indicated above, the Hinayana pledge to ahimsa appears as the First of the Ten Precepts that both the laity and monks follow. The vow of noninjury is a core value of Buddhist ethics in all of its forms. Compassion leads to respect and the intent not to harm. Like Hinduism, the Buddhist commitment to noninjury is an extension of the Buddhist belief that all life is interconnected. Injury or premature death interferes with every being's movement toward enlightenment and disrupts the web of relationships that comprise the universe.

In recent years, the Buddhist ethics of compassion has expanded beyond the traditional goal of helping others achieve nirvana and has focused increasingly on the struggle for social justice. This new form of "engaged Buddhism" centers on human rights struggles in those parts of the world that experience widespread poverty or where repressive politicians prevent the public expression of new ideas. In India, Buddhists have protested against the caste system. Throughout Sri Lanka, Thailand, Burma, and Vietnam, Buddhists are actively seeking to transform their societies in ways that benefit everyone. For many decades, the Dalai Lama has spearheaded the movement to liberate Tibet from Chinese control. In Japan, Soka Gakkai Buddhist laity works passionately to protect the environment through international agreements and to put and end to war.[6]

The fundamental aim of Engaged Buddhism is nothing less than the development of a global ethic. The natural starting point is the first five of the Ten Precepts: no killing, no stealing, no sexual misconduct, no lying, and no drinking of intoxicants. These five have constituted "a minimum ethical standard for all Buddhists throughout time. The five precepts have always been understood as the minimum one must accept and work with as a Buddhist."[7]

Just as Gandhi's religious views and nonviolent politics reflected his Hindu heritage, engaged Buddhism of the late twentieth and early twenty-first centuries embodies ethical ideals that can be traced back to the start of the Buddhist movement. Modern engaged Buddhism retains its direct connection to the past while at the same time it adapts the strengths of its moral tradition to current circumstances. Engaged Buddhism does not just turn inward in order to achieve spiritual liberation from the endless cycle of suffering. It also faces outward in order to bring greater peace and justice, that is, social as well as spiritual liberation, into the emerging global village by transforming political and economic structures. Thus, Buddhism shares many of the same values of noninjury, compassion, and empathy for suffering of the Hindu spirituality from which it sprang.

JAINISM

In Jainism, the doctrine of ahimsa is carried to its extreme. The Jain founder Mahavira became the conqueror whose detachment from all worldly desires, including food and water, led to death by starvation. The liberation of the soul or jiva from its entanglement with matter or ajiva requires the conquest of cravings of all kinds. Only then can the soul be liberated from the cycle of rebirth that leads only to more suffering and death. Like Buddhism, Jainism began as a protest movement against the Brahmin-controlled caste system of Hinduism. Also, like Buddhism, the ethics of Jainism serve as a stepping-stone to enlightenment. It is not possible to advance to the higher stages of spiritual discipline without first mastering the moral prerequisites.

Like Buddhism, the followers of the Jain philosophy can be divided into monks and laity. The Jain parallel to Buddhism's Ten Precepts is the Five Vows. They involve the renunciation of:

1. Killing—ahimsa.
2. Lying in all its forms especially when aroused by emotions like anger, greed, fear, and so on.
3. Taking anything not given whether little or much, small or great.
4. Sexual pleasures of every kind and with any god, human, or animal.
5. All attachments whether little or much, small or great.[8]

All Five Vows apply to the minority of monks who are able to accept their rigorous demands. Among the nearly 4 million Jains in the world, the majority of laity follows only the first three. Like their Buddhist counterparts, Jain laypersons marry, raise families, and engage in worldly vocations that do not conflict with the first three Vows. The expression of sexuality for the laity is restricted to fidelity in marriage.

Among the laity, adherence to the lower Vows leads to a higher reincarnation and greater potential to commit to all five of them as a dedicated monk. The fifth Vow is the most challenging of all because it requires total detachment from any and all desires, which only conquerors like Mahavira were able to accomplish. Dedicated Jain monks exercise great caution not to harm any living creature, including insects. They carry brushes and sweep the roadway in order not to crush any form of life. They practice straining water so as to not accidentally kill any living creature that might be living in it. As vegetarians they refuse to eat meat of any kind because this involves the killing of animals.

Like all of the great religions of the world, the devotees of Jainism have split into factions over doctrinal disagreements. The first of the two main Jain groups are the "sky clads" (Digambaras) who practice nudity in order not to squash insects that might live in or under garments. The second group, called "white clads" (Svetambaras) from northern India, wear clothing. They reject the notion that nudity is a requirement for enlightenment. Unlike the conservative sky clads, white clads allow women into their monasteries and accept that women may be liberated from rebirth without first having to be reborn as a male.

While Jainism numbers only 4 million followers worldwide, Jain morality has exerted a significant influence throughout the world primarily in two ways. First Jains avoid occupations that involve violating the norm of ahimsa, including farming, the military, animal slaughter, tanning, and so on. Jains are concentrated mainly in urban areas and enter business and professional vocations where they achieve high levels of financial success. Respected for their honesty and hard work and, as a result, they achieve high education levels and social class standing.[9]

The Jain commitment to ahimsa has also left its mark on modern politics, especially through Gandhi and Martin Luther King, Jr. As stated earlier, Gandhi was deeply influenced by the belief in noninjury, which all of the religions of South Asia share in common. Jainism represents the most extreme interpretation of this doctrine. For the sky clad monks, this means wandering the world naked. For the laity it means pursuing occupations that steer clear of potential harm to any living being, however small or seemingly unrelated to the daily conduct of life. Along with detachment from worldly desires, inculcating the value of respect for all life is a central virtue in the Jain view of character development. Not only does it serve as a prerequisite to a higher spirituality, but it also has a profound effect on daily life.

CONCLUSION

Despite their ancient origins, the Asian religions continue to thrive as three of the twenty-first century's most enduring systems of beliefs and behaviors. Hinduism and Jainism inspired Gandhi whose extraordinary spiritual and political achievements mark him as one of the twentieth century's outstanding leaders. All of the Asian spiritualities tie their ethical expectations to the common goal of achieving enlightenment. Character development is central to all forms of Asian morality in which the core value is ahimsa or noninjury. Virtues such as kindness, compassion, gentleness, peacefulness, patience, empathy, and concern for the sufferings of others, are also linked to religiosity. The Asian coupling of spirituality with morality creates a common foundation for fostering interfaith cooperation that is readily adaptable to the changing circumstances of the modern world.

CHAPTER 7

Middle Eastern Religions

The sacred scriptures and traditions of all the Middle Eastern religions define their essential ethical norms. For devout believers, conforming to God's moral mandates, as each religion perceives them, carries the promise of an eternal reward no matter what happens on earth.

ZOROASTRIANISM

Nowhere is this more clearly demonstrated than in Zoroastrianism. For Zoroastrians, Ahura Mazda is the Wise Lord of the Universe. Zoroaster is the prophet whom Ahura Mazda commissioned to reveal the ethical norms that Ahura Mazda requires humanity to follow and that will be used as the measuring stick for determining each person's destiny after death. The overarching image that Zoroastrians use to define the nature of moral righteousness is "good thoughts, words, and deeds," as the following passage from the Zoroastrian Scripture, the *Avesta*, makes clear.

> Oh Lord Protector! In obedience to your command I am firm in the pure religion and I promise to think and speak and do every righteousness. Forgive me of my many sins. May I keep my conduct pure and, in accordance with your wishes, keep my six powers of the soul uncontaminated: work, speech, thought, reasoning, memory, and intellect.
>
> And, in order to obtain the riches of the next world through good thoughts, good words, and good deeds, I will worship you, that I may thus open for myself the path to the shining paradise. By this, the heavy punishment of hell will not be inflicted upon me.

There are five best things in religion. These are: truthfulness, generosity, being possessed of virtue, diligence, and advocacy. This truthfulness is best: One who acts (in such a manner) to the creatures of Ahura Mazda that the recipient of his action has so much more benefit when he acts like that to him. This generosity is best: One who makes a present to a person from whom he has no hope of receiving anything in reward in this world, ... This possession of virtue is best: One who makes battle against the non-material demons, whatever they may be, Greed, Envy, Lust, Wrath, and Shame. This diligence is best: One who does the work which he is engaged in doing in such a manner that at every moment he has certainty in himself, ... This advocacy is best: One who speaks for a person who is inarticulate, who cannot speak his own misery and complaint; that person speaks out the voice of his own soul and of that of the poor.... Wisdom is manifest in work, character in rule, friend in hardship.[1]

It is clearly seen in this quotation that the pathway to heavenly eternal life after death depends on high moral conduct during earthly temporal life.

In the cosmic struggle between the forces of good and evil, at the end of time Ahura Mazda will prevail and decide each soul's destiny according the net balance of good versus evil. The *Avesta* contains the moral criteria that the Lord of the universe will use to make such judgments, as revealed by the prophet Zoroaster. These include the development of virtuous character traits, such as truthfulness, generosity or seeking to benefit others, diligence, speaking on behalf of the poor or justice and avoiding such vices as Greed, Envy, Lust, Wrath, and Shame. The coupling of theology and ethics is straightforward—measure for measure: You get (your place in the afterlife) what you deserve (what you do during your earthly life).

JUDAISM

The core of Jewish ethics is found in the *Torah*, which contains a total of 613 laws that comprise the complete ethical code that the faithful Jews believe Yahweh revealed to Moses during the 40 years that the Jewish people lived in the desert after they escaped from Egyptian slavery. Although the *Torah* narrative credits Moses with authoring the Law, most Hebrew Scripture scholars believe that the *Torah* actually contains three distinct but overlapping moral codes that developed during different time periods of ancient Israelite history.

The first is the Covenant Code that is found in Exodus 20:1–23:33. This portion of the *Torah* dates from the time of Moses and becomes the model for the other two codes. This Code contains the best-known moral mandates of the Hebrew Scripture, the Ten Commandments. The first three cover

Israel's relationship to Yahweh by commanding faithfulness, shunning idols, and revering the sacred name. The fourth sets aside the Sabbath as a day of worship. The next six contain the specific ethical injunctions that create harmony throughout the Israelite community. They prescribe parental respect and proscribe murder, adultery, theft, lying, and envy. The most general principle of justice is also found in 21:23–24 of the Covenant Code: "life for life, eye for eye, tooth for tooth, hand for hand, foot for foot, burn for burn, wound for would, stripe for stripe."

The second Moral Code woven into the *Torah* is the Holiness or Priestly Code that the Israelites created after they returned from the Babylonian exile starting in 538 BCE. This Code is found in chapters 17 through 26 of the book of Leviticus. It contains many of the same moral requirements of the Covenant Code and adds other worship rules related to priestly rituals. Like the original Covenant Code, the Holiness Code rests on the belief that the Israelites would fulfill their call to righteousness by obeying Yahweh's commandments. In turn, Yahweh will show favor on them by bestowing blessings both now and in the future.

Like the Covenant Code, the Holiness Code summons the ancient Israelites to treat each other and their neighbors with fairness. "You shall not render an unjust judgment; you shall not be partial to the poor or defer to the great; with justice you shall judge your neighbor. You shall not go around as a slanderer among the people." (Leviticus 19:15–16) "You shall not defraud your neighbor; you shall not steal; and you shall not keep for yourself the wages of a laborer until morning; you shall not revile the deaf or put a stumbling block before the blind." (Leviticus 19:13–14)

The third and final Code appears last in the *Torah* in the book of Deuteronomy, although it emerged historically before the post-exilic Holiness Code. The Deuteronomic Code inspired King Josiah's reforms in 629 BCE. Like the Covenant and Holiness Codes, the writers of the *Torah* wove the Deuteronomic Code into the Moses narrative. Deuteronomy summarizes many of the events that appear in the previous four books of *Genesis*, *Exodus*, *Leviticus*, and *Numbers*. The Deuteronomic Code appears in chapters 12 through 26. It restates the justice norms of fair treatment toward neighbors and foreigners and adds some additional rules that cover dress codes, and building safe houses, among others.

In addition to the written Torah Codes, Jews also developed an extensive Oral Torah tradition that began when they were relocated away from Jerusalem either by force due to military conquest, as in the case of military defeat by the Assyrians, Babylonians, Greeks, or Romans, or by choice. The Oral Torah grew out of the need for the Jewish community to preserve its historical identity and continuity amidst changing circumstances away from their homeland. Over time during the Diaspora, the rabbis wrote down the Oral Torah in order to preserve for later generations the updated applications that they derived from the written *Torah*.

This vast, multivolume collection of oral interpretations of the written Torah Codes became known as the *Talmud* or "teachings." The *Talmud* incorporates Oral Torah teachings that arose in geographical settings as diverse as Palestine and Babylonia and that span hundreds of years from exile to the Medieval Era in Europe. The tradition of rabbinical oral reflection of the relevance of the ancient Torah Codes to the challenges of contemporary society continues to this day. The diversity that exists among the three major branches of modern Judaism, namely, Reform, Conservative, and Orthodox, turns on which aspects of both the written and oral traditions they accept as authoritative—from *Torah* to *Talmud*.

Like Zoroastrianism, Judaism recognizes the essential role that virtue plays in the development of moral character. In Judaism, this is expressed fully in the Wisdom tradition. Like character ethics in general, the Israelite position on Wisdom looks to the inner motives that lie behind behavior. Whether in their Eastern or Western forms, all of the world religions understand that human beings are self-determining moral agents whose deeds flow from either virtues or vices. While the inner dispositions of individuals are formed through social influences such as family, social class, gender, nationality, ethnicity, race, and so on, sooner or later all persons must willfully decide for themselves which ethical course of action they will follow.

Israel's ancient King Solomon is the main originator of the Jewish Wisdom tradition. After his father King David died in 960 BCE, Solomon ascended the throne and formed political alliances with the surrounding nations of Babylon, Egypt, Greece, and Mesopotamia, which possessed an extensive literature of wise sayings. Through these international arrangements, Solomon gained access to many Wisdom writings that he gathered together into ancient Israel's Wisdom tradition.

The *Book of Proverbs* provides the major point of entry into this tradition. Along with *Proverbs*, *Job*, and *Ecclesiastes* also qualify for inclusion in the Wisdom writings that appear in the Hebrew Scripture. Proverbs in particular identifies the types of virtuous character traits that the ancient Israelites believed Yahweh expected them to internalize and demonstrate as the chosen people. Becoming wise starts by honoring Yahweh's holiness, that is to say, by standing before the Creator of the universe with an attitude of respectful awe. "The fear of the Lord is the beginning of wisdom, and the knowledge of the Holy One is insight." (Proverbs 9:10) "The Lord by wisdom founded the earth; by understanding he established the heavens." (3:19). Finally, "Trust in the Lord with all your heart, and do not rely on your own insight. In all your ways, acknowledge him, and he will make straight your paths. Do not be wise in your own eyes; fear the Lord, and turn away from evil." (3:5–7)

The authors of the Hebrew Scripture understood that ancient Israel could become Yahweh's righteous people only if they chose to internalize the virtues that lead to wisdom. "Keep sound wisdom and prudence, and they will be life for your soul and adornment for your neck. Then you will walk on your way securely and your foot will not stumble." (3:21–23) The Lord "is a shield to those who walk blamelessly, guarding the paths of justice and preserving the way of his faithful ones. Then you will understand righteousness and justice and equity, every good path; for wisdom will come into your heart." (2:7–10)

Like all other aspects of ancient Israel's existence, the Wisdom tradition, especially *Proverbs*, links fidelity and virtue to the reward and punishment promises of the Covenant with Yahweh. Choosing wisdom is not optional. It is obligatory. If the Israelites do not walk on the pathway of wisdom, Yahweh will judge them harshly. "Do not let loyalty and faithfulness forsake you; bind them around your neck, write them on the tablet of your heart. So you will find favor and good repute in the sight of God and of people." (3:3–4) If wisdom does not prevail throughout the nation, then the future will be filled with dire consequences. "Therefore walk in the way of the good, and keep to the paths of the just. For the upright will abide in the land and the innocent will remain in it; but the wicked will be cut off from the land, and the treacherous will be rooted out of it." (2:20–22)

Solomon's reign proved to be a mixed blessing for ancient Israel. On the one hand his international political agreements enabled Israel to remain at peace with its neighbors for several decades. At the same time, his expansionist policies led him to enslave fellow Israelites in order to secure the labor necessary for the completion of his many building projects, including the construction of Israel's first Temple. As a result, he created the conditions that launched Israel's gradual decline as the region's dominant political power.

After Solomon's death, the nation splintered into two hostile groups with ten tribes consolidating into the northern kingdom of Israel and the remaining two into the southern kingdom of Judah. Their mutual acrimony never diminished, and it sealed their long-term fate. In 722 BCE, the Assyrians swept in from the north and destroyed Israel forever. In 587 BCE, the Babylonians sent the inhabitants of the remaining southern segment of Judah into exile and destroyed the Solomon-built Temple. After nearly 50 years of adjusting to life away from their native soil, in 538 BCE the Zoroastrian King Cyrus, whose Persian armies defeated the Babylonians, permitted the Jews to migrate back to Jerusalem.

Prior to their return to their homeland, the Babylonian exile created a crisis of confidence in the Jewish self-understanding as Yahweh's chosen people. The political autonomy that they took for granted since the days of King David disappeared with little hope of recovery. The God of their ancestors, who showered them with untold blessings, took the promised land from them and heaped curse after curse upon their heads. The Proverbial warning that the lack of wisdom would bring forth Yahweh's harshest judgment came to pass. For the writers of the Hebrew Scripture, the chosen people turned their backs on the virtues that would have enabled their transformation into a people of sustained righteousness. As a result, Yahweh pulled them out of the promised land and hurled them into Babylon.

Despite this tragic turn of events, the ancient Israelites never lost hope in Yahweh's abiding love. Nowhere is this better expressed than in the writings of Jeremiah, who envisioned that a brighter day for the Jewish people loomed ahead on the far side of exile. After Judah's demise, Jeremiah reminded the nation that Yahweh would remain true to the Abrahamic promise. At some future point in time, Yahweh would restore the Covenant but with one exception. Speaking for Yahweh, Jeremiah proclaims, "I will write it on their hearts." (Jeremiah 31:33) No longer would Wisdom be mere words written on the pages of sacred Scripture. It would issue forth naturally from the depths of each person's heart and permeate the entire community. The Israelites would become Yahweh's people in their inner being, that is, in the quality of their character and the virtuous traits that emanate from it. As a result, they would become the righteous nation Yahweh called them to be through the promise given to Abraham.

CHRISTIANITY

Christian morality also stresses the importance of developing the virtuous character, which reflects its Jewish origins. Jesus' earliest followers were Hebrew converts who created their new Faith out of their Israelite heritage. Just as Jeremiah used the metaphor of the heart to define the inward nature of character development, writers of the Christian Scripture employ this same image to define the source of all good and evil. This is especially noticeable in two of the Gospels, Matthew and Luke.

Matthew depicts Jesus as the new lawgiver, whose Sermon on the Mount replaces the Torah Commandments that Moses gave the Israelites during their 40 years of wandering in the desert. Jesus embodies the ideal person to perfection. When Jewish leaders accused his disciples of impurity because they failed to wash their hands before eating, Jesus replied, "Do you not see that whatever goes into the mouth enters the stomach, and goes out into the sewer? But what comes out of the mouth proceeds from the heart, and this is what defiles." (Matthew 15:17–18) Defilement comes in many forms. "For out of the heart come evil intentions, murder, adultery, fornication, theft, false witness, slander. These are what defile a person, but to eat with unwashed hands does not defile." (Matthew 15:19–20) Immorality springs from an immoral character.

Luke's Gospel parallels Matthew's in accenting the effect that inner motivations have on morality. Luke's allegory of the tree and its fruits encapsulates the nature of virtue. "No good tree bears bad fruit, nor again does a bad tree bear good fruit; ... The good person out of good treasure of the heart produces good, and the evil person out of the evil treasure produces evil; for it is out of the abundance of the heart that the mouth speaks." (Luke 6:43–45)

In addition, the author of the book of Hebrews reminds the Jewish convert to Christianity of the adverse consequences of unfaithfulness by referring directly to Israel's 40 years of wandering in the desert during which time they weakened and backslid into worshipping the false gods of Egypt. Hebrews caution Christians not to harden their "hearts as in the rebellion, as on the day of testing in the wilderness." (Hebrews 3:8) His admonition is direct and decisive. "Take care, brothers and sisters, that none of you may have an evil, unbelieving heart that turns away from the living God." (Hebrews 3:12)

While some writers of the Christian Scripture employ the heart imagery to define the nature of the virtuous character, it is the Apostle Paul who provides the most thorough listing of desirable traits. His conversion, which occurred on the road to Damascus shortly after Jesus' death, filled him with passion to spread the new faith throughout Asia Minor. During his three major missionary ventures he established many budding Christian communities. As a result, when the Romans destroyed Jerusalem and the Second Temple in 70 CE and drove the Jews in Diaspora, Christianity had already taken root well beyond the borders of Palestine.

As these many new church groups grew, numerous internal disagreements arose and threatened their very survival. On those occasions when the word of congregational discord reached Paul, he wrote a series of letters that offered solutions to internal conflicts. Many of his letters include lists of the kinds of traits that Christians should internalize as they develop their virtuous characters. At no point did he ever provide a comprehensive list of all possible Christian virtues or write a definitive theological or ethical treatise. Rather, he aimed his letters at the specific needs that his parishioners were encountering in their separate locations and circumstances.

Paul's letters typically include both theological and ethical components. He always connects morality to faith. His most basic spiritual assumption is that anyone who accepts Christ as a personal savior because of his atoning crucifixion and resurrection becomes a new creation. The sins of the past are forgiven, which creates a sense of inner freedom for converts to live fully in the future. His letters to the churches in Galatia and Corinth convey as keenly as any of his epistles how character development flows from faith. In the process of expressing the relationship of one to the other, he enumerates the virtues that he believes all Christians ought to have.

His letter to the Galatians includes the following passages. "For freedom Christ has set us free. Stand firm, therefore, and do not submit again to the yoke of slavery." (Galatians 5:1) "The fruit of the Spirit is love, joy, peace, patience, kindness, generosity, faithfulness, gentleness and self-control. There is no law against such things." (5:22–23) "Let us not become conceited, competing against one another, envying one another." (5:26) In contrast, Paul also lists several detrimental traits that tear apart the fragile fabric of community. The destructive fruits of the flesh encompass "fornication, impurity, licentiousness, idolatry, sorcery, enmities, strife, jealousy, anger, quarrels, dissensions, factions, envy, drunkenness, carousing, and things like these." (5:19–21)

In his first letter to the Corinthian church, he composed the most widely quoted of all his virtue passages. For Paul, love sits at the center of the Christian character, and all other positive traits stem from it or in one way or another relate to it. "Love is patient; love is kind; love is not envious or boastful or arrogant or rude. It does not insist on its own way; it is not irritable, or resentful; it does not rejoice in wrongdoing, but rejoices in the truth." (1 Corinthians 13:4–6) "And now faith, hope and love abide, these three, and the greatest of these is love." (Verse 13)

Taken together, the metaphor of the heart that Jesus uses in the Gospels of Matthew and Luke, and Paul's lists of virtues that appear throughout his letters, most notably Galatians and 1 Corinthians, comprise the foundation of the Christian conception of character. When combined with Proverb's wisdom insights and Jeremiah's view that one day Yahweh's law will be written on the heart, the first two of the Abrahamic faiths (Judaism and Christianity) point to the kinds of virtues that it is desirable for any person to have in the development of moral character. The compatibility of both Judaism and Christianity with the Zoroastrianism view of virtue, as described above, is self-evident.

The Apostle Paul's virtue lists reflected his acquaintance with Greco-Roman philosophy and in particular Stoicism. As the unity of Roman Civilization began to disintegrate under the onslaught of warring barbaric tribes and as Islam expanded, many of the Greek manuscripts fell into the protective hands of Muslim scholars. The initial success of the Crusaders in wresting control of Jerusalem from Islam enabled European universities to gain renewed access to Greco-Roman philosophical writings.

As a result, European theologians began integrating ancient ideas into their religious and ethical treatises. Nowhere is this more evident than in the writings of Thomas Aquinas, who found in Aristotle's works a philosophical framework for his entire multivolume *Summa Theologica*.[2] In the middle of the thirteenth century, Aquinas created an intellectual synthesis of Christian, Jewish, Greek, and Roman ideas that paralleled the Catholic Church's domination of a largely unified Medieval European Civilization. Aquinas discovered in Aristotle's writings and temperament an outlook compatible with his own.

Like the legendary Greek predecessor, Aquinas maintained that human character consists of a combination of virtues and vices. Like Aristotle, Aquinas viewed virtue as a habit that leads a person to will good outcomes. Continuing along the thought line laid down by Aristotle, Aquinas held that humanity's chief purpose in life (*telos*) is the pursuit of happiness, the achievement of which depends on developing a virtuous character and avoiding vice. From this point of departure, Aquinas created his lists of seven virtues that believers ought to embrace and the seven vices that they ought to shun.

Aquinas included among his seven virtues four from Greco-Roman philosophy and three from Christian writings. The first four, called the cardinal virtues, consist of wisdom, justice, courage, and moderation. The last three, or theological virtues, come from Paul's first letter to the Corinthians: faith, hope, and love. This list of seven represents a culmination of character ethics as it evolved from ancient Greco-Roman/Judaic-Christian times to the Medieval Era. Aquinas' seven virtues personify the dispositions of the inner self at the highest level of character formation. In essence, they embody a way of being in the world by internalizing traits that it is desirable for every person to have.

In contrast, the seven vices epitomize the character traits that prevent progress toward the achievement of human happiness. Aquinas' seven vices are sloth, lust, anger, pride, envy, greed, and gluttony. The major negative consequence that derives from vice is, at a minimum, arrested self-development as an ethical being or, at most, self-destruction. In addition to emphasizing the importance of personal moral development, Aristotle and Aquinas viewed humans as inherently social. For both writers, the idea of the individual, understood as an abstract entity, does not exist. Each person attains an identity as a result of membership in social groups. This means that the development of virtue enhances not only each individual self but also society as a whole, whereas the expression of vice leads to an entire community's moral deterioration. That is to say, acting in a virtuous manner creates goodness at both the personal and communal levels and thereby contributes to a society's overall happiness, whereas vice undermines it.

ISLAM

Islam more closely parallels Judaism than either Zoroastrianism or Christianity because like the Jewish emphasis on following the laws of the *Torah*, Islam stresses the necessity of obeying the mandates of the *Qur'an*. For both Judaism and Islam, the moral laws revealed in their respective sacred Scriptures provide the framework for character development. For Muslims, the entire *Qur'an* contains Allah's all-inclusive moral laws as revealed to the prophet Muhammad.

Islamic ethics involves submission to the will of Allah. While humans are free to choose an ethical course of action for their lives, this freedom is not to be understood in the sense of satisfying one's personal or ego needs. Rather, freedom in Islam means that each person may choose to live or not to live by Allah's laws. The choices one makes in life determine where one will go after death: paradise or hell. For Muslims submitting to the moral laws of

Allah is an urgent necessity connected to an immediate destiny after death as well as on the Day of Judgment.

This radical stress on submission stems from the exclusivist belief that the *Qur'an* contains Allah's perfect will for all times and places and that no improvements or future revelations are necessary. Allah's word as conveyed in the *Qur'an* is final. Therefore, all that the faithful need to do is submit to Allah's divine commandments as conveyed in the *Qur'an*. The submission mandate has remained the central feature of Islamic beliefs and behavior from the earliest days of the Faith.

After Muhammad's death in 632 CE, successive leaders continued Muhammad's goal of aggressive and rapid territorial expansion. This brought Islam into contact with many separate societies located throughout the Middle Eastern region, northern Africa, and the Iberian Peninsula across the Strait of Gibraltar. As the Muslim Empire expanded and Islamic leaders encountered diverse cultural practices, the need to clarify the sources of religious authority grew. The most basic source of religious authority for Islam is, of course, the *Qur'an*. Virtually all Muslims everywhere agree that their sacred Scripture contains the revelations that Muhammad received directly from Allah during his lifetime.

If the *Qur'an* does not include specific laws that guide believers' choices on any given ethical issue, then they turn to the next level of authority. This involves the traditions or hadiths that stem from Muhammad's life and times, also called the sunna of the prophet. Unlike the *Qur'an*, whose authenticity Muslims take for granted, debate among legal scholars over the historical validity of the traditions existed from the beginning. During the height of leadership struggles in the eighth and ninth centuries in particular, many Muslims fabricated hadiths to support their competing political or theological positions. Over time legal scholars gathered the hadiths into two collections and ranked them on a scale from sound to weak depending on their perceptions of the degree of validity of each tradition. Today, Muslims believe that together the *Qur'an* and hadiths reveal the true nature of Muhammad and his era in every respect—from word to deed.

The third level of authority consists of community consensus or *ijma*. This source is a direct outgrowth of procedures that led to the development of the second level. In the process of authenticating the traditions related to Mohammad's life, Islamic scholars created a bridge between the early decades of the seventh century when Islam began and the future. As time passed, changing circumstances confronted Islam, as it does all faiths, with the challenge to remain vibrant and relevant. Each new occasion brought forth the often-repeated questions of "How does this relate to the *Qur'an* and/or hadiths?"

As in the case of the Jewish rabbis who created the vast written Talmud out of the Oral Torah in order to insure historical continuity, Muslim clerics and scholars connected the past to the ever changing present by creating a third level of authority: community consensus. As one of his main legacies, Muhammad assured his followers that Allah would never lead them astray or cause them to fall into false beliefs. Allah would provide for the continuation of the Muslim community across future generations.

The task of fashioning widespread agreement on a broad range of issues, many of them novel, fell on the shoulders of legal and religious scholars. As an essential aspect of the process, Muslim leaders made sure that any new consensus would remain consistent with Muhammad's original revelations and the traditions that grew up around him. Over time, these new applications to changing circumstances based on community consensus became a third source of authority along with the Qur'an and the hadiths.

The fourth source of authority involves the use of analogy (giyas) or human reason to arrive at decisions on issues that the Qur'an, hadiths, and consensus do not cover. Many Muslims view reason as a fourth source of authority for making moral judgments in new circumstances. For example, many of today's harmful narcotic drugs did not exist during Muhammad's lifetime. Through the use of analogy and reason, contemporary Muslims have concluded that their use is forbidden today in the same way that Muhammad forbad the use of alcohol and other injurious intoxicants during his day.

As the fourth source of authority, applying reason to current innovations often affects Islam in ways that differ dramatically from the other three. The Qur'an, hadiths, and consensus reinforce Islam in a conservative direction. They look primarily to the past for clues about how to respond to changes that are occurring in the present. However, many Muslims use reason as a means for adapting to changes that are occurring in the present or that might occur in the future, including the acceptance of many modern political, economic, scientific, and technological innovations.

Over the centuries, Islamic scholars ranked and combined these four sources of authority in different ways, which in turn led to the creation of four distinct Legal Schools that vary from liberal to conservative. Today's Sunni Muslim societies can be divided according to which of these four traditions they follow. The most liberal of the four is called the Hanifite School that was named after the eighth century legal scholar Abu Hanifa who emphasized the importance of analogy and reason in moral and legal matters. The Hanifites are the largest of the four groups and exert the greatest influence in parts of Iraq, Pakistan, and India.

At the other end, the most conservative is the Hanbalite School that emerged in the ninth century and is named after Ibn Hanbal who stressed submission to the Qur'an above all else, including the hadiths. Modern Wahhabism as practiced in Saudi Arabia found its inspiration in the Hanbalite School. The Malikite and Shafi'ite Schools combine the traditions of Muhammad with various compilations of legal decisions. Both arose in the eighth and ninth centuries and occupy middle ground between the liberal

Hanifites and conservative Hanbalites. The Malikite and Shafi'ite Schools influences are strongest in Egypt and Indonesia respectively. In short, the liberal to conservative diversity that exists among modern Muslims depends on how each nation ranks and applies the four legal traditions of Hanifites, Malikites, Shafi'ites, and Hanbalites.

The combined moral and legal traditions are called the Sharia, which means path to the watering hold. In the same way that Jews accept the *Torah* and *Talmud* as Yahweh's Law, Muslims view the Sharia as Allah's Law. However, just as Jews accept or reject various aspects of their heritage, so do Muslims depending on which of the many moral and legal mandates they consider to be (1) required; (2) recommended but not required; (3) neutral; (4) discouraged but not forbidden; and (5) forbidden.

All Muslims accept that some moral actions are required and others are forbidden. Performing the five pillars is required of all Muslims. Adultery and the consumption of pork and alcohol are forbidden. The major differences that prevail among Muslims pertain to categories (2) through (4). For example, disagreements exist over the types of dress codes that both men and women should follow while in public. Ought twenty-first century Muslims adhere to the clothing traditions that existed in Muhammad's time according to the *Qur'an* and/or hadiths? Or should they be able to choose their own attire? What is required, recommended, discouraged, or forbidden? Or is it neutral in the sense that it does not matter one way or the other?

While Islam affirms as a theological tenet that men and women are equal in the eyes of Allah, how does this translate at the social level? Are all economic, political, and educational rights equally available to both men and women? Or should men and women be treated differently in the arena of domestic and nondomestic roles? The answers to these questions vary widely among Muslims according to which aspects of the Sharia each nation accepts or rejects. Islamic communities disagree in their perceptions of what is required, recommended, neutral, discouraged, or forbidden according to the *Qur'an*, hadiths, consensus, or analogy/reason.

Thus, like Judaism, the legal traditions of Islam are a central feature of Muslim Faith. In addition, like Zoroastrianism, Judaism, and Christianity, Islam emphasizes the development of the virtuous character as one of its major moral goals. While the legal traditions provide Muslims with frameworks for integrating the actions of individuals into a collective identity, Islamic ethics also underscores the importance of motives.

In Sura 3:104, the *Qur'an* instructs the following: "Let there become of you a nation that shall speak for righteousness, enjoin justice, and forbid evil." As in the case of Zoroastrianism, Islam accentuates the importance of the heart's internal motivations and the tongue's kind words. Islam shares with all religions the perception that good or evil speech and conduct emanate ultimately from the self's deepest moral motivations. While Muslims expect external submission to the letter of the Law, Islamic ethics remains incomplete unless each believer internalizes the spirit of the Law as well.

If for some reason, circumstances prevent a Muslim believer from performing acts of submission, then Allah who is all-knowing and compassionate will judge as worthy the inner commitments of the heart. To this end, Islam advocates cultivating the virtues of honesty, modesty, wisdom, courage, and justice and the avoidance of vices such as greed, theft, anger, lust, adultery, and so on. Sura 70, called The Ladders, provides relevant passages: "Therefore conduct yourself with becoming patience." Worshippers who remain "steadfast in prayer; who set aside a due portion of their goods for the needy and dispossessed; . . . who restrain from carnal desire (save with their wives: . . . he that lusts after other than these is a transgressor); . . . These shall be laden with honours and shall dwell in fair gardens."

CONCLUSION

Paralleling the South Asian religions, for the Middle Eastern religions, worldview warrants ethics. All four of them hold that each person has only one life, and not many, to accept the right beliefs and to engage in mandated behaviors that will guarantee safe passage into heaven or paradise after death. The alternative is hell. The believer must get it right while alive or face the dire consequences after death.

All four of the Middle Eastern religions go to considerable length in identifying the norms upon which the ultimate power of the universe, whether this is called Ahura Mazda, Yahweh, Lord, Jehovah, Allah, or other, will judge each person's earthly accomplishments. Like the Asian faiths, the Middle Eastern religions demonstrate the capacity to adjust to changing circumstances even though they have adopted different strategies. Most Catholic, Orthodox, and Protestant Christians have adapted to scientific and technological innovations that emerged during the Renaissance and Enlightenment. Judaism and Islam expanded through a process of interpretation and accumulation. Both religions perceive that Yahweh and Allah revealed to Moses and Muhammad respectively the divine commandments for regulating earthly life.

For the ancient Israelites, the experiences of living in exile and in Diaspora led the rabbis to reflect on the Legal Codes of the *Torah* in light of new conditions. As indicated above, this process created the multivolume *Talmud* that served to preserve the past and adjust to the present and future. Unlike Judaism, Islam's adaptation to social change did not arise through expulsion from their homeland or by living as a minority group amidst many dominant host cultures.

Most important of all, the four Middle Eastern traditions share overlapping values that provide a common ground for constructive interaction. All of them spotlight the importance of developing the kinds of virtuous character traits that it is desirable for persons of all faiths to have, irrespective of theological differences. The two most common are compassion and justice. All of the sacred scriptures of the Middle Eastern religions counsel their followers to show empathy, kindness, and generosity toward the dispossessed of the world and to act justly on their behalf.

All four Middle Eastern religions place Wisdom at the center of their understanding of character development. In no particular order, they pile virtue on top of virtue, such as devotion to God, truthfulness, righteousness, diligence, knowledge, prudence, faith, loyalty, hope, peace, sexual fidelity, and so on. The metaphor of the heart symbolizes the importance that intention plays in the Middle Eastern Ethics of Virtue. It is the source of both faithful belief and righteous behavior.

CHAPTER 8

Ethical Comparisons: Search for Common Ground

CHALLENGES TO FINDING COMMON ETHICAL GROUND

Relationship of Worldview to Ethics

The major challenge to finding common ethical ground between Hinduism, Buddhism, Jainism, Zoroastrianism, Judaism, Christianity, and Islam applies to the various ways in which they connect worldviews to ethics. Of particular importance is the degree to which the followers of any particular religious faith perceive that their view of truth embodies The Truth and, stemming from this, how they understand their faith's moral imperatives. Another way of saying this is that the followers of every religion must decide how they will relate ethically to the world as this is commanded by their faith. This operates at two levels.

The first involves their depth of commitment, that is, the degree to which they believe they have been commissioned to transform the world according to their truth. Of equal importance, the second entails their openness to the truths of others and how they will adapt to diversity once they encounter it. Will they seek to convert or impose their views on others who hold different positions? Or will they adapt to the reality of difference and learn to live with it at some level of acceptance and possibly even appreciation? The ability of the various world religions to find common ethical ground depends on how all of them perceive their moral mandates in relationship to the dissimilarities that exist between themselves and others.

In the final analysis, the believers of every religion will place themselves somewhere along a continuum of being open or closed to the world's variety of viewpoints. In turn, this will determine the extent to which they are willing either to join with others in the search to find common moral ground or remain opposed to this possibility. From a historical perspective, this is not new because for centuries all of the world's major religions emerged within a context of pluralism. As discussed in earlier chapters, Buddhism grew out of Hinduism; Christianity started as an offshoot of Judaism; Islam emerged amidst polytheism, and so on.[1] In the process each of these religions either rejected and replaced many existing ideas or synthesized their new insights with older ones.

Second, anyone who has studied the history of the world religions knows that the current global arrangement of religious diversity and dominance in various geographical regions correlates closely with past patterns of political extension, conquest, and domination. The dynamics of Muslim development during the first century and beyond after Muhammad's death, and the spread of Christianity in conjunction with colonialism were described earlier. What is new about the twenty-first century is that there are no more "unknown worlds" to be discovered and conquered.

Thus, as a result of past patterns of political expansion, the world is now, in a very real sense of the word, "all filled up." Geographical regions are no longer isolated from each other but rather, as indicated at the outset of this book, are inextricably bound together through webs of electronic communication and mass transportation systems. Military assaults still occur as in the case of the United States invasion of Afghanistan and Iraq; and the pattern of terrorist attacks against civilian and military targets could continue in the foreseeable future. As the twenty-first century unfolds, the world is sadly nowhere near ridding itself of the sufferings that accompany violence and its tragic consequences.

Nonetheless, the opportunity to bring greater peace and justice into an increasingly integrated and growing global village is greater now than at any other time in the history of humankind. Much of what happens in the next several decades will be determined by how the believers of the various religions perceive each other and the patterns of interaction that develop between them.

EMBEDDING CURRENT PRACTICES
IN HISTORICAL PRECEDENTS

Two areas in particular present major challenges to the world religions for finding common ethical ground. The first is the perception that specific social arrangements are embedded in the structure of the universe and are unchangeable. The second involves assuming that religious or legal commandments that arose at some point in the past remain binding forever. Both of these tendencies are found to a greater or lesser extent in all of the world religions. Many of their most basic beliefs contain images and references that are unique to their historical development.

For example, traditional Hindu morality involves adherence to the caste and life cycle duties that the sacred *Laws of Manu* connect to each person's spiritual destiny through karma and reincarnation. In order to transmigrate toward enlightenment, Hinduism requires obedience to divinely sanctioned social behaviors that are associated with the station in life into which one is born. While many modern Hindus reject altogether the caste system, the majority continues to follow its regulations in the hope of achieving a higher rebirth. In the most popular of all Hindu Scriptures, *The Bhagavad-Gita*, Lord Krishna reminds Arjuna of the necessity of doing his duty as a member of the kshatriya or warrior caste even if it means he must kill his kinsmen in battle or lose his own life in the process.

While Buddhism and Jainism began as protest movements against the Brahmin-dominated system of Hindu caste and life cycle regulations, they also locked into their traditions many of the practices that prevailed at the time of their origins. For Buddhists, the lotus position not only epitomizes the moment of the Buddha's enlightenment, but it also symbolizes that in the midst of modern life's raging uncertainties, calm and tranquility are equally available to anyone who pursues the practice of disciplined meditation.

As was Mahavira's custom, many of the modern followers of Jainism continue to carry brushes and sweep the sidewalks as they walk from place to place in order not to harm the innocent life that might be resting on the ground in front of them. The unpretentious dress of both Buddhists and Jains signifies the life of simplicity and detachment from the desires and temptations of life. For Jains who stand in the more conservative "sky clad" tradition, nudity is preferred over wearing any clothes at all.

As the behaviors of the believers of all three of the South Asian religions demonstrate, the past and the present are inseparably joined together. For many of the devout followers of Hinduism, Buddhism, and Jainism, questions involving what to wear or eat, where to live, or what behaviors are appropriate under what circumstances are all regulated by many of the customs that existed at the time of their origins.

This is equally true of the four traditions that arose in the Middle East. Zoroastrian worship requires covering the mouth with a white cloth as a symbol of purity and to avoid polluting sacred space. The three Abrahamic religions also contain distinctive normative practices that stem from the past and separate them from each other. Support for the current state of Israel is widespread among the world's Jewish population because of the perception that the Abrahamic Covenant promises them the ancient land of Canaan as a permanent homeland. Coupled with this ancient belief is the modern Zionist desire to create and maintain a Jewish homeland where Jews finally can be free from the endless cycles of persecution that came with living for almost two millennia in the Diaspora.

Roman Catholics make up about half of the world's more than 2 billion Christians. While many Protestant and Orthodox groups permit the ordination of women and/or support the use of artificial birth control as an acceptable practice for family planning, Catholic Officialdom does not. The Roman hierarchy cites the historical continuity of Church traditions as embedded in morality and law as the basis for maintaining many present policies. From its earliest days, the Catholic Church viewed procreation as the primary purpose of marriage and that nothing should interfere with the possibility of conception after sexual intercourse. In modern times the Church has expanded its view of marriage by adding conjugal love as a second purpose along with procreation. The Catholic Church continues to base its position on the nonordination of women on the historical precedent that none of Jesus' original disciples was female.

Modern Islam parallels the other two Abrahamic religions by incorporating numerous ancient customs into present practices. One of Islam's earliest reactions to its loss of empire during the past four centuries was to speculate that as a group Muslims had either unknowingly or intentionally strayed from living by the Qur'an's divine commandments. Some speculated that Allah had withdrawn support and was using European colonial expansion as punishment for disobedience. For many Muslims, looking to the future means bringing the past into the present by turning to the Qur'an for guidance in virtually all areas of private and public behavior—from dress codes; to the morality of male-female relationships; to the organization of economic, political, and other social structures.

Thus, one of the main challenges to finding common ethical ground between the religions that arose both in Asia and the Middle East is to deal with the disparate practices that arose in the past and persist into the present. At the heart of this challenge is the issue of the extent to which contemporary believers imbue their traditions with a sense of the sacred. It is typical of the followers of all the world religions that they connect their dedication to following "in the footsteps" of the founder. As in the case of worldview differences, unwavering adherence to tradition-based moral standards may impede constructive cooperation among the devotees of the world's diverse religions.

THE STATUS OF LEGAL AND ETHICAL CODES

In addition to retaining in the present traditional practices from the past, many adherents of the world religions convert historical norms into unchangeable legal codes. For example, as indicated earlier, Hinduism embeds the caste system and stages of the life cycle into the divine structure of the universe. Once legitimized by The Laws of Manu, Hindus elaborated the caste system framework into a multilevel spiritual system that remains consistent with the Brahmin-dominated social arrangement.

Within the Middle Eastern religions, Judaism and Islam parallel the Hindu lawmaking approach more than Zoroastrianism and Christianity. For Jews, Yahweh revealed the *Torah* to Moses on Mount Sinai. The multivolume *Talmud* contains interpretations of *Torah* laws that rabbis applied over many centuries to diverse circumstances in foreign countries away from the Jewish homeland. The entirety of the Jewish legal code stems from Yahweh's original commandments. For Muslims, the Sharia embodies the laws of Allah even though Islamic societies vary according to the extent of their acceptance of one or more of these sources of authority (*Qur'an*, hadiths, consensus, and analogy).

Both conservative and orthodox Judaism and Islam in general surpass both Zoroastrianism and Christianity in the extent to which their legal codes apply comprehensively to every aspect of society from clothing to economic practices. Roman Catholic Christianity also contains a major Moral Law perspective, but unlike Judaism and Islam it did not emerge during Jesus' lifetime or among his early followers. Instead, it surfaced much later, especially during the thirteenth century through the writings of Thomas Aquinas, one of Catholic Christianity's most articulate advocates of the Moral Law tradition.

Many practices that currently divide followers of the three Abrahamic religions originated in very different historical circumstances. As faithful followers interpreted their ethical imperatives as either revelations from God or rational principles derived from the Natural Law, they instilled them with a sense of the sacred. Since all ethical and legal codes emanate from the worldviews that warrant them, disconnecting them from the theological or philosophical beliefs that justify them is virtually impossible. Devoted members of the Asian and Middle Eastern religions adhere to the standards of right and wrong that they perceive are structured into the universe. To disobey them is to place one's eternal destiny at risk.

Thus, as a result of (1) embedding current practices in unalterable historical precedents, and (2) instilling legal and ethical codes with divine status, finding common ethical ground across the boundaries of the world religions remains a formidable challenge.

POSSIBILITIES FOR FINDING COMMON ETHICAL GROUND

As noted earlier, the world's major religions hold very dissimilar worldviews, perpetuate different practices that date back to their origins, and adhere to varied normative standards that their sacred scriptures and moral traditions sanction. Conflicts inevitably arise when each tradition claims priority for its positions as the relationship between the world's religions in the early twenty-first century demonstrates. Despite these diverse perceptions, the possibilities for finding common ethical ground between the Asian and Middle Eastern spiritualities are substantial.

COMMON VIRTUES—LOVE, COMPASSION, AND MERCY

The area where finding common ground is most noticeable involves emphasizing specific virtues as they relate to each religion's image of ideal character development. For example, two of the most important virtues found in all three of the Asian religions, Hinduism, Buddhism, and Jainism are ahimsa or noninjury to biological and physical life forms and respect for the planet's ecosystem that serves as the very foundation of life itself. Ahimsa and respect are closely coupled with other traits such as kindness, gentleness, compassion, mercy, self-restraint, and placing spiritual values ahead of material ones. Within Mahayana Buddhism, the bodhisattva ideal of freeing all beings from suffering is nothing less than compassion personified. In sweeping the sidewalk as they travel from place to place, Jains imitate their beloved founder Mahavira's deep reverence for every form of life, including the most lowly and vulnerable insects that creep along the ground. Kindness stands at or near the top of the list of virtues that flow from all of Asia's abiding spiritualities.

The same can be said of the Middle Eastern religions. Zoroastrianism counsels kindness in thought, word, and deed. In ancient Judaism, the prophet Micah proclaimed that pleasing Yahweh did not require the sacrifice of thousands of rams but rather to love mercy. (Micah 6:8) The Wisdom sayings of Hebrew Scripture as contained in books such as *Proverbs* reflect the high opinion that the ancient Israelites held toward the development of the virtuous character. For Jeremiah, the heart symbolized the importance internalizing *Torah* values as a prerequisite to becoming Yahweh's devoted servant.

For Christianity, love is the dominant virtue. It is the principle trait by which the followers of Jesus understood their relationship to God and God's supreme act of mercy in offering Christ as the Messiah, the Savior of the world's sins. Christ's compassion for the downtrodden and dispossessed parallels the Buddhist's bodhisattva vow to strive without end to rid the world of its suffering. The early Apostle Paul added peace, patience, kindness, gentleness, and others, to the list of virtues that characterize becoming a new creation in Christ. Aquinas included love among his seven most important virtues. Every Sura within the *Qur'an* begins by acknowledging Allah as compassionate and merciful. Islam counsels its members to imitate in their attitudes toward others, with heart, tongue, and deed, what Allah has so generously bestowed upon them.

In short, the amount of common ground that advocates of all the world's major religions share on the centrality of virtues such as love, compassion, mercy, kindness, gentleness, and respect for others and for the world at large is remarkable in spite of the worldview differences that separate them.

COMMON VIRTUES—JUSTICE

This applies to other values as well, especially the call for justice or getting one's due. At the same time, the issue of justice is not as uniformly interpreted as are the virtues enumerated in the preceding paragraphs. Differences on questions of justice relate primarily to worldview differences that lock specific social structures or legal codes into the "nature of things" as either inherent in the design of the universe or as revealed by the Supreme Creator.

For example, within Hinduism, each person's caste position is determined by karmic consequences of a previous lifetime. The prerequisite for advancing into a higher caste during the next rebirth is conformity to caste obligations in this lifetime. In the language of justice, each person got his or her due in the present because of the past and will receive a fitting rebirth in the future because of beliefs and actions in the present. Imbuing the hierarchical Brahmin-dominated caste system with divine status enabled Hinduism to provide society with a stable social structure that (1) defined each person's proper place, that is, how they got their due; (2) combined material and spiritual values; and (3) provided alternative pathways to enlightenment. The penalty for failure to fulfill the expectations associated with one's caste duties in this lifetime is bad karma and transmigration away from the goal of liberation. Breaking "out of the mold," so to speak, is strictly forbidden. Brahmins, or priests, ought to act like priests, Kshatriya, or warriors like Arjuna, should behave like warriors, and so on down the line.

Buddhism and Jainism rejected this caste system classification of who gets what and why. At the same time, they retained the doctrines of karma, reincarnation, detachment from desire, and enlightenment. As a result, they radically redefined the notion of getting one's due. Whereas Hinduism wove the transition from material to spiritual values into the advanced forest dweller and world renunciation stages of the life cycle, Buddhism and Jainism democratized the pursuit of enlightenment.

Both religions disconnected their images of attaining liberation from conformity to caste and life cycle norms. By making detachment from all desires an irreducible prerequisite for advancing to the higher stages of meditation and liberation, Buddhism and Jainism abolished the need for adherence not only to the norms of the Hindu hierarchy but also to any social system at all. In all three Asian faiths, karma determines who gets what and why. In this sense they are identical. Their differences turn on alternative views of how to accumulate good or bad karma and the resultant rebirth consequences.

The emergence of Engaged Buddhism in the twentieth century represents the recognition that justice issues in the larger community are tied inextricably to spiritual goals. Turning inward in search of enlightenment and outward in pursuit of social justice are complementary. Poverty is a condition not to be ignored along the road to liberation. The elimination of poverty, as well as the establishment of political freedom, enables individuals to focus their energies on life's religious journey rather than merely on physical survival. In addition, during the past 200 years, many Hindu reformers have decried the ill-treatment of the lower castes, especially the "untouchables," and have sought actively to better their earthly lot. As a result of these and other changes, the traditional Asian religious perceptions of the means for distributing the burdens and benefits of society, that is, of justice are being stretched in new directions.

Within the Middle Eastern religions, the virtue of justice also plays a prominent role. As stated in the last Chapter, Zoroastrianism places advocacy for the poor among "the five best things in religion." In the afterlife, Ahura Mazda apportions rewards and punishments according to each person's lifetime balance of good versus bad thoughts, words, and deeds. Getting one's due on Judgment Day rests in large part on taking care of the needs of the most vulnerable members of society—the downtrodden poor. All persons will be judged by their ethical acts and the content of their characters. The virtue of justice stands at center stage in the Zoroastrian view of the universe where the struggle between good and evil will continue to the end of time.

Starting with Judaism, all three of the Abrahamic religions parallel Zoroastrian morality by placing justice at the top of their lists of virtues. Deuteronomy, the last of the five books of the *Torah*, pulls together many of the justice commandments that appear in the preceding books. During the 40 years that the Jews wandered in the wilderness after their escape from Egyptian slavery, Moses delivered to them the revealed Law of the Covenant that enumerates Yahweh's moral directives as well as the formula of blessing and curses that come with them.

In the *Book of Joshua*, Chapter 8, Joshua places six of the twelve tribes in front of Mount Gerizim and the other six in front of Mount Ebal. Appealing to Moses, he reads the Law to the assembled Israelites. Joshua reminds them that God's curse will fall on those who disobey the Ten Commandments: dishonor parents; mislead the blind; deprive foreigners or widows of their rights; commit murder or bribery; and so on. As indicated in Chapter 4, from Joshua through Two Kings, ancient Jewish writers interpreted the rise and fall of Israel as a regional power from the perspective of violating the justice standards of their Covenant.

Throughout the period that Israel existed as an independent nation, an entire line of prophets that stretched from Amos to Jeremiah repeatedly warned the Jews of their impending doom due to the steady deterioration of their commitment to be a just and righteous people. In the end, Joshua's warning came to pass. Yahweh punished the Jews by expelling them from the promised land and exiling them to Babylon. Israel's success or failure as a chosen people who enjoyed more than four centuries of political autonomy rested entirely on their shoulders. From Moses to the Babylonian exile, the justice commandments of the Covenant remained the measuring rod by which Yahweh blessed and ultimately cursed the ancient nation. In the emerging global village of the twenty-first century, these commandments continue to occupy a central position in the moral practices of modern Jewish people.

As Christianity emerged from its Jewish ancestry, it retained and reinterpreted the justice norms in light of the Christ event. In the Christian Scripture, Luke's Gospel and book of the *Acts of the Apostles*, more than any of the others' writings connects justice to Jesus. By Luke's account, Jesus revealed his concern for justice at the onset of his movement. After his baptism by John and temptation struggles in the wilderness, Jesus went on the Sabbath to a Nazareth synagogue where he read aloud from the *Book of Isaiah*, "The Spirit of the Lord is upon me, because he has anointed me to bring good news to the poor. He has sent me to proclaim release to the captives and recovery of sight to the blind, to let the oppressed go free." (Luke 4:18–19)

This is the language of justice applied to the person of Jesus. The Jewish and Christian parallel is clear. Just as Moses set the ancient Israelites free from Egyptian slavery, Jesus came to liberate the downtrodden of his time. In another passage, Luke's Jesus proclaims, "Blessed are you who are poor, for yours is the kingdom of God. Blessed are you who are hungry now, for you will be filled." (Luke 6:20–21)

The parable of the Rich Man and Lazarus dramatically combines the justice imperative with one's destiny after death. (Luke 16:19–31) When the Rich Man dies, he goes to Hades. When Lazarus dies he joins Abraham in heaven. When the Rich Man begs Abraham to "dip the tip of his finger in water and cool my tongue," Abraham replies that it is only Lazarus who merits heaven's comforts while the Rich Man deserves the agonies of hell. Abraham reminds the Rich Man, "Between you and us a great chasm has been fixed." In short, Luke aims Jesus' message of justice directly at the wealthy: Take care of the poor when you are alive or suffer the consequences after you die.

Luke's Gospel transforms the pattern of blessings and curses that the Hebrew Scripture writers applied to ancient Israel's rise and fall as a worldly power to an image of rewards and punishments in life after death based on a person's just or unjust treatment of the poor in life before death. For Luke, Jesus not only lives by the *Torah* code of justice, but he also embodies it in his being. As Christianity expanded over the centuries, Jesus' followers and Church leaders carried forward this early vision of justice and applied it to a broad range of changing circumstances.[2] Like Judaism, contemporary Christianity incorporates within its understanding of character development a major emphasis on the virtue of justice.

This is equally true of Islam. From the beginning until the present day, the last of the three Abrahamic religions has placed justice at the center of its understanding of morality. The Qur'an counsels the followers of Allah's revelations to practice justice in all their relationships. The often-quoted Sura 107 makes this clear. "Have you thought of him that denies the Last Judgment? It is he who turns away the orphan and does not urge others to feed the poor. Woe to those who pray but are heedless in their prayer; who make a show of piety and give no alms to the destitute." Islam's Third Pillar reinforces the justice imperative by urging support for the poor and sick by distributing 2.5 percent or more of one's wealth.

Like Zoroastrianism, Judaism, and Christianity, the core value of Islam involves doing good deeds and avoiding evil. "Let there become of you a nation that shall speak for righteousness, enjoin justice, and forbid evil. Such men shall surely triumph." (Sura 3:104) Allah requires that each Muslim "pass judgment upon men with fairness." (Sura 4:58) Building on this general justice norm, the Qur'an includes many specific applications, especially as it applies to treating neighbors with honesty. Cheating is strictly forbidden in personal and business-related exchanges. "Give full measure, when you measure, and weigh with even scales. That is fair, and better in the end." (Sura 17:35) "Keep your promises; you are accountable for all that you promise. (17:34)

Like the founders of all the world's great religions, Muhammad understood that the best moral motivations come from within each person's character. While obedience to external laws is required of all Muslims, internalizing the highest ethical standards and assuming personal responsibility for one's actions is one of humanity's highest goals. Sura 5:105 forewarns, "Believers, you are accountable for none but yourselves; he that goes astray cannot harm you if you are on the right path. You shall all return to Allah, and He will declare to you what you have done."

Within the Abrahamic tradition of sacred texts, the Qur'an's consistent reference to justice norms corresponds to both the Jewish and Christian Scriptures. Starting with the Torah Commandments and stretching to the Gospel of Luke's portrayal of Jesus, concern for the poor, sick, orphans, widows, or other disadvantaged groups sits at the center of Jewish, Christian, and Muslim ethics. In the twelfth century Muslim theologian al-Ghazali emphasized that faithful living according to the Qur'an involves a lifelong commitment to nurture virtue and avoid vice. In the thirteenth century, Aquinas included justice as one of the seven most important virtues.

Thus, it can be concluded that many possibilities exist for finding common ethical ground across the boundaries of the major world religions. This includes both the Asian and Middle Eastern spiritual traditions. Despite major worldview differences, there are ample opportunities for constructive interfaith interaction in the area of the Ethics of Virtue. The greatest amount of overlap involves the norms of kindness, compassion, mercy, noninjury, empathy, gentleness, moderation, and self-restraint. Equal emphasis is placed on avoiding destructive vices such as anger, pride, greed, gluttony, envy, sloth, and lust, among others.

On questions of justice, considerable consensus prevails within each of the two families of religions. Differences turn on how "getting one's due" is determined by doctrines such as karma, dharma, and reincarnation (as in the case of the Asian religions) versus the belief in human sinfulness, heaven, and hell (as found among the Middle Eastern traditions). At the same time, the growing concern over economic and political issues among many leaders of the Asian religions has resulted in greater convergence on the importance of social justice as necessary to the pursuit of spiritual goals among all of the great world religions.

The creation of greater peace and justice within the emerging global village will be determined in part by the ability of the leaders and laity of the world religions to cooperate at many levels. Whereas worldview differences all too often separate believers of the diverse traditions from each other, their ethical similarities can serve to bring them together. In the final analysis, a peaceful and just global village must rest on a global ethic. During the latter third of the twentieth-century, many scholars focused their inquiries on the quest for such an ethic.

THE SEARCH FOR A GLOBAL ETHICS

In the midst of the religious pluralism that divides humanity into distinct communities, numerous authors have looked beyond the diversity of beliefs for the unity of values. Their search dovetails with one of the main claims of this book. *All of the major religions of the world share a common core of values such as truth, love, compassion, mercy, fairness, and justice.*

Starting in the post-World War II period, the global ethic quest gained steady momentum. The impetus for this movement began with the United Nations' Universal Declaration of Human Rights. While the majority of countries endorsed the broad individual rights framework of the Declaration, critics pointed out that it remained incomplete for lack of equal emphasis on social rights and responsibilities. In addition to the United Nations' political-legal approach, other authors turned to culture as the source for discovering a core of shared values. Some writers identified one ethical principle from which all others have their origin.

Despite these different approaches, the global ethic quest begins with one question. Given the worldview diversity that exists among the world religions, how far is it possible to go in identifying the common values of a universal ethic? This question is really all about "minimum versus maximum." What constitutes a minimum global ethic? What does it take to stretch a minimum global ethic to the maximum?

The Universal Declaration of Human Rights is the starting point in any discussion of a global ethic. In December 1948, the United Nations approved the Declaration in order to protect and promote the human rights of every individual around the world irrespective of nationality or political philosophy. Even though several members of the Communist world, South Africa, and Saudi Arabia voted to abstain, forty-eight nations supported the world's first Universal Declaration. While widespread praise greeted its passage, the Declaration left unanswered a multitude of questions.

The original wording served well the purpose of protecting the rights of individuals, but it said very little about group rights, right to collective determination, economic and political rights, rights of women and children, and other historically unprotected groups. Subsequent revisions and expansions of the original Declaration have addressed many of these and other criticisms. Several critics pointed out that the Declaration embodies the secular humanist philosophy of Western culture with its central emphasis on the individual rather than the welfare of society as a whole.

Even though the Declaration excludes the explicit use of religious language and references to the religious foundations of its underlying values, it is often assumed that religions that stress the importance of the individual believer rather than collective conformity helped create the cultural context from which the Declaration sprang. Despite the controversies that surrounded it, the 1948 Human Rights Declaration produced the first truly international global ethics framework. The additions and modifications that the United Nations has made since approving the original text provide ample evidence of the ongoing interest in the universality of human rights issues.

Not everyone follows the UN's approach. Rather than focus on the legal Declarations of international politics, others dig deeper into the diverse cultures of the world to find the common values that cut across all of them. Those who employ this method usually begin with a critique of cultural relativists who contend that universal values do not exist. Well-known sociologist and futurist author Wendell Bell writes that today we know "cultural relativism is a misleading doctrine."[3] Many of the early anthropological studies that gave rise to this doctrine have been refuted or reversed upon restudy, including Margaret Mead's classic research on *Coming of Age in Samoa* and *Sex and Temperament in Three Primitive Societies*. This also holds for Bronislaw Malinowski's work on *Sex and Repression in Savage Society*. Dissimilarities among cultures are superficial compared to their similarities.[4] For centuries, from ancient to modern times and in all fields of study, writers from philosophy to modern social science have created lists of humankind's common values.

In 1990, widely known ethics writer Rushworth Kidder founded the Institute for Global Ethics for the purpose of promoting ethical behavior in individuals, institutions, and nations through research, public discourse, and practical action. His moral agenda for the twenty-first century involves identifying shared human values that can serve as the basis of a universal code. In the early 1990s he interviewed twenty-four prominent world citizens, which led him to identify eight core values that all interviewees held in common. They are love, truth, fairness, freedom, unity, tolerance, responsibility, and respect for life.[5]

These broad values lend themselves to creative adaptation in a variety of situations. They have cross-cultural appeal. Compared to the United Nations' 1948 Declaration of Human Rights that was written in the legal language of international lawyers and focuses on individual rights, this list of eight core values engages the moral imagination at a broader level. Values like love, fairness, tolerance, and responsibility, to name four, can be adapted to an unlimited number of circumstances that cut across a wide range of social settings. Legal documents are specific. Value lists are more general. In this sense, the two do not stand in opposition. Instead, they operate at different levels and complement each other.

A third approach to creating a global ethic starts by identifying only one overarching universal moral principle that appears in all cultures around the world. Leonard Swidler, who founded the Center for Global Ethics (not to be confused with Kidder's Institute for Global Ethics) at Temple University, employs this method to develop and promote the acceptance of a viable and sustainable global ethic. A global ethic "could well start with—though not limit itself to—elements of the so-called 'Golden Rule': Treat others as we would be treated."[6]

The Golden Rule appears in all of the religions described in this book, Hinduism, Buddhism, Jainism, Zoroastrianism, Judaism, Christianity, and Islam. It can also be found in Confucianism, Baha'i, and in the writings of one of the Western World's greatest philosophers Immanuel Kant, who described it as the Categorical Imperative.[7] Underneath the heterogeneity of diverse worldviews, "We propose the Golden Rule, which for thousands of years has been affirmed in many religious and ethical traditions, as a fundamental principle upon which to base a global ethic."[8]

Once established, this common ground principle can serve as a broad global platform for identifying middle range values or for delineating even more specifically the areas where universal rights apply as defined in the UN Declaration of Human Rights. In effect, the three approaches thus far described represent different points along a continuum that ranges from the most general Golden Rule to the most specific Declaration of Human Rights with middle range values falling in the middle.[9]

The last approach to developing a global ethic stretches beyond the UN's emphasis on individual rights. In addition to preserving the United Nations' high regard for such rights, it incorporates respect for social rights as well. The UN's protection of individual rights is only a minimal starting point that needs to be expanded in order to move the quest for a global ethic toward a vision of maximum inclusion. A universally viable global ethic should "focus on economic and social rights as deserving priority and serious attention. Unless this happens, it will always seem to most of the peoples of the world that human rights are little more than a luxury of the affluent."[10]

There exists a range of social areas into which the concept of rights can be expanded. These include protection of indigenous peoples and their right to self-determination, minority nationalities and religions, women, lower economic classes, gay and lesbian persons, young people, and so on. At its 1993 worldwide conference in Chicago, the Parliament of the World's Religions created one of the most comprehensive statements of a global ethics to date, The Declaration of a Global Ethic. A new global order cannot exist without a global ethic. As the following excerpt shows, not only does the Parliament's Declaration embody the earlier minimalist vision of protecting individual rights found in the UN's Declaration, but it also encompasses broad social rights that stretch toward maximum inclusion.

> We are interdependent. Each of us depends on the well-being of the whole, and so we have respect for the community of living beings, for people, animals, and plants, and for the preservation of Earth, the air, water and soil.
>
> We take individual responsibility for all we do. All our decisions, actions, and failures to act have consequences.
>
> We consider humankind our family. We must strive to be kind and generous. We must not live for ourselves alone, but should also serve others, never forgetting the children, the aged, the poor, the suffering, the disabled, the refugees, and the lonely. No person should ever be considered or treated as a second-class citizen, or be exploited in any way whatsoever. There should be equal partnership between men and women. We must not commit any kind of sexual immorality. We must put behind us all forms of domination and abuse ...
>
> We must strive for a just social and economic order, in which everyone has an equal chance to reach full potential as a human being.... Therefore we commit ourselves to this global ethic, to understanding one another, and to socially beneficial, peace-fostering, and nature-friendly ways of life.
>
> We invite all people, whether religious or not, to do the same.[11]

CONCLUSION

The more that each religion emphasizes that its traditions, moral mandates, and legal codes are grounded in the structure of the universe or incorporate God's perfect revelations, the more difficult it is to create a common ground of cooperation. The diverse worldviews that provide the broad theological or philosophical framework for each religion's ethical standards can block forward-looking dialogue.

At the same time, it is clear that there is widespread consensus among the world religions on the universality of certain values. Despite diverse and often isolated patterns of historical development, the same virtues appear repeatedly. These include truth, love, compassion, mercy, kindness, fairness, justice, respect for life, and so on. It is ironic that the modern electronic and transportation systems that are creating the communication web of the global village are enabling humankind to discover the core of universal values that have always existed across the boundaries of once isolated societies and the religions that helped create them.

The 1948 UN Declaration of Human Rights unleashed a torrent of initiatives to develop a global ethic. The minimal vision of individual rights laid the foundation for further expansion into the realm of maximum social rights. Numerous organizations and their leaders have created global ethics positions papers and Declarations that complement each other in their overarching visions and detailed descriptions of baseline values. In 1993, the Parliament of the World's Religions produced a Global Ethic Declaration that embodies the very universal values that they hold in common.

As the world continues to evolve toward greater global integration in the twenty-first century, a growing number of religious and other global ethics advocates have moved beyond worldview differences. They are drawing from a reservoir of values that Hindus, Buddhists, Jains, Zoroastrians, Jews, Christians, Muslims, and others, whether religious or not, share—and it would appear have always shared. Herein resides the common ground for bringing greater peace and justice into the global village.

SECTION IV

Applications—Confronting Global Dilemmas

CHAPTER 9

Violence and the World Religions

Sooner or later, all religions get blood on their hands.[1] The only issue is when it occurs in their history. For some, it begins early in their evolution and is instrumental in spreading their faith. For others, it happens later by either defending the faith and the way of life connected to it against an outside aggressor or in disseminating more widely an already well-established faith. This is to say, despite the existence of shared values such as respect for life, kindness, compassion, love, justice, and so on, all religions have violated these norms by resorting to violence at various times during their history. Why should this be so?

The answer to this question is complex because religion does not exist in a social vacuum. Its very survival is always tied to outside forces that imperil, permit, or promote its existence. These include cultural norms, economic and political structures, demographic patterns, and the unique historical circumstances in which the religion arose. No two religions travel the same road in their development from the embryonic impulses of their founders to the long-term support they garner among millions of loyal followers generation after generation.

Second, in addition to external factors, the internal worldview commitments of the followers of any religion determine the extent to which they become aggressive in trying to win over others to their points of view. Each religion differs in the degree to which it perceives that it has a spiritual mandate to spread its faith to nonbelievers. Internal motivation is an essential contributing factor in predisposing religious and political leaders to employ violence as a means of changing the world.

In the history of religions, for centuries the two most aggressive convert-seeking faiths have been, and continue to be, Christianity and Islam. In the emerging global village of the new millennium, the ability of religions to expand through political conquest is far more limited than in the past. Now, because of the emergence of a worldwide web of electronic communications, religious ideas must compete in a global marketplace for the allegiances of believers and nonbelievers alike. In the midst of this give and take, the extent to which the world religions will contribute to increasing peace and justice or greater hostility in the twenty-first century will depend on the extent to which they emphasize their joint heritage of shared values or maneuver to gain advantage through stressing the superiority of their worldviews over others.

ASIAN RELIGIONS

Hinduism

Hinduism incorporates ambivalence between duty or dharma and non-injury or ahimsa. The earliest Hindu Scriptures are the *Vedas,* which date from the third millennium BCE and consist of hymns dedicated to various gods that embody nature's forces. The most important deity in the *Vedas'* polytheistic belief system is Indra—the creator and sustainer god who is also the god of war and who will bring success in battle.[2]

As Hinduism evolved from its early polytheistic to later pantheistic stage, Indra worship merged with the caste system as defined in *The Laws of Manu,* which tied it to the warrior caste. Because traditional Hinduism anchored the caste system into the structure of the universe, performing military duties as a member of the warrior caste became a religious obligation that resulted in progressing toward enlightenment through the accumulation of good karma. As we indicated in our earlier summary of the *Bhagavad-Gita,* Lord Krishna explains to Arjuna that he must go to war against his beloved kinsmen if he wants to achieve the spiritual goal of release from reincarnation. Only one course of action is open to him: he must wield the sword even if it results in his own death or the deaths of others.

The *Gita* does not stand alone as a sacred text but is included in a massive epic called the *Mahabharata,* which ancient Hindu scholars wrote and compiled over 800 years from 400 BCE to 400 CE. The Hindu position on the appropriate uses of violence is developed in this lengthy story about the struggles for political control between two blood-related families, the Pandavas and the Kauravas. The account of their battles and maneuvering is really an extended narrative on the conflict between good and evil. Arjuna is a renowned warrior prince of the Pandava family, which represents the forces of goodness. The Kauravas embody evil and greed and are responsible for provoking the wars that engulf the two families. When Arjuna instructs his charioteer Krishna to drive him onto the pending field of battle so that he can catch a glimpse of the enemy he is about to fight, his challenge as a member of the warrior caste is not merely to perform his individual spiritual duty but also to defend what is right and good.

Even though the Pandavas ultimately prevail over the Kauravas, the *Mahabharata* recognizes the waging war is messy, brutal, and filled with deceptions on both sides. It is not simply a contest between the forces of pure light and pure darkness. Goodness and evil are intermixed in ambiguous ways, and it is not always easy to distinguish where one leaves off and the other begins. The victors often resort to the same kind of deceit and dishonesty they experience in the attitudes and actions of their enemies.

In the final analysis, the *Mahabharata* lays out a vision of violence in religion and society that is complex and layered. Almost any position can be found. On the one hand the *Mahabharata* views all war as evil, although it does not espouse pacifism in either passive or active form. On the other hand, it glorifies the courage and heroism that war inspires in the bold combatants who engage in it. The Pandava King Yudhisthir personifies the propeace outlook when he affirms, "In all cases war is evil." "Peace is preferable to war. Who, having the choice, would prefer to fight?"[3] Arjuna stands on the opposite end of the violence continuum. The *Gita* portrays him as a celebrated hero warrior who combines the dual commitments of spiritual dedication and military skill second to none.

In-between these two extremes, the *Mahabharata* sets forth two other conditions related to the decision to go to war and the killing that always results from it. First, wars should be fought only for the purpose of self-defense. No group should resort to war as an offensive tactic to conquer or destroy others. Such premeditated action is inherently evil. Every group has a right to defend itself when attacked without provocation and for the purpose of military conquest or destruction. It is Arjuna's duty as a Pandava from the inherited nobility caste of warriors to defend his people from the Kauravas despite the inevitability of interfamilial bloodshed.

Second, those who engage in war ought to be guided by moral principles that keep carnage and killing within clearly defined boundaries. The *Mahabharata* projects an image of warring where only armed combatants should engage in violent behavior that leads to damage or death. This means that all noncombatants, including unarmed or captured soldiers, animals, and plants, should not intentionally be injured or destroyed. The conduct of war should always be confined to warriors engaged in armed conflict. Placing civilians in harms way must be assiduously avoided. Warfare should be as brief as possible, and peace should be reestablished as quickly as possible.

Thus, from the beginning, the *Mahabharata* in general and the *Bhagavad-Gita* in particular accepted warring as an integral part of human behavior, although the Hindu sages approached the topic of warfare with many minds. They preferred peace but accepted the inevitability of war given the human tendency of some to desire domination over others. At the same time, they sought to keep communal disruptions to a minimum by developing moral guidelines that regulated the conduct of war and confined the carnage to armed combatants. They assigned the soldiering task to an inherited caste of noble warriors and made armed fighting for the purpose of self-defense a spiritual and social obligation. They admired the military prowess of fighters like Arjuna, whose skills they celebrated as a safeguard against aggression and as indispensable to restoring the peace.

Despite the preference for peace, the ancient Hindu writers were not pacifists unlike Mahatma Gandhi whose nonviolent resistance to British occupation led to India's independence in 1947. The modern Hindu Gandhi embraced the principle of noninjury or ahimsa as an integral part of his personal spirituality and political philosophy. Given the long-standing Hindu tradition of resort to arms as a means of self-defense against military aggression, Gandhi could have easily opted for violence. He chose not to do so.

Buddhism

Buddhism and Jainism emerged during the sixth century BCE as spiritual alternatives to Hinduism. The founders of these new religions were members of the warrior caste that stood on the second step of the caste ladder that the priestly Brahmins dominated. Although much scholarly speculation exists over why these two religions emerged at about the same time, both Buddha and Mahavira brought new spiritual insights to the ancient inhabitants of South Asia. Both of these new faiths demonstrated a strong dedication to the doctrine of ahimsa.

In its original Theravada form, the Buddhist worldview begins with the First Noble Truth that life is suffering. Over time, this evolved into an ethic of compassion and kindness. The nondestruction of life anchors Buddhist morality as an extension of Steps 3 through 5—Right Speech, Conduct, and Livelihood. In developing the original Ten Precepts, Buddha placed the noninjury principle of ahimsa at the top of the list for both monks and the laity to follow. The Mahayana branch puts limitless compassion at the center of the bodhisattva vow.

Nonetheless, as Buddhism expanded beyond the original simplicity that monastic isolation made possible, it encountered many of the complexities and ambiguities that integration into the larger structures of social life entails. In contrast to the integration of religion and society, which existed in Hinduism from the start, Buddhism began as a spiritual movement set apart from the world. However, its very success brought it into the larger arena of political and economic challenges.

Like Christianity under King Constantine, the spread of Buddhism throughout most of ancient South Asia stems from the fierce conquests of one person, King Asoka, who ruled the Mauryan dynasty from 265–238 BCE. There are two distinct phases to his leadership, his pre-Buddhist ruthless militarism and his post-Buddhist conversion that led to a complete transformation of attitude and policies. After nearly a decade of ruling by carnage that resulted in tens of thousands of deportations and deaths, King Asoka succumbed to remorse over the senseless loss and dislocation of so much life.

As legend has it, a humble monk convinced him of the superiority of Buddha's doctrine to the ways of the world that resulted only in endless suffering. After his profound conversion, Asoka declared that he would no longer follow the path of violence but instead would govern according to Buddhist morality and the principle of noninjury. As a result, he carved new rulings into stone pillars and placed them at strategic locations throughout his empire for all to observe and obey. Asoka, the once virulent monarch whose violent manner seemed second nature, became the virtuous king who established nonviolence as the cornerstone of his reformed regime.

After his conversion to Buddhism, Asoka ceased warring and turned to managing his empire according to the Buddhist moral standards that he etched into his rock edicts. He sent ambassadors to surrounding dynasties to promote peace. Although he maintained a standing army to protect from invasion and retained the death penalty, he earnestly labored to extend Buddha's ethical principles throughout his kingdom. He founded monasteries and supported missionary ventures to new territories to spread Buddhist beliefs and morality. He did for Buddhism in Asia what Constantine did for Christianity in Europe, and what Mohammad and his followers did for Islam in the Middle East and Northern Africa.

Asoka's conversion took Buddhism beyond the doors of serene monasteries where monks meditated for nirvana and into the dynamic world of politics where kings and nobility fought for advantage. In such a world, the commitment to nonviolence confronts its greatest challenge: the use of violence by those who go to war in order to conquer others. For all religions, this is the greatest threat to peace. In Hinduism, while peace is preferred, the warrior caste stands prepared to protect against violent aggressors. In his original teachings, Buddha adopted the principle of noninjury to all forms of life as a precondition to advancing to the higher stages of the Eightfold Path. Under Asoka's rule, Buddhism became the official religion of the empire.

Thereafter, like its Hindu parent and predecessor, Buddhism became entangled in the political fortunes of those societies that adopted it. The historical patterns of Buddhism and violence parallel those of other religions. When threatened by outside forces, Buddhist monks arose to defend the faith. On others occasions, they joined armies to expand the faith to new territories. As Buddhism spread throughout Asia, the doctrine of nonviolence gave way to participation in war. The Tibetan king Glan Durma, who was a fierce opponent of the Buddhist faith, was killed by a monk who faked going to him out of compassion.[4]

In addition, in Korea in the twelfth, fourteenth, sixteenth, and seventeenth centuries, kings recruited monks into their armies by the thousands to defend against attacks by various enemies such as the Mongols and the Manchus. In China, in 515 CE, Fa-ch'ing assembled an army of 50,000 troops and proclaimed (contrary to the vow of compassion) that anyone who killed an enemy in battle would become instant *bodhisattvas*.[5] In 619, 5,000 Buddhists rebelled against and killed a government official after which one of the monks, Kao T'ao Cheng, declared himself emperor with the title Mahayana. In modern Maoist China, radical political Buddhists justified killing those who opposed the revolution by arguing that Buddha took the side of the oppressed.

The most extensive interlocking of Buddhism and war occurred in Japan with the introduction of Zen Buddhism toward the end of the twelfth century. From 1192 until 1868, the shogun political class controlled Japan. Shortly after their rise to power, they adopted Zen as their religious preference, and for nearly seven centuries they maintained control through the soldiering strength of the legendary samurai warriors who integrated Zen discipline into their rigorous military training. Zen austerity appealed to the soldier's combat readiness that helped warriors prepare for battle by focusing the mind on the pending battle.

Thus, the original South Asian Buddhist faith that began with a premise of noninjury evolved into a far distant East Asian form that meshed with a military mindset. This does not mean that the original impulse of compassion that motivated the Buddha and became the cornerstone of the bodhisattva vow disappeared. The contrary is true as all forms of Buddhism continue to incorporate this core value. It means simply that like all religions Buddhism has made its concessions to the world of politics. Starting with Asoka, it joined in the exercise of power that lies at the heart of it.

At times Buddhists resorted to war in order to defend their faith against those who would seek to destroy it. At other times Buddhists took up the sword in league with aggressors who would extend their control over new territories. No doubt, the original impulse for peace pulls devout Buddhists back to their core values. At the same time, worldly compromises that seemed compelling at the time caused peace-loving Buddhists to kill.

Jainism

The doctrine of ahimsa is more pronounced in Jainism than in either Hinduism or Buddhism, although the value of noninjury is central to both. For Jainism, it is the supreme virtue as Mahavira embraced it through starvation unto death. Jains who sweep the street as they walk in order to avoid destroying even the most vulnerable insects that others define as pests exemplify this trait in extreme measure. The Hindu Gandhi, whose nonviolent leadership led modern India to national liberation, put the principle of ahimsa at the center of his political philosophy and personal spirituality.

At the same time, like Hinduism and Buddhism, Jainism produced its share of violent warriors. Even though Gandhi integrated the precept of noninjury into his political ideology during the twentieth century, early Jains did not create a pacifist ethic as an alternative to the view of war as expressed in the Hindu Scriptures. Jain monarchs stressed the necessity to protect themselves and their subjects, by war if necessary, from corrupt Brahmin influences.[6] No doubt, Mahavira's birth into a warrior/nobility family and his rebellion against the older Brahmin-dominated caste system combined to place Jainism in a position of self-defense from the beginning. Like Hindus and Buddhists, early Jains preferred peace to war. At the same time, they combined without seeming contradiction the doctrine of noninjury to all life with the need for military defense.

Over centuries Jainism produced numerous battle commanders whose military prowess became legendary. Like the Hindu Arjuna in the *Bhagavad-Gita*, heroic Jain warriors were celebrated for their military successes in defending the faith, while maintaining an attitude of detachment from worldly passions and possessions. In addition to self-defense Jain warriors engaged in offensive aggression to spread their religious convictions to new populations. During the tenth and twelfth centuries, Jain commanders terrified their enemies by their aggressive tactics.[7] Just as Zen Buddhism contributed to the creation of Japan's austere Samurai soldiers, spiritual asceticism helped craft a class of disciplined Jain warriors.

Thus, at the purely spiritual level, Jains alongwith Hindus and Buddhists prefer life without war and raise the norm of noninjury to the highest levels of their moral convictions. At the same time, a study of these three Asian religions shows that human spirituality does not exist in a social vacuum. The more these religious movements matured into successful organizations and established a formidable social presence, the more they depended on politics, and if necessary the choice of violence, to survive and expand. History shows that ancient Asia's religious and political leaders offered ample justification for both defending the faiths as well as spreading them to new populations that they perceived would benefit by having them. No doubt, these motives were mixed with greed and the desire to dominate.

At the same time, despite the role of religion in justifying war for whatever reason, a vision of ahimsa sits at the center of the three Asian religions. This vision condemns war as a human failure to live by the highest ideals of the faith. Despite the killing and carnage that war inevitably produces, it is this vision that pulls believers back to their spiritual center as Gandhi's life and convictions demonstrate. In the final analysis, for Hinduism,

Buddhism, and Jainism, a vision of peaceful existence trumps the impulse to war.

MIDDLE EASTERN RELIGIONS

Zoroastrianism

Zoroastrianism views the universe as a cosmic struggle where the battle between the good spirit Spenta Mainyu and evil spirit Angra Mainyu will culminate on a dramatic Day of Judgment in the triumph of Light over Darkness. In the apocalyptic worldview of Zoroaster, at some unknown point in the future the Wise Lord and Creator of the universe, Ahura Mazda, will intervene on the side of goodness and destroy all of the wicked forces that prowl the universe. Through conflict and battle, Ahura Mazda will overthrow the powers of darkness.[8]

From the beginning, Zoroastrianism was associated with an aggressive nationalism. It was the religion of the conquering Persians in the sixth century BCE and beyond. As devout followers of the teachings of Zoroaster, kings Cyrus I and Darius I, and their subjects, were not pacifists. They saw in the symbol of the sun the light that pushes out the darkness. They viewed the sun's rays as burning arrows that press forward the cause of war, and they construed their conquests as the triumph of good over evil. They pursued war as a sacred cause to seek converts. In the revelations of Zoroaster, the most fundamental religious symbol, the sun, became the inspiration for the development of a military mindset that eventually cost even Zoroaster his life. He was killed at age 77 during one of the holy wars that his ideas inspired.

All of the paradoxes of the Middle Eastern religions are found in Zoroastrianism. On the one hand, it contains a demanding code of behavior that rests on the highest virtues and moral standards of good thoughts, words, and deeds. On the other hand, its worldview allows for the conduct of war as a holy cause especially when combined with militant nationalism.

Judaism

Like Zoroastrianism, Judaism embodies all the peace and war paradoxes. From the time of Yahweh's call to Abraham to build a great nation until the deadly destruction of Jerusalem and the Temple by Romans soldiers in 70 CE, the entire ancient accounts of the Israelites reveal the cyclical nature of this paradox. Like the Law of the Torah and the Covenant with Yahweh, the repeated pattern of violence and concord are etched into the hard stone of Israelite history.

The Hebrew Scripture and sacred writings narrate how violence accompanied all major phases of the ancient Jewish story. These include escape from

Egypt under Moses, punishments for apostasy in the desert, the conquest of Canaan, the period of the judges and the creation and sustaining of the monarchy from Saul to Solomon, the acrimonious split between the northern and southern kingdoms, the Assyrian destruction of Israel, the Babylonian captivity of Judah and exile, the return to Jerusalem that followed Cyrus' military defeat of the Babylonians, the Greek occupation from Alexander to expulsion by Judas Maccabee and his followers, and the Roman conquest that ended in a devastating defeat of the Jewish rebellion.

The "chosen people—promised land" theology and tribal existence made violence in ancient Hebrew society inevitable. With myriad deities leading numerous tribes into combat, proof of the superiority of each tribe's god or gods rested solely on success in battle. The Hebrew Scripture is filled with stories of Jews marching to battle carrying the Ark of the Covenant that housed the Ten Commandments and Yahweh who led the charge, provided the protection, and assured the victory.[9] In no other narrative is Yahweh's safeguarding the chosen people more vividly portrayed than in the account of youthful David's killing of the Philistine Goliath with a single stone (I Samuel 17:1–54).

Clearly, the Yahweh of ancient Israel is a God of War. The resort to violence not only repelled unprovoked aggression but it also served to fulfill Yahweh's gift of giving the promised land to the chosen people as well as later in taking it away from them. The ancient Hebrews engaged in war both to defend against and to conquer their enemies. Life during the era of ancient tribal conflict was precarious at best. In particular, the military prowess of Joshua, the Judges, Saul, David (Saul has slain his thousands, David his tens of thousands—I Samuel 21:11), and Solomon led ancient Israel to the height of regional independence and national political power. In equal measure, for the Israelites of old, the military might of outside forces such as the Assyrians, Babylonians, Greeks, and Romans resulted in defeat, exile, return, relative autonomy, and eventually Diaspora. The violence that helped raise them up also brought them down. In keeping with the ancient Hebrew proverb, they not only lived by the sword but also died by it.

In addition to the earthly war tradition of political Israel, a new image of apocalyptic war arose during the period of Greek domination as described in the *Book of Daniel*. For the pre-Davidic Israelites, the resort to violence was integrated with a vision of earthy war as the means of securing Jewish control of the promised land. David used violence to consolidate the twelve tribes into national unity. With the decline of Israel-Judah's political independence and subordination by outside military forces, the role of violence became subsumed under an image of apocalyptic war that would occur at the end of time when Yahweh, like the God Ahura Mazda in Zoroaster's worldview, would destroy the reign of evil.

In the vision of Daniel, the faithful would not be rewarded through Yahweh's reestablishment of the old political dynasty but with everlasting life after death when the wicked would be punished with eternal damnation. The metamorphosis of earthly war to end-of-the-world-as-we-know-it apocalyptic war occurred during a period of political powerlessness that gave rise to the feeling of personal and collective hopelessness. For Daniel, the vision of apocalyptic war was an end-of-history projection in lieu of earthly war that was no longer possible. As Israel's political fortunes changed, so did its view of war. Whether in worldly or apocalyptic form, the ancient Israelites envisioned that the will of Yahweh would prevail, either in time or at the end of it.

The story of ancient Israel does not end with accounts of past wars and images of future battles. The other side of the peace-war paradox is the Jewish perception of peace or *shalom*. The well-known image of turning swords into plowshares stands in direct opposition to Joel's directive to "Beat your plowshares into swords, and your pruning hooks into spears." (Joel 3:10) Despite the cyclical recurrence of violence throughout the highs and lows of ancient Israel's history, in the final analysis the Hebrew perception of Yahweh's purpose in bringing the chosen people into being is to establish shalom on earth. The ultimate goal is peace not war.

The theme of shalom appears throughout the Psalms in passages such as, "Let me hear what God the Lord will speak, for he will speak peace to his people, to his faithful, to those who turn to him in their hearts." (Psalm 85:8) In addition to the narrower view of shalom as the absence of war, it also implies a broader understanding of emotional and physical wellness, stability, and the absence of fear related to military threats. Shalom means wholeness, inner calm, and social prosperity under Yahweh's protective hand.

The above discussion makes clear that there are multiple positions on the issue of violence in the traditions of ancient Israel. These range from a preference for peace to both defensive and offensive war relative to the perceived purposes of Yahweh at any given point in time—past, present, and future. The ancient Jewish views of violence and peace apply not only to life before the Diaspora but after it as well. With the development of the rabbis' Talmudic commentaries on the Torah during the Diaspora, the theme of peace moved to the center of Hebrew thought. Surviving for centuries as a dispersed minority group amidst dominant, and frequently hostile, host cultures became a priority of the highest order. Stressing the centrality of shalom became the cornerstone of Jewish morality when other options simply did not exist, especially the possibility of returning to Israel. It was either peaceful coexistence away from the promised land or no existence at all.

At the same time, the Jewish emphasis on shalom during the Diaspora did not guarantee that they would be allowed to live peacefully with their non-Jewish neighbors. For nearly two millennia, discrimination and recurring violence against Jews became one of Europe's harshest realities. The

Jews could never assume that life in the Diaspora would lead to permanent security because even extended periods of peaceful coexistence with non-Jewish Europeans always eroded into violence and death. Jews became Europe's scapegoats for every imaginable form of political, social, or economic failure.

By the late nineteenth century, many Jews concluded that they would never be free from persecution until they had an independent nation of their own. The vision of returning to the ancient homeland fired the imagination of an Austrian Jew, Theodor Herzl, who founded modern Zionism. For Herzl, real assimilation and equal rights in Europe were impossible as nearly 2,000 years in Diaspora demonstrated.[10]

In the 1890s political Zionism emerged as a nationalist movement based on the belief that the Jewish people would never be secure without a homeland of their own in which they could prosper as a distinct race and culture. Over the next several decades thousands of Jews peacefully migrated to Palestine and purchased land of their own. Others resorted to violence to drive Palestinians from their homes. After nearly two millennia of European dispersion and abuse, many twentieth century Zionists adopted violence as a means of reoccupying the ancient promised land. Their principle goal was the creation of a Jewish state in the heart of the Palestine region that Muslims had inhabited for 1,300 years.

At the end of World War II, the world became aware of the horrors of the Nazi Holocaust. As a result sympathy for the Zionist quest to create an independent nation rapidly gained momentum. In 1948, the newly created United Nations established the modern state of Israel. From the beginning, the hope of creating a modern, peaceful Israel remained a distant dream. Modern Israel's very survival amidst hostile Palestinians and Arabs rested on the superior use of violence.

Instead of peace, the Zionists got into constant war with their Muslim neighbors who view modern Israel as one of the last vestiges of western colonialism. While peace may eventually come to Israel and Palestine, in the process much blood has been and no doubt will continue to be shed on all sides. Bringing the Israeli-Palestinian conflict to a peaceful and just resolution is one of the greatest challenges of the twenty-first century.

Christianity

Christianity's view of violence can be summarized into four distinct doctrines: no war, apocalyptic war, just war, and holy war. One of the major Hebrew Scripture passages that the earliest Jewish converts to Christianity applied to Jesus comes from Isaiah 9:6–7, "For a child has been born to us, a son given to us; authority rests upon his shoulders; and he is named Wonderful Counselor, Mighty God, Everlasting Father, Prince of Peace. His authority shall grow continually, and there shall be endless peace."

For the first-generation core of disciples and apostles who joined the Jesus movement, the long-awaited Messiah of Israel had arrived on earth. The proclamation that Jesus was the resurrected Christ who died for the sins of the world became the cornerstone belief of the embryonic peace-oriented church.[11]

The oldest images of Jesus depict him as a Savior who eschewed war as a means of creating the Kingdom of God on earth or in heaven. All of the pacifistic no-war traditions of Christianity[12] stem from this perception of Jesus. His Sermon on the Mount (Matthew, Chapters 5–7), his "turn the other cheek" sayings, and his refusal to defend himself through violence when he was arrested, tried, convicted, and executed point to the priority of pacifism in his perception of God's peace-loving Kingdom. Despite Jesus' violent death through a gruesome crucifixion, his early followers chose his way of nonviolence and did not resort to retaliatory war against those who killed him.

In addition to images of Jesus the no-killing pacifist, like Daniel in the *Old Testament*, the *New Testament* is filled with visions that visit eschatological havoc on nonbelievers. In the Book of Revelations, the historic Prince of Peace becomes transformed into an end-of-history warrior who rewards the faithful and punishes the wicked. In the *Gospel of Matthew* the end days are depicted as a time of turmoil when nations will war against each other, famines and earthquakes will abound, and persecutions will be widespread. "For at that time there will be great suffering, such as has not been from the beginning of the world until now, no, and never will be." (Matthew 24:21) On the final Day of Judgment, the book of life will be opened. Anyone whose name is "not found written in the book of life" will be "thrown into the lake of fire." (Revelations 20:15) Apocalyptic war stands at the opposite extreme from pacifism.

Like the *Book of Daniel* that was written during the Greek domination of the Jews, the apocalyptic images that appear in the *New Testament* reflect the status of the early Christians as a powerless minority group. In the face of total vulnerability to persecution at the whim of the Roman rulers, projecting a final victory for the faithful at the end of time when chaos and violence would descend upon the earth, brought an assurance that their sacrifices were not in vain. These canonized images of Jesus' Second Coming served to inspire "end-of-the-world-in-our-generation" millennial groups during almost every decade of Christian history.[13] The images of Jesus the Pacifist versus Jesus the apocalyptic warrior represent the extremes of early Christianity's view of violence as recorded in the *New Testament*.

The Just War and Holy War traditions occupy the middle ground between the extremes of the "no violence"—"end-of-the-world apocalyptic violence" continuum. Both apply to the Church's view of the appropriate use of violence in history. Both are inextricably tied to Christianity's growth as a religious, cultural, social, and political force during the first 1,200 years of its history. By the end of the thirteenth century, all of the four views of war had found expression. At the start and end of the Era of Medieval Christendom, Augustine and Aquinas respectively formulated and expanded on the doctrine of the Just War. Others contributed to its development as well during this time. The Holy War tradition is tied most dramatically to 200 years of Christian Crusades that the Popes launched between the end of the eleventh and the end of the thirteenth centuries in order to wrest control of the Holy Land from the Muslims. The Reformation also gave rise to Holy Wars between Protestants and Catholics as well as between Protestants and Protestants.

Among the historical four views of violence, the Just War doctrine dominates the other three. Even though Christians engaged in Holy War throughout different eras, it is viewed as the least justifiable because it stands in such stark opposition to Jesus' beliefs and behavior. For many, the very concept of Holy War represents a corruption at the heart of the Faith. Jesus' commitment to nonviolence inspired untold generations of pacifists to follow in his footstep. During the first 130 years after Jesus' death, Christians refrained from participating in Rome's wars. No evidence exists that Christians joined the Imperial army before 170 CE.[14] Thereafter Church members began to view soldiering as a legitimate form of Christian vocation. While Church leaders regarded the defense of public order as a social good, many refused to sanction killing as a part of it. By 300 CE, just 12 years prior to Constantine's vision to conquer in the name of the Cross, a substantial number of Christians had joined the Roman military.

The transformation from pacifism to the doctrine of the Just War accompanied the changes that occurred in Europe in a relatively short time period from Constantine's conversion in 312, which stimulated the Church's rapid expansion, until the Gothic leader Alaric conquered Rome in 410. During this transition of nearly 100 years, Christianity expanded as the ancient Roman Empire disintegrated under the relentless invasions by the surrounding tribes. As Christianity grew, the Church's imperative to defend the Empire that it was helping to shape and that the pagan attacks were increasingly threatening also grew. It was in the midst of the barbarian wars against Rome that Augustine gave voice to the doctrine of the Just War.

After witnessing the viciousness of the invading Germanic tribes as they marched toward Rome, Augustine rejected pacifism because of its inability to prevent the senseless slaughtering of thousands of innocent citizens. At the same time, he rejected the crusader's call to arms as a holy cause. For Augustine, going to war was tragic—a last resort when all else failed—but under certain circumstances utterly necessary. The only justification for the evil that killing in battle produced was to prevent a greater evil. For Augustine, war was always immoral even though the purpose for engaging in it could be just.

Augustine spelled out the criteria that warranted military intervention, which later writers, including Aquinas, elaborated into the Just War doctrine. During the Medieval Era the Church condensed its position on involvement in war and the resort to violence into seven principles.

1. The cause must be just.
2. The war must be declared and waged by a lawful authority.
3. War must be a last resort.
4. War must be the only possible means of securing justice.
5. War must be conducted by the right means: respect for noncombatants.
6. There must be a reasonable chance of victory.
7. The good to be achieved must be greater than the evil effect of war.[15]

From the time of Augustine forward, the position of "war as a justified last resort" remained Catholic and Protestant Christianity's dominant doctrine on the use of violence when all other nonviolent means of keeping the peace became exhausted.

This shift from the pacifist commitments of Jesus' early followers to the evolving doctrine of the Just War does not imply that Christianity came to prefer war to peace. The contrary is true. First and foremost, the Christian Church proclaimed from the start that its commitment to Christ as the Prince of Peace both in this life and in heaven mandates establishing peace on earth. Christianity is not unique in this regard. All of the major religions of the world prefer peace to war, and nonviolence to violence, despite their historical involvement in actions to the contrary.

At the same time, when religions become more deeply invested in the civilizations that they help to create they become more enmeshed in the world of politics. When threatened by hostile forces that would seek to subjugate or destroy them, their followers inevitably rise to defend their way of life according to the doctrine of the Just War. If they take a further step into the realm of envisioning that the Creator of the Universe has commissioned them to convert the world according to their revelations, Just War can give way to Holy War.

From the Medieval Church forward, "no war pacifists" and "holy war crusaders" stood at the opposite ends of the no violence-violence "bell curve," so to speak, while support for the Just War doctrine occupied the broad middle. By the time of Aquinas in the thirteenth century, the specific guidelines related to the justifiable uses of defensive violence had been worked out in considerable detail. By its very nature, nonhistorical, apocalyptic war is always projected to occur at the end of time even though many generations of Christians have falsely assumed that this meant "in their time."

Prior to the emergence of the modern world, the idea of war was limited to fighting individual battles under specific rules of engagement. With the rise of nationalism and modern science and technology, the concept and conduct of war changed dramatically. While there are many reasons for Europe's colonization of the world from the sixteenth through the mid-twentieth centuries, in part this dominance rested on superior military strength brought about by technological improvements in weaponry. Both Roman Catholic and Protestant branches of Christianity permeate North, Central, and South America because Spain, Portugal, England, and France conquered, destroyed, and converted native populations. The same holds true for sub-Saharan Africa and parts of Asia.

As the Colonial Era began to decline near the turn of the twentieth century, on every continent, Christianity had fulfilled Jesus' Great Commission as recorded in the Gospel of Matthew. "All authority in heaven and on earth has been given to me. Go therefore and make disciples of all nations, baptizing them in the name of the Father and the Son and of the Holy Spirit, and teaching them to obey everything that I have commanded you." The only areas of the world that Christianity did not convert were regions that the outstretched hand of the Church did not touch or where the devotees of other religions, most notably Islam, Judaism, Hinduism, and Buddhism, rejected the missionaries' message. In large measure, Christianity owes its current status as the world's largest religion to the Colonial Era that opened new opportunities for expansion and to the European nations that enabled it.

A comparative study of the history of religions teaches us that the combination of religion and politics has opened the door on numerous occasions to geographic and demographic expansion. In turn, this has led followers to an uncritical acceptance of war as inevitable. Nowhere is this better demonstrated than in the bloody conflicts of the twentieth century when the total amount of violence that erupted between World War I and the year 2000 was greater than the combined violence of all prior centuries.

Two factors in particular contributed to the heinous nature of war in the twentieth century. The first was nationalism and the second was development of the ideology of total war. Advances in airplane technology took warring to unimaginable heights of death and destruction as exemplified in the saturation bombing of entire cities such as Hamburg and Dresden in Germany and Tokyo in Japan, during World War II. When the United States dropped atomic bombs on Hiroshima and Nagasaki in early August 1944, and killed over 200,000 Japanese, the twentieth century science of killing had reached its apex. For the next 50 years until the end of the century, the threat of mutually assured destruction (MAD) kept Cold War antagonists from launching annihilating nuclear strikes against one another.

It is ironic that the dominant religion of the European countries that launched the Crusades and the Reformation wars, colonized the world for over four centuries of military aggression, and took warring to the high point of brutality during two World Wars and a Cold War, was Christianity. By the end of the twentieth century, the pacifist religion that the Prince of Peace started nearly two millennia earlier had become totally transformed and subordinated to nation-state conflicts in which millions of patriotic Christians from different countries fought each other to death. "The historic association of the Christian faith with nations of commercial enterprise, imperialistic expansion and technological advancement has meant that Christian peoples, although their faith is one of the most pacifistic in its origins, have a record of military activity second to none."[16]

Islam

What is the role of violence in the history of Islam? First, despite the current wave of terrorism that Al Qaeda and similar terrorist groups have launched around the world, the vast majority of Muslims prefer peace to war. No doubt, widespread media coverage of Muslim political terrorism has contributed to stereotyping Islam as an inherently proviolence religion. It is not. It would be incorrect to conclude that all the devoted followers of any religion are premeditated killers because of the behavior of some members. Just as all Christians were and are not crusaders, all Muslims were and are not terrorists.

At the same time, it would be naïve to dismiss modern Radical Muslim terrorism, or any other form of terrorism for that matter, as the isolated work of a few insane religious extremists. Modern terrorism is planned and purposeful; terrorist networks exist worldwide with one goal in mind: to kill massively and indiscriminately by the most lethal means available. By any measure of global morality, terrorism is a scourge that needs to be abolished. In the emerging global village of the twenty-first century, much political energy from individual nations to the United Nations will be spent in trying to contain and defeat it.

Given that much of today's systematically organized terrorism is linked to Islam, it is essential to examine carefully the Muslim view of violence. To begin, while Islam favors peace over war, it is not a pacifist religion, although a small segment of Islamic mystics called Sufis are pacifists.[17] From the start, Mohammad and his successors spread the Muslim faith through political-military expansion, conquest, and conversion. Islam's attitude toward violence developed over time as the Muslim community or umma expanded from its Medina origin to its empire status throughout the Middle East, Northern Africa, and parts of Asia and Europe.

On the Arabian peninsula of the sixth century, intertribal conflict was common and military skill was admired. Many tribes survived by attacking merchant caravans and sharing the spoils. Mohammad participated in these raids. War occurred frequently as the various tribes fought each other for control of territory and economic advantage. As Mohammad matured, he became a smart and shrewd warrior. He also developed an exceptional ability to help squabbling tribes resolve their differences. He fled Mecca to Medina in 622 not only to escape from the assassins who tried to kill him but because the leaders of the local tribes in Medina implored him to become their town administrator, which he did successfully and which culminated in the Medina Constitution that helped foster intertribal cooperation.

At the same time, Mohammad's Medina experience set the stage for later interpretations of virtually every aspect of Islam's view of war. Two experiences in particular shaped the Muslim norm related to the appropriate uses of violence. Even though Mohammad fled to Medina to save his life, the army from Mecca relentlessly pursued him. In 624 at the battle of Badr, the Muslims of Medina defeated a force from Mecca that was three times its size. As recorded in Sura 8:7–10, Mohammad construed the Badr battle as proof that Allah was on the side of the Muslims victors.

However, soon thereafter in 625, Mohammad's forces experienced their first major setback at Uhud, which resulted in the deaths of numerous Muslims. This disaster led Mohammad to reflect more deeply on why Allah would permit success on one occasion and defeat on another. The *Qur'an* addresses this issue: Suffering and loss can be seen as a test of faith and a challenge to remain loyal to the unfathomable will of Allah. (Sura 3:121–130; 14:27) The Muslim answer to the question of "why victory or defeat" is that only Allah knows. For Mohammad, it was far worse to retreat from battle over the fear of death than to die while defending the faith. The former leads to eternal retribution on the Day of Judgment, while the latter results in eternal life in paradise. (47:4–9, 20–21)

As a result of Mohammad's warring experiences against the forces from Mecca, which he eventually conquered in 630, all of the pieces of Islam's view of peace, war, and violence came together. These include the distinction between the dar al-Islam and dar al-harb, the doctrine of *jihad*, and the Sharia or Muslim Law.

The cornerstone of Islam consists of the creation, defense, and expansion of the umma or Muslim community. All Islamic beliefs and behaviors serve this one overriding goal. Dar al-Islam refers to the territory that Muslims control, whereas dar al-harb is the territory that Muslims do not control. The former is called frequently the land of peace and the latter the land of war. As the history of warring among Muslims shows from the earliest days of the faith, the image of a peaceful dar al-Islam is an ideal that has been and continues to be violated in reality, as current terrorist acts that involve Sunnis and Shi-ites in Muslim countries demonstrate.

After Mohammad conquered Mecca in 630, he spent the remaining 2 years of his life extending the dar al-Islam across the Arabian Peninsula. He was convinced that Allah had commanded him to convert the world. After Mohammad's death in 632, his followers continued his vision of territorial expansion even as they fought each other over control of the growing Muslim Empire. Within 150 years after his death, the Ummayad and Abbasid dynasties had captured vast territories that spread from Spain to India. Subsequent Muslim leaders pushed the dar al-Islam across northern Africa and as far away as Indonesia.

The successful expansion of the dar al-Islam depended on jihad, which means "to strive" or "to struggle." Although the doctrine of jihad is not one of the Five Pillars of the faith, it plays a central role in the life of every devout Muslim. It would not be far from the truth to say that the concept of jihad has been analyzed and subdivided *ad infinitum* by Muslim jurists over the centuries. Islamic scholars have distinguished between the jihad of the heart, tongue, hands, and the sword. They have written about jihad against polytheism, apostasy, dissension, bandits, People of a Book—Jews, Christians, Zoroastrians, Hindus, Buddhists, and so on.[18]

In the final analysis the many interpretations of the doctrine of jihad can be reduced to its greater and lesser forms. The greater jihad consists of the internal struggle of every Muslim to remain faithful. The lesser jihad involves defending the umma when confronted by either internal or external threats. Much controversy exists over whether jihad sanctions offensive war against nonbelievers or like Christianity's Just War Theory pertains only to defensive actions. Muslims disagree among themselves over the correct understanding of this doctrine. The *Qur'an* can be cited to support either position, and Mohammad's life reflected both. Either way, the doctrine of jihad serves the goal of protecting and promoting the umma that Mohammad believed Allah had instructed him to spread around the world.

Last but not least is the Sharia or Muslim Law. The Sharia consists of the combined legal codes related to Islam's four sources of authority that include the *Qur'an*, hadith, consensus, and analogy. Modern Islamic societies vary to the extent that they emphasize one or more of these sources over the others. Irrespective of these differences, starting with the *Qur'an* Muslims around the world understand their codes and laws as the means for organizing the umma. In this sense, the umma has not been left without guidance. Allah revealed to Mohammad the *Qur'an* that Muslims believe is Allah's perfect book. Therefore, like devout Jews who bind themselves to the *Torah*, committed Muslims live according to the moral and legal mandates of the *Qur'an*. The differences that exist among Muslims relate to their diverse perceptions of the extent to which the various laws of the Sharia are required, recommended, neutral, discouraged, or forbidden.

The internal striving to submit to Allah's commandment, that is, the greater jihad, is directly related to faithful adherence to the Sharia, which in turn strengthens the dar al-Islam. No doubt, the goal of peace on earth sits at the center of the Islamic moral vision. At the same time, the motivation of modern-day Muslims to extend the dar al-Islam into the dar al-harb depends on how they interpret the doctrine of jihad. Will it be understood as the commandment to engage in offensive war in order to establish the Sharia wherever possible or simply as a justification for defending the faith? The role of Islamic violence in the emerging global village of the twenty-first century will turn on how Muslims around the world answer this question. On this issue, the future is open ended.

CONCLUSION

It has been shown repeatedly in this chapter that political and religious leaders everywhere throughout the history of every society have used their religion to justify the use of violence despite the vision of peace that lies at the center of all of them. During warring times prior to the emergence of twentieth century total war, religion kept the brutalities of wartime killing to a minimum. The rules of war regulated the conduct of war. The policy of saturation bombing and the development of atomic weapons resulted in unprecedented levels of real and potential destruction.

While debate exists over which of the world religions is worst based on the amount of killing that their followers have perpetrated, in the final analysis this is like arguing over whether hurricanes or earthquakes are worse because of the relative damage and/or death they produce. At this level, this debate is merely academic. Just as all natural disasters are bad, all killing in the name of religion is immoral. In this sense, despite their collective adherence to the value of universal peace, all religions have engaged at one time or another in appalling acts of violence. At this most fundamental level, they are all equal.

At the same time, despite the use of violence from which no religion can claim exemption, all of the world religions have demonstrated a capacity for creating extended periods of peace and for bringing countless benefits to humanity in the form of justice, education, health care, and so on. While the historic circumstances differ widely regarding religious warring, the core values of peace and justice have sustained all of the world religions for centuries. On balance, vastly more people live under conditions of peace than die as a result of war; and all of the societies that the various religions helped create have enjoyed far more years of relative social tranquility than outbursts of warring behavior.[19]

In addition, in spite of every religion's historical connection to violence, all of the world religions include persons and groups who refuse to resort to killing under any circumstances. These range all the way from (1) individual pacifists like the Hindu Gandhi, the Buddhist Dalai Lama, and the Christian Martin Luther King, Jr., to (2) peace groups such as modern Israelis who pursue peaceful paths of reconciliation with Palestinians, Christian churches such as the Mennonites, and the Islamic group started by Uztaz Mahmoud Mohamed Taha who sought to bring Sudan's civil war to an end through Gandhi-like strategies of nonviolence. No doubt, a vision of a peace inspires a minority of followers of all the world religions to use only nonviolent strategies for political change. At the same time, as history shows, the majority of the adherents will respond to the call to arms when the nations where they live come under attack.

The global challenge for the world religions in the twenty-first century is clear. Can they rise above the cultures into which they are fully integrated and the political processes that they defend and promote? Is it possible for the devout leaders and followers of all the world religions to develop a common vision of peace that transcends the powerful forces that separate them? Can they build on the peace and justice values that cut across all of their distinct worldviews and reduce or eliminate the suspicions that separate them?

CHAPTER 10

Sex, Sexuality, and Gender and the World Religions

Among the world religions, the area of sex, sexuality, and gender is undergoing major redefinition. The term "sex" refers to being born with either male or female reproductive organs.[1] Sexuality refers to an individual's sexual orientation, that is, heterosexual, homosexual, bisexual, or transsexual, as well as to the forms of sexual activity that emanate from sexual orientation—both inside and outside of marriage. In all religions, sex is linked inseparably to acceptable and unacceptable expressions of sexual orientation and activity. Gender refers to the social roles and statuses that are tied to sex. They involve private, family, or domestic roles as well as public, economic, or political roles. As in the case of sexuality, all societies differentiate gender roles according to sex.

The relationship between sex, sexuality, and gender in the world religions is connected closely to worldview assumptions about Ultimate Reality. Since the male-female duality is inherent in all earthly species, every religion must address the human male-female duality from its worldview perspective. The religious interpretations of the relationship between sex, sexuality, and gender differ widely depending on whether Ultimate Reality is defined in either personal or impersonal terms. At this level, considerable disparity exists between the Asian and Middle Eastern religions.

At the same time, despite multiple perceptions, there are only four major ways to conceptualize how worldviews connect to sex, sexuality, and gender. This fourfold division starts by defining how Ultimate Reality relates to the male-female distinction. At this level, two possibilities exist. Religions that define Ultimate Reality in personal-creator terms must decide whether as created beings males and females are equal "in the eyes of God," so to speak. In the heavenly blueprint from which God created the universe, males and females are either equal or they are not. If males and females do not possess equal status at the level of the Ultimate, then it becomes necessary to explain why God would make such an unequal delineation. For religions that define Ultimate Reality in impersonal terms, such as Brahman, emptiness, or other, the same issue exists. Is the ultimate spiritual status of males and females that of equality or inequality?

The next level involves the position of males and females "on earth," after they are born. Once this occurs, sex differences translate into socially sanctioned expressions of sexuality and gender. In the area of sexuality, the main issue involves whether heterosexuality is the only legitimate form of sexual orientation and activity or whether other forms such as homosexual, bisexual, and transsexual are acceptable as well. Other issues involve sexual activity inside or outside of marriage, monogamy or polygamy, divorce procedures, and so on. Earthly sexual orientations and activities are always tied to spirituality. Or, stated differently, all religions sanction human sexuality in terms of their worldview definitions of how sex relates to Ultimate Reality.

In addition, religions also legitimize the gender roles that are acceptable or unacceptable for both males and females. Here two possibilities exist. In the first alternative, males and females have equal access to both domestic and nondomestic social roles. In the second alternative, males and females do not have equal access to all social roles. Instead, women are confined to domestic roles and men are restricted to nondomestic ones. In none of the world religions does an inverse gender role arrangement exist where men are identified with domestic roles and women with nondomestic ones.

In light of the preceding discussion, four combinations are possible. First, males and females are equal at both the worldview, that is, theological or philosophical, and social levels. Second, males and females are equal, but only at the worldview level and not at the social level where gender roles are defined in complementary rather than egalitarian terms. Third, males and females are not equal at either the worldview or social levels. Fourth, males and females are not equal at the worldview level but are equal at the social level. The first three of these four options appear in one form or another throughout the world religions. The fourth combination does not exist for the simple reason that no religion accords social equality to males and females if it defines them as unequal at the worldview level.

In addition, all of the world religions define heterosexuality as the normative form of human sexuality. At the same time, every religion must deal with the nonheterosexual forms of sexual orientation and activity. A continuum of responses exists ranging from vehement rejection to tolerance and accommodation depending on how each religion connects its view of

Ultimate Reality to the male-female sex duality. Religions that view hetero-sexuality as inherent in God's plan for creation are more inclined to view sexuality and gender roles from a complementary rather than an egalitarian perspective.

Enormous changes are occurring in the each religion's understanding of the nature of sex, sexuality, and gender. Historically, all societies and the religions that helped create them have based their understanding of human sexuality and gender roles mainly on the criterion of sex. Women give birth to babies. Men do not. Women breast-feed babies. Men do not. In the past, each person's sex at birth was the most important determinant of his or her social destiny.

With the advent of modern techniques of birth control and abortion, this is no longer the case. Many contemporary adherents of the world religions are redefining the relationship between sex, sexuality, and gender. They reject the traditional idea of using male-female physical differences as the sole criterion for determining acceptable expressions of human sexuality and gender role allocation. They are also offering new interpretations of their religious traditions as the basis for their alternative views.[2]

Modern feminists from all the world religions are spearheading the challenge to traditional religious views, which they critique as male-dominated. At core they are calling for a major shift from patriarchy to egalitarianism at both the spiritual and ethical levels. In terms of the four ways of combining equality or inequality at the worldview and social levels, modern female critics accept only one: males and females are equal in all regards except for biological differences related to childbirth. They reject all notions of gender inequality based on sex differences. In particular, they reject the idea that males and females are equal at the level of Ultimate Reality but not at the level of sexuality and gender.

Historically, men have determined the status of men and women at both the spiritual and social levels. At the worldview level, men have defined women as either equal with males or as unequal with them. At the social level, men have always envisioned women's roles as either complementary or subordinate to those of men. What men have socially constructed as complementary social roles according to some divine plan or cosmic structure, feminists critique as forms of discrimination based on the disproportional distribution of power. Since men have been able to control women, through violence if necessary, men have determined where both males and females fit into the social scheme of things based on their perceptions of the divine nature of things.

Males also wrote all the scriptures upon which all the world religions rest. As a result, the images that appear in these sacred texts are given divine sanction as the way God or the universe intended creation to be. In short, because of their power over women, men have defined where both men and women fit into the world and why. Part of the critique of male-dominated religious traditions involves the claim that the authority to define the place of women spiritually and socially belongs either to women and not to men or to both women and men.

Thus, language plays a very important role in terms of how men and women view their respective religious traditions. What traditionalists call complementary, modern detractors label discriminatory. For female and male critics and their sympathizers, it is a form of discrimination when women are not allowed to pursue nondomestic social roles and men domestic ones or when neither sex is permitted to express any other form of sexuality except heterosexuality. Double standards that give men access to privileges women do not have both inside and outside of marriage are also labeled as discriminatory and designed to keep men in control of women at virtually all levels—including self-definition, reproduction, and control over their bodies, and social behaviors.

How do the world religions differ on these issues? What contemporary challenges are leading leaders and laity to look at sex, sexuality, and gender in new ways?

ASIAN RELIGIONS

Hinduism

Traditional Hinduism combines spiritual equality with social inequality, which is also the dominant historical pattern, although not the exclusive one, that has permeated all the world religions. It is this pattern that is being challenged by modern writers who argue that the belief in spiritual equality lays the foundation for male-female equality in the areas of human sexuality and gender roles as well.

Classical Hinduism defines Ultimate Reality as the impersonal Brahman that permeates the whole of existence. At this level, males and females are equal by virtue of the atman that pervades all living creatures. For many Hindus, male superiority over women does not exist.[3] Despite the belief in male-female spiritual equality, Hindu attitudes toward the relationship between men and women are both multiple and contradictory. The writers of sacred texts (men only) did not translate the doctrine of spiritual equality into gender role equality for men and women. Rather, ancient Hinduism developed a rigid code of social inequalities.

In actual practice, women were not treated as equals with men. In *The Laws of Manu*, females were expected to be subordinate first to their fathers, then their husbands, and finally to their sons. The primary duty of women was to be obedient to her husbands, reproduce sons, and care for their homes. In addition, the female dowry tradition led to the practice of female infanticide because females were thought to be a financial burden to the families who could not afford the gifts that marriage required. Women were taught to think of their husbands as gods. For centuries, in the practice of *sati*, widows threw themselves on the funeral pyres of their deceased husbands to express the view that their lives as separate persons ended with their husbands' deaths.

Hindu sacred doctrines incorporated contradictory positions of female sexuality. On the one hand, some texts defined men and women as spiritual and sexual equals. Ancient Hindu sages described this as one soul (Brahman) in two bodies (male-female). This doctrine combines sexual union as the supreme act of spiritual liberation. This tradition is expressed in the *Kama Sutra* and related texts.[4]

On the other hand, proscriptions against attachment to worldly desires led other ancient writers to view female sexuality as source of all evil because it lured men away from focusing on the goal of spiritual liberation. This viewpoint is depicted vividly in *The Laws of Manu*. "It is the nature of women to seduce men in this world; for that reason, the wise are never unguarded in (the company of) females. For women are able to lead astray in (this) world not only a fool, but even a learned man, and (to make) him a slave of desire and anger." Furthermore, "Manu allotted to women (a love of their) bed, (of their) seat and (their) ornaments, impure desires, wrath, dishonesty, malice, and bad conduct."[5]

Thus, Hindu views of male-female duality, sexuality, and gender vary along a continuum. At one end stands the belief that the spiritual essence of all men and women transcends gender because of the inner atman-Brahman connection. The sharp delineation of males and females into gender roles based on sex and sexuality stands at the other. Some conservative interpreters of the doctrine of reincarnation held that males only could reach enlightenment. Females could only hope for a good rebirth as a male through the proper performance of their sexual, caste, and gender duties.

However, *The Laws of Manu* does not support this position. The dominant view holds that upon death dutiful women who perform their religiously defined social roles while alive join their deceased husbands in heaven. "A virtuous wife who after the death of her husband constantly remains chaste, even if she has no sons, reaches heaven, just like those chaste men." (chapter 5:160) In a later verse, "She who, controlling her thoughts, words, and deeds, never fights her lord, lives (after death) with her husband (in heaven) and is called virtuous." (5:165) It is clear in these passages that equal spiritual status is readily combined with unequal (or complementary) social status.

Thus, the Hindu view of male-female, sexuality, and gender roles is best described by the word diversity. Two conclusions are of particular importance. "A serious student of Hinduism can find a paradigm for nearly all possible sexual relationships."[6] The first conclusion is inseparably linked to the second. Multiple perspectives on the relationship between sex, sexuality, and gender are closely tied to various Hindu doctrines.

At the same time, the caste system also plays a major role in defining sex, sexuality, and gender expectations. Because the ancient sages viewed the caste system as sacred and tied it to the doctrines of karma and reincarnation, they believed that each person received his or her "due" in this life according to the accomplishments of a previous life. Unfairness does not exist because all persons get their just desserts according to karma. Anyone who attempts to change the caste system and life duties that sacred scriptures specify accumulates bad karma. Males and females accrue good karma by obeying the *Laws of Manu* and thereby insure themselves of a better rebirth. In a very real sense, reincarnation through karma is the very definition of justice in traditional Hinduism.

Many modern Hindus hold a different view of justice based on modern democratic and egalitarian ideals. British occupation for nearly 100 years from the mid-nineteenth to the mid-twentieth century left a deep impression on many Indians. The Gandhi-led movement for independence emphasized equality for both females and males. The 1947 Constitution that created India's secular state granted to women the same social, economic, and political rights that for millennia had been the exclusive domain of men. As a result, women have entered into all arenas and in some cases have risen to the top, as in the case of Indira Gandhi who held the position of Prime Minister from 1966 until 1984, when she was assassinated by a Sikh bodyguard who was distraught over India's military's suppression of the Sikhs' struggle for political freedom.

Dramatic cultural changes do not occur overnight. Modern India is a society in transition as issues of sex and sexuality undergo redefinition and as more women enter into social roles traditionally reserved for men. Many long-established patriarchal structures continue, especially throughout rural areas isolated from urban and secular influences where the shift toward egalitarian norms is more pronounced. As the twenty-first century unfolds, the only question is how far India will go in replacing the caste-based pattern of "spiritual equality-social inequality" with one that emphasizes both spiritual and social equality.

Buddhism

When Buddha rejected the caste system as an essential component of religiosity, he opened new possibilities for women to redefine themselves as spiritual and social beings. Whereas Hinduism justified social and gender inequalities by divinely sanctioning the caste system and reinforcing it through the concepts of atman-Brahman, karma, and reincarnation, Buddha's doctrines of no soul (anatta) and emptiness moved ancient Asian spirituality in the direction of equality. At the spiritual level, no essential differences exist between men and women. Maleness and femaleness are merely different bundles (skandas) of reincarnated karmic energy. All humans are equal by virtue of being able to accept the Four Noble Truths and Eightfold Path and of achieving nirvana that results from the discipline of meditation.

This does not mean that in the original Hinayana form Buddhism translated male-female spiritual equality into social role equality. Hinduism also viewed men and women as spiritual equals through the doctrine of one soul (atman-Brahman) in two bodies (male-female). Nonetheless, Hinduism spiritualized the caste system that reinforced inequalities, whereas Buddhism negated it. For purposes of liberation, the caste did not matter. Potentially anyone could enter the monastery (sangha). The road to spiritual liberation did not go through the caste hierarchy but rather by withdrawing from it.

Given the harsh realities of the male-dominated Brahmin social order of ancient South Asia, it was only a matter of time before women approached Buddha about becoming members of the monastery. Mahapajapati Gotami, the woman who raised Buddha after his mother died, was the first woman to seek access to the sangha. This request put Buddha on the horns of a dilemma. On the one hand, his doctrine opened the doors of the monastic life to both men and women. On the other hand, separate facilities for men and women did not exist. Because of the power of sexual desire that Buddha had known as a younger married man prior to his enlightenment, he knew that placing both sexes in close proximity would create temptations and earthly attachments that might undermine the pursuit of spiritual goals.

When Buddha's personal assistant Ananda interceded on Gotami's behalf, Buddha created a separate order of nuns with the provision that Gotami and other women who joined it would accept eight rules that permitted male supervision. This "middle ground" solution gave women a legitimate social alternative to their traditional domestic roles even though they did not possess complete autonomy as homeless nuns. According to Liz Wilson, "By taking up the homeless life as followers of Buddha, women opted out of confining systems of control over women prevalent in India in the early centuries before the Common Era."[7]

In addition, many wealthy and well-educated women were able to live independently apart of male domination. However, for the vast majority of women born into poverty, few social options existed outside of obedience to male authority within the confines of family. Even though Buddha's doctrines did not cause widespread alteration of the caste system, his belief in the spiritual equality helped men and especially women define themselves apart from mainstream Hindu society.

Separate orders of nuns spread throughout many parts of Asia but eventually many of them disappeared due to lack of support. Buddha's creation of an order of nuns under male authority gave women a non-domestic social alternative, on the one hand, while, on the other hand, it restricted their autonomy. In the early monastic system of Buddhism, women became second-class citizens. Males created the rules for both men's and women's monasteries. Women could leave the patriarchal domestic mainstream

provided they accepted the male authority over their order. Male domination did not disappear. It merely assumed a different form. No doubt, this
left the impression that female virtue could not be guaranteed apart from
male supervision. Over time this double standard undermined support for
the order of nuns.

Also, many Buddhists throughout much of Asia assumed that they could
accumulate more good karma by giving contributions to monks rather than
nuns. This male preference eroded the material and financial backing that
the nuns needed to sustain their separate orders. Over time, the lack of
support resulted in the demise of many Buddhist convents that could not
become self-sustaining.

Mahayana Buddhism offered women opportunities to move beyond traditional gender roles. Both women and men could take the bodhisattva vow
and become earthly embodiments of spiritual wisdom. In Japan, the popular
goddess of mercy, Kannon, is a reincarnation of the heavenly Buddha Aval-
okitesvara. The *Lotus Sutra* incorporates wise female deities who, like their
male counterparts, have achieved nirvana. In Tibetan Buddhism, women
serve as teachers who care for those in need.[8]

Despite the unrelieved emphasis on male authority throughout Buddhist
history, it is correct to conclude that both the Hinayana and Mahayana
branches of Buddhism took significant steps in the direction of reconceptu-
alizing the relationship between males and females as one of equality in the
spiritual realm. Even though Buddha's original doctrines and the variations
that spun out of them had a marginal effect in reforming gender roles in the
larger society in his time and during many centuries thereafter, his religious
legacy provided women with genuine alternatives.

This legacy continues to serve as a foundation for making significant
social changes in modern times. In the area of sex, sexuality, and gender,
many current critics use Buddhist ideas to challenge traditional patriarchal
views in favor of egalitarian ones. Buddhism rises above the need to support
any arbitrary gender hierarchy that defines acceptable relationships between
women and men.

The well-known Buddhist writer Rita M. Gross holds that three Buddhist doctrines lay the foundation for both spiritual and social equality in
Buddhism. The first relates the Buddha's early teachings about egolessness.
Ego-based personality models reinforce male-female differences, whereas
the Buddhist doctrine that all selves are essentially egoless dissolves gender
duality. Second, the Mahayana ethic of compassion for all sentient beings is
available to everyone. Both men and women are equally capable of taking
the bodhisattva vow. Late twentieth century engaged Buddhists not only
continued their historic quest for spiritual liberation, but in the name of social justice, they also began actively working for the political and economic
transformation of society. Third, all sentient beings, including humans, possess an inherent Buddha nature even though it remains veiled. When the veil

is removed and wisdom is attained, then each person discovers his or her innate spiritual nature.[9]

Like Hinduism, Buddhism is undergoing radical redefinition regarding how belief in spiritual equality lays the groundwork for the pursuit of social equality. Hinduism's doctrine of one soul in two bodies and Buddhism's philosophy of Buddhahood in all beings opens the door to reordering the norms and structures of society away from traditional patriarchal patterns and toward egalitarian ones.

Jainism

Jainism is the second major derivative religion from Hinduism. Between the time that Mahavira achieved liberation and his death 30 years later, he attracted nearly 500,000 followers of laity, monks, and nuns. The majority of these were female: 36,000 nuns compared to 14,100 monks and 310,000 women laity in contrast to 150,000 men. Like Buddhism, the Jain rejection of the Brahman dominated caste system appealed to women. Throughout Jain history, many learned women distinguished themselves as teachers and disciplined role models for their faith despite the persistence of patriarchal norms and structures.

Like the adherents of both Hinduism and Buddhism, not all Jains accept men and women as spiritual and social equals. According to the Digambara sacred writing *Sutraprabrita*, wearing clothes is a form of attachment to an earthly desire. "The path to liberation is that of nakedness, and all other (paths) are wrong paths." (Verse 23) By definition, women are incapable of achieving enlightenment.

Digambara monks hold that women are emotionally fickle and therefore cannot commit to the kind of long-term, uninterrupted concentration that leads to liberation from rebirth. In addition, their bodily processes lead to the growth and destruction of small organisms, which is contrary to the norm of noninjury or ahimsa. "In the genital organs of women, in the area between their breasts, and in their navels and armpits are extremely small living beings, so how can women be ordained (since their bodies make them unable to keep the first vow of nonviolence)?" (Verse 24)

The more liberal Shvetambara branch of Jainism rejects this position. Both men and women are capable of achieving liberation, as referenced in an alternative Jain Scripture, *Strinirvana-Pariccheda*. "The cause of liberation from the sickness of cyclic existence is the non-deficiency of the (three Jewels): correct view, knowledge, and conduct." "It is not reasonable (to assert) that any of the three jewels are incompatible with womanhood, and so it is not the case that there is no liberation for women." (Verse 2)

Like Hinduism and Buddhism, modern Jainism is also undergoing change from within in the direction of greater equality for both males and females.

This transformation is leading to the development of new orders of "semi-monks" or "seminuns," which exist between the traditional monasteries and convents and the laity. Unlike the ancient orders, the new orders permit their members to spread Jainism to other countries. Once they complete their rigorous monastic training in India, groups of men and women are commissioned to travel to foreign nations where they teach their spiritual practices to others. Like the devotees of other world religions in the twenty-first century, groups of Jain followers are extending Mahavira's ancient message of spiritual liberation around the globe.[10]

MIDDLE EASTERN RELIGIONS

Zoroastrianism

Within Zoroastrianism, there exist tendencies toward both equality and inequality in the area of human sexuality. On the one hand, the traditional religious leadership or (*mobeds*) has remained largely male-centered. On the other hand, certain Zoroastrian rituals treat males and females equally. For example, five times each day, devout Zoroastrians tie a sacred cord called a *kutsi* around their waists to signify their faithful allegiance to Ahura Mazda and to keep from submitting to evil.[11]

Zoroastrian theology does not rank females below males in the orders of creation. The cosmic struggle between good and evil apply to women as well as men. Since Zoroastrianism does not include the doctrine of transmigration, females are not defined as deficient males who must reincarnate as males in order to improve their spiritual chances to achieve enlightenment. Each person has only one life to lead. The forces of darkness tempt both males and females alike. Ahura Mazda will be judged both according to their accumulated lifetime balance of good versus evil thoughts, words, and deeds. Despite their small numbers worldwide (less than 150,000 living mostly in India but increasingly in other nations as well), the Zoroastrian worldview easily promotes equality at both the spiritual and social levels in the area of sex, sexuality, and gender.

Judaism

Judaism is more ambiguous on this topic. As is well known, two creation stories are woven together in the first three chapters of the book of *Genesis*. In the first account recorded in Chapter 1, Verse 27, God creates man and woman together presumably as equals. In the second account in Chapter 2, Verses 18–23, God first creates the man Adam who names all the animals. Then God creates the woman Eve out of Adam's rib because "It is not good that man should be alone; I will make him a helper as his partner."

In Chapter 3, it is Eve who first eats the forbidden fruit and then gives it to Adam who also eats it.

From the moment of creation, the Hebrew Scripture sends two different messages, one of equality and the other of inequality. The latter position dominated the Jewish understanding of the relationship between males and females throughout the long sweep of Jewish history. At the same time, the Hebrew Scripture contains stories of strong women like Ruth and Naomi who demonstrated extraordinary courage and cleverness in the face of adversity. During the past 150 years Jewish writers have begun to challenge the male-centered interpretation of Judaism starting with the first creation story that sets forth powerful images of equality. Clearly, depending on who chooses what verses and who interprets them, like all sacred texts, the Hebrew Scripture contains diverse and frequently conflicting points of view.

On the whole, however, the Hebrew Scripture embodies a bias toward male superiority over females. This is particularly noticeable in the *Torah*, the first five books that contain the 613 Jewish Laws that comprise the Mosaic Covenant with Yahweh. Written by men, the *Torah* takes men's authority over women for granted. Given that all of the world religions took shape in patriarchal settings, many of the sacred scriptures that emerged in different cultures contain similar views. For example, like the Hindu *Laws of Manu*, the *Torah* gender laws define the status of girls under the ownership of their fathers, that is, as their fathers' property. When a woman marries, ownership transfers to her husband. In the area of sexuality, a woman could be stoned if her husband could prove she was not a virgin when they married. (Deuteronomy 22:13–21) Men were not subject to the same test.

The rabbinical traditions of the Talmud expanded on the *Torah's* assumption of male superiority. A woman's primary purpose is defined as obedience to her husband and sons and faithful observance of dietary and other regulations pertaining to spousal conduct. Her sex defined her sexuality and gender expectations in terms of heterosexual marriage and dutiful motherhood. According to the gender norms of the Jewish community, a woman's greatest fear was infertility, because it negated her primary purpose in life, which was to bear children. Like other world religions, sons were preferred over daughters. The *Talmudic* view of women is summarized in the phrase, "Happy is he whose children are sons and woe to him whose children are daughters."[12]

Unlike some branches of the three Asian religions and the monastic tradition of Christianity, Judaism does not view sexual desire as an impediment to the pursuit of spiritual goals. Human sexuality is a gift from God for the purpose of procreation and shared intimacy. The main issue was assuring that sexual passions were properly integrated into righteous living. Rabbis emphasized that sharing sexual pleasures in marriage was consistent with the will of God.

At the same time, their scriptural heritage includes the legacy of Eve the temptress. Medieval rabbis developed the legend of Lilith to explain why the Hebrew Scripture contained two different creation stories, one in which man and woman were created together and the other in which woman was created from the rib of man. According to the Lilith legend, the two creation stories are about two different women. Lilith was the first even though she is not mentioned in the *Genesis* narrative, and Eve was the second. Being born together with Adam according to the first creation story, Lilith demanded equality with him and wanted to be on top during sex. According to the strict sexuality norms of the patriarchal rabbis, this angered God who exiled Lilith from Eden and created a second woman, Eve, out of Adam's rib to be his supportive partner. In the medieval era, Lilith became popularized as a demon that killed children because of her rage at being expelled from the Garden of Eden. Jewish mothers tied red ribbons on cradles to keep her away from their infants.[13] The legend of Lilith epitomizes extreme female denigration within the male dominance traditions of Judaism.

In all fairness, the *Torah* and *Talmud* also stress the duties of men as loving and faithful providers and protectors of their families. The Jewish male role of "caring provider-protector" parallels men's primary domestic function in the other world religions as well. Nonetheless, as in the case of the other world religions, the classic pattern of spiritual equality and social inequality dominates Jewish history. From this perspective, both males and females are equal in the "eyes of God," although they are not equal in society. God created them to be complementary partners. God created women to perform primarily monogamous domestic roles and created men to function in nondomestic ones. God gave males authority over females in both domestic and nondomestic settings. This is the classic pattern that sacred books or other writings reinforce.

In 1885, Reform Jews met in Pittsburgh and wrote their Declaration of Principles that recognized Judaism as "a progressive religion, ever striving to be in accord with the postulates of reason." Since then many modern Jews have offered alternative ways of thinking about the relationship between worldview and morality. As Reform Judaism grew throughout the twentieth century, new views of the relationship between sex, sexuality, and gender began to emerge. As in the case of the other world religions, women spearheaded these new interpretations.

Women are taking an active role in asserting their right to full participation in all aspect of Judaism. They call for the elimination of language that refers to God in masculine terms and for revisions that are gender-neutral and inclusive. They seek full empowerment in all areas of leadership, worship, and prayer. Starting in 1972 the Reform branch of Judaism began ordaining women as rabbis. For many twenty-first century Jews, nothing short of full membership for both women and men at all levels is acceptable. Jewish feminist author Judith Plaskow writes that "Beginning with the conviction of our presence both at Sinai and now, we rediscover and invent ourselves in the Jewish communal past and present, continuing the age-old process of reshaping Jewish memory as we reshape the community today."[14] The historical coupling of spiritual equality and social inequality is giving way to both spiritual and social equality.

Christianity

Like its parent Judaism, Christianity settled early into a pattern of male superiority despite some initial egalitarian tendencies (Galatians 3:28—"in Christ there is neither male nor female" and the *Book of Acts*) that grew out of the Jesus movement. Also, like contemporary Judaism, twenty-first century Christianity is undergoing tremendous change in the area of sex, sexuality, and gender. The historic origins of female subordination in Christianity are well known along with their worldview justification. They began with *New Testament* writings such as the first letter to Timothy. "Let a woman learn in silence with full submission. I permit no woman to teach or have authority over a man; she is to keep silent. For Adam was formed first, then Eve." (2:11–13)

In both Scripture and tradition and among all Christian branches, the pattern of male domination persisted and continues to persist for nearly two millennia of Christian history. In the post-New Testament Era, writers like Tertullian looked upon women as the "Devil's gateway." He defined every woman as an Eve whose temptation of Adam brought sin and death into the world, which only Christ could overcome through his redemptive death on the cross. Augustine, who is arguably the greatest of all the early Christian writers, believed that sexual desires *per se* resulted from the sins of Adam and Eve. Only married couples were permitted to engage in sexual intercourse for the purpose of procreation only.

As a result of these early views of sex and sexuality, the Catholic Church defined the gender relations between men and women as complementary. The most significant Catholic teaching involves the "complementarity of the sexes." Men and women are equal in God's sight but have complementary social roles.[15] This doctrine of equal but different permeates every aspect of Catholic teachings on sex, sexuality, and gender from religious leadership to marriage roles. Women are forbidden from becoming ordained clergy. While there are no proscriptions against serving in a variety of occupations outside the home, child rearing and domesticity are still honored as women's highest calling.

The Protestant Reformation reinforced this pattern. Despite the doctrine of the priesthood of all believers, Luther believed that the blight of original sin weighed heavier on women than men because Eve tempted Adam and not the reverse. Like his Catholic counterparts, Luther held that women's roles ought to be limited to the home—under the control of men—because only they could bear children. Patriarchal marriage served the purpose of regulating sexual behavior and rearing children in socially acceptable ways. Unlike Luther, John Calvin held that Adam and Eve were responsible jointly for the fall into sin. At the same time, Adam was the dominant partner in the Garden of Eden as well as after being expelled from it. Like Luther, Calvin accepted that men and women were equal spiritually but that women were subordinate to men socially.[16] As in the case of the other world religions, in Christianity patriarchy became pervasive from the start.

Like Reform Judaism, Christian challenges to traditional male-dominant views of sex, sexuality, and gender began during the middle to late nineteenth century and gained momentum during the twentieth. What is at stake is nothing less than a paradigm shift. Many female writers are redefining the place of both men and women within all major branches of Christianity. For many theologians, the concept of complementarity is inherently incompatible with the modern view that women's roles not be based on their sexual nature alone. Complementarity has meant inequality, and this is what needs to be changed.

This is the heart of the matter. Those who hold traditional views always turn to their scriptures for support of male authority over females. Since men wrote all the sacred scriptures of the world religions, the male point of view will always be the reference point for measuring women's status as spiritual, sexual, and social beings. By appealing to scripture, men will always hold power to define the nature of both males and females and the proper ordering of their relationships. At the same time, all of the scriptures contain egalitarian themes and images that critics of male-dominant views, whether Asian or Middle Eastern, invoke as alternatives to patriarchy. Many feminists are expanding their traditions to include women's voices and interpretations. Thus, the issue is not only "what to say and include" but "who gets to do it."

A second issue involves combining historical with contemporary witness. On this point many observers note that women's voices are mostly absent from the scriptures that define the major faiths of the world. In order to offset this silence, several writers appeal to balancing men's viewpoints by adding women's experiences and perspectives. They hold that until the sacred traditions of all the world religions include both male and female interpretations and not just the male point of view regarding men and women, an unfair male bias will persist.

Because Christianity is the world's largest religion and is present on every continent, the Christian critique of patriarchy has emerged as a global movement. Fairness motivates the call for change not only in the West but also around the world. Well-known theologian Rosemary Radford Ruther identifies Christian feminist movements in the United States and Europe as well as throughout the "Two-Thirds World" of the Middle East, Africa, Asia, and Latin America. "Christian feminism across ethic and national boundaries is developing many voices and styles, as it is rethought in the distinct cultural and socioeconomic realities of each context. And yet these are, in many ways, variants of a common language."[17] This is the language of justice. It is nothing short of a universal call for the equal treatment of women and men at both the spiritual and social levels.

Islam

Like Zoroastrianism, Judaism, and Christianity, Muslim female writers are also challenging the historic male-centered perspectives of Islam by reinterpreting in new ways inherited doctrines and sacred beliefs. Muslim women, like their counterparts in the other world religions, are searching for ways to separate centuries of accumulated male interpretations from authentic Muslim teachings that foster fairness and equality for both women and men. This task is probably more difficult for the followers of Islam than for those of the other world religions.

The reason is clear. The Renaissance, Reformation, and Enlightenment occurred in Western culture over several centuries. Despite the many conflicts that arose among Jews, Catholics, and Protestants and across the boundaries of religion and science, both Judaism and Christianity eventually adapted to the separation of society into sacred and secular realms. Except for minor fringe groups who remain intolerant of others' views, Jews and Christians are well adjusted to the modern norms of liberty, equality, democracy, respect for individual rights of conscience and free speech, and religious pluralism.

The developing awareness of religious pluralism that accompanies the spread of globalization confronts the followers of all the world religions with the challenge to their exclusivist truth claims. Jews and Christians have been responding to this challenge over a longer period of time than Muslims. As Colonialism waned throughout the twentieth century, Muslim nations became deeply divided over how to respond to the rise of the Western forces that led to their subordination. Whatever the form, from Turkey's liberal secularism to Saudi Arabia's conservative Wahhabism, Islam's resurgence in the twentieth century gave it a powerful worldwide presence.

Amidst Islamic renewal, Muslim women began to reexamine the traditions that define the place of males and females within Islam. Unlike the feminist writers of other religions that have already adjusted to modernism, Muslim women must confront male-dominated views of sex, sexuality, and gender within their own traditions as well as Western views of individual rights, democracy, liberty, and equality, which many conservative Muslims reject. This is no easy task for the following reasons.

Like all religions, the traditions of Islam are steeped in patriarchy. In addition, all religions have blessed their male-dominated norms and structures with spiritual sanctions of one kind or another. The worldview perspective of the *Qur'an* conveys the perfect will of Allah according to Muslim beliefs.

On the one hand, it offers Muslims a comprehensive religious plan for ordering every aspect of community life from what to wear to how to govern. On the other hand, it challenges, and in some cases hinders, Islam's ability to adapt to many of the dynamic changes that have occurred over the past four centuries.

The modern world confronts Muslims, as it does followers of all the world religions, with questions about what to keep, what to discard, what to modify, and what to add. The process of deciding how far to go in adapting to the modern ideals of freedom, equality, liberty, democracy, and religious pluralism is proceeding more slowly in many Islamic states than in most non-Islamic countries. This is because most non-Islamic nations have been and continue to be deeply influenced by religions that have already adjusted to the modern ideals that came out of the Renaissance, Reformation, and Enlightenment. Nowhere are these differences more in evidence than in the Islamic view of sex, sexuality, and gender.

Depending on who is quoting what text, Islam contains images of male-female equality and/or male superiority. Like all world religions, traditional Islam combines spiritual equality with social complementarity or unjust power inequalities, depending on one's point of view. The feminist challenge within Islam parallels that of the other world religions: to change this pattern to a new combination of spiritual and social equality.

Traditionalists typically quote from the fourth *Sura* to support the view that Allah created men to have authority over women "because Allah has made the one superior to the other, ... Good women are obedient. ... As for those from whom you fear disobedience, admonish them and send them to beds apart and beat them. Then if they obey you, take no further action against them. Allah is high, supreme." (4:34) Inheritance rules of the *Qur'an* specify that a man should receive twice as much as a woman. (4:10–11) Men may marry up to four wives (Muhammad had fifteen), whereas a woman may not have more than one husband. Divorce rules make it easier for a man to dissolve an unhappy marriage than a woman. In short, for traditionalists, the *Qur'an* reveals that Allah intended for men to have authority over women in the orders of creation.

For Muslim feminists such as Riffat Hassan, this interpretation is a male corruption of the *Qur'an* that left women in a subordinate position. This occurred because the male hadith biases that permeated Islam during the early centuries after Muhammad's death undermined the *Qur'an's* intent to free women from their inferior chattel status and to make them free and equal to men.[18] In order to reclaim the original norm of male-female equality in contemporary Islam, it is necessary to reject the patriarchal prejudice that appears in the hadiths. Men and women are equal in Allah's eyes at the spiritual level.

At the social level, however, Allah created men and women to complement each other sexually. In traditional Islam, Allah created the world with an inherent biological dualism. Allah "gave you wives from among yourselves, that you might live in joy with them, and planted love and kindness in your hearts." (30:20–21) Muslim feminist Aysha Hidayatullah maintains that "although the two sexes are distinct, the origin of both is the same, and their creations are complementary . . . the nature of the sexes is cause for religious reflection and prayer. The *Qur'an* addresses the sacred and the sexual as part of one another."[19]

Reconciling the "equality-complementarity" dualism of the *Qur'an* with the call for greater equality in the areas of sex, sexuality, and gender is a major challenge for Muslim feminists. If women and men are equal spiritually but have been created to complement each other sexually, how does sex complementarity keep from slipping into male superiority in the realm of gender roles? This is an issue that women from all the world religions confront when men, who hold power over women, believe that the doctrine of male-female dualism (that many read as male-female hierarchy) is divinely ordained.

In addition, unlike women of the other world religions, Muslim feminists confront a challenge that is unique to their faith. They must not only engage Islam's patriarchal traditions, but they must also come to grips with wearing public attire, that is, covering and veiling, that symbolizes their allegiance to Islam but does not simultaneously communicate an image of female inferiority.

For women accustomed to making their own decisions about what to wear and when, the practices of head covering or complete body veiling except for eyes and hands appear to perpetuate the historic custom that gives men the right to define what is proper for women to wear. For many Western feminists, it is a sign of women's continuing subordination to men within Islam and a male projection that blames females for male sexual arousal that males by themselves cannot control or refuse to take responsibility for controlling.

For women like Aysha Hidayatullah this is a false perception for two reasons. Muslim women wear headscarves and veils as symbols of resistance against the legacy of colonial repression and as an expression of modesty that rejects the West's vulgar clothing styles that turn women into dehumanized sex objects.[20] While this explanation is clear and understandable, Muslim feminists confront a tough challenge to persuade non-Muslims that male-female equality in society is compatible with covering and veiling, for any reason, especially in nations that allow men and women complete freedom to dress as they want within the broad boundaries of public decency.

CONCLUSION

It is clear that historically all religious views of sex, sexuality, and gender emerged in patriarchal cultures where males, who wrote their traditions' scriptures, defined the spiritual and social status of both men and women. This led to four possible combinations: (1) spiritual equality and social inequality or complementarity; (2) spiritual inequality and social inequality or complementarity; (3) spiritual inequality and social equality; and (4) spiritual and social equality. Critics of patriarchy favor the fourth option over the others. The most problematical option involves combinations that include the word "complementarity." On the one hand, the coupling of spiritual equality with sexual complementarity need not lead automatically to gender inequality or unjust social relationships between men and women. On the other hand, if men and women are defined as sexually complementary, it is but a short leap of the imagination to consider that men hold positions of authority over women both inside and outside domestic settings.

Here then is one of the twenty-first century's bottom line challenges: to combine the concept of sexual complementarity with gender equality in all social realms except procreation where this is not biologically possible. Except for a minority of traditionalists, it is relatively easy for adherents of all the religions to reject the doctrine of male-female spiritual inequality. For all intents and purposes then, the main challenge that confronts all the world religions is to combine the belief in spiritual equality with gender equality—by building on the doctrine of either sexual complementarity or sexual equality. On this issue, the extent to which adherents of the world religions can contribute positively to increasing justice in the global village will depend on their success in transforming traditional patriarchal patterns into alternatives that define equality for men and women in both domestic and nondomestic domains.

CHAPTER 11

The Sacred and the Secular and the World Religions

THE SACRED, THE SECULAR, AND SECULARIZATION

All religions connect their views of ultimate reality to society; or stated differently, they relate the sacred to the secular. For the world religions, this is the mega issue that envelops all lesser issues. In a very real sense, how the leaders and followers of the world religions define the scope of their authority over nonreligious areas determines their views of war and peace and of male-female relationships.

In defining the terms, the sacred refers to the internal spiritual dimension of human existence and the secular to the external social dimension. At one level, this distinction seems obvious. At another level, the relationship between the inner and outer aspects of human experience can be complex and downright confusing. This is because some religions combine the sacred and the secular as if no distinction exists at all, while others delineate strict boundaries between the two. These differences among the world religions grew out of their unique historical circumstances. Their dissimilar world-views also contributed greatly to their distinct sacred-secular combinations.

For example, within the Asian religions, traditional Hinduism spiritualizes the caste system. The sacred and secular are identical. Hindus make progress toward liberation by obeying the rules (dharma) of their castes, life cycle stages, and gender roles. For traditional Buddhism, the sacred and secular are different. Theravada Buddhists progress toward liberation apart from society by joining the monastery (sangha) for the purpose of following the Eightfold Path. The separate monastic (sacred) and laity (secular) callings of the Middle Eastern religions, most notably within Roman Catholicism, parallel those of Theravada Buddhism. Islam makes no distinction between the sacred and the secular and views the Sharia or totality of Muslim Law as the rulebook for organizing every aspect of personal and social life.

The above examples show clearly that no single pattern prevails in combining the realms of the sacred and the secular. However, when viewed in their totality, these diverse combinations can be lined up along a continuum that ranges from complete separation at one end to complete integration at the other end. As globalization continues to blanket the planet during the twenty-first century, many of the peace and justice conflicts that occur in the areas of war and peace and in sex, sexuality, and gender link directly to changing perceptions of how the realm of the sacred connects to the secular.

In order to grasp fully the changes that are occurring in perceptions of how to combine the sacred and the secular, it is useful to begin with a discussion of secularization and its relationship to modernism. Prior to the gradual rise of what is now called the modern world, most societies for centuries remained agrarian. The dominant institutions of economics, politics, and religion were largely undifferentiated. The royalty owned the land and exercised political control over their economic domains. The power to rule was usually inherited through family lineage and was exercised from the top-down.

Religion defined the origin and nature of all aspects of life from beginning to end and created the sacred canopy through which all inhabitants defined their place in the universe both now and after death. In essence, religious elites defined reality and exercised control over as many aspects of society as possible, being limited only by countervailing political or religious forces. In many circumstances, political and religious leaders were identical, as in the case of the Brahmin priests' domination of the Hindu caste system, the Imams' influences in Muslim territories, and the Roman Catholic Church's control over much of Medieval Europe.

All this changed with the rise of modern science, technology, and urbanization. The story of the transition from agrarianism to urbanism is well known. Virtually every aspect of society changed as factories replaced farms and as the peasants migrated to the crowded cities in search of manufacturing and other nonagricultural jobs. As a result, a new type of secular society was born and continues to spread throughout the developing nations of the world.

In addition, modern science, as it advanced throughout Western nations, gradually undermined the authority of religious elites to define the nature of reality. Rational-empirical methods for discovering new knowledge replaced revelation as the basis for determining truth about the universe. Galileo's solar system discoveries and Darwin's ideas about evolution undermined the *Biblical* story of a 7-day, divine command, earth-centered creation, and humanity's special status within it.

Also, Adam Smith[1] redefined economics according to independently operating laws of supply and demand. Building of the Social Contract theories of the seventeenth and eighteenth centuries, John Locke[2] and Jean-Jacques Rousseau[3] held that political power resided in a nation's citizens as a whole rather than in a single monarch or small group of royalty. Government should be accountable to the citizens who create it from the bottom-up just as the buying and selling of goods and services should result from unfettered exchanges among individuals or groups in the market place.

As the process of differentiation continued, the once largely integrated social institutions of economics, politics, culture, education, and religion became divided into separate social spheres that could operate by their own internal laws or processes independent of religious definition or oversight. Religious leaders lost direct control of all the areas of society that existed outside the boundaries of their increasingly shrinking spheres of influence. Thus, the twin dynamics of secularization and differentiation led to social and personal privatization in the realm of religion.

This does not mean that secularization did or will lead to the eventual disappearance of religion, as many writers have incorrectly predicted, or that religions cease to be influential. The contrary is true. It is readily apparent that the world religions thrive around the globe and will continue to do so throughout the twenty-first century. The real issue is what the world's religious leaders will do to creatively adapt to secularization or to resist it in the hope of regaining their dominance over nonreligious areas of society. The future of religion and violence and of sex, sexuality, and gender turns on how they and their followers respond to this issue. Some of the early twenty-first century signs are already visible.

ASIAN RELIGIONS

Hinduism

Any analysis of the relationship between Hinduism and the separation of the sacred from the secular must begin with India, which is inhabited by more Hindus—900 million—than any other nation. India's political Constitution formally defines the nation as a Secular Democratic Republic.[4] At the official level, the state of India takes the position of secular neutrality with regard to religion. Modern India is a democratic secular state not a Hindu state that recognizes only one official religion. At the formal lawful level, India separates the sacred from the secular and legally allows for the expression of religious pluralism.

Contrast India's sacred-secular division with the comments of Saudi Arabia's new monarch King Abdullah, who replaced his deceased brother in August 2005. During his inauguration, he announced to the assembled tribal chiefs, princes, clerics, and citizens, "I promise God and you that I will adopt the *Koran* as the constitution and Islam as the course and that all my concerns will be to establish righteousness and justice."[5] The difference could not be clearer. India is a secular state, whereas Saudi Arabia is an Islamic State that is controlled by followers of the conservative Wahhabi branch of Sunni Islam. India and Saudi Arabia represent both ends of the sacred-secular spectrum: separation versus integration.

Despite its official secular position and internal religious pluralism, since independence in 1947 India has walked a tolerance-intolerance tightrope between interreligious violence and peaceful coexistence among its diverse religions. When India first achieved independence, many Hindus and Muslims, who had inhabited India for centuries, found it impossible to live together peacefully. In 1947, the same year as India's independence, Muslims were partitioned from Hindus through the creation of West Pakistan (now Pakistan) and East Pakistan (now Bangladesh). During the hastened migration of Hindus from Pakistan to India and of Muslims from India to Pakistan, interreligious hatred led to terrible killings by both groups.

Conflicts between Hindus and Muslims have plagued both India and Pakistan for decades. Border disputes have led to five wars, two full-scale, since 1947. Now that both nations possess nuclear weapons, they threaten each other with annihilation as well as catastrophe for the entire region and beyond. In all probability, the creation of Pakistan-Bangladesh and India into separate states gave the vast majority of Muslims and Hindus homelands of their own. While this has not eliminated all hostility and hatred, it has created the geopolitical conditions that enable two of the world's largest and dissimilar religious groups to maintain an uneasy coexistence that is reinforced by a Cold War mentality of mutually assured destruction (MAD).

Not all Muslims migrated out of India after independence. Currently, while only 5 percent of Pakistan's population consists of non-Muslims, Muslims are 12 percent of India's population. As a result, traditional Hindu-Muslim intolerance erupts sporadically into outbursts of violence. For example, on December 6, 1992, several thousand loyal Hindus destroyed a 450-year old mosque in the north central city of Ayodhya, because they considered it an offense that an Islamic mosque stood on the birthplace of their god Rama. Muslims countered with violence against Hindus. The conflict that started at Ayodhya spread quickly to other cities, including Bombay, where riots resulted in some 1,700 deaths and 6,000 injuries.

The periodic violence that has afflicted India since independence demonstrates that an officially democratic-pluralistic state that separates the sacred from the secular does not always give rise to tolerance within or between religious groups. A year after liberation from British rule, even Gandhi, the leader of India's independence, on January 30, 1948, became the victim of a violent assassination by a fellow Hindu who perceived that he betrayed Hinduism through his nonviolent approach to religious pluralism. In 1984, Indira Gandhi's Sikh bodyguards assassinated her after the Indian military damaged the Sikh's sacred Golden Temple at Amritsar in northern India and quelled the Sikh quest for political liberation. Indira's son Rajiv succeeded her as Prime Minister. He also was assassinated—at a political rally in southern India. A radical Tamil Hindu woman, who was protesting Buddhist rule in nearby Sri Lanka, stood next to him and detonated explosives that she had wrapped around her body killing both herself and Rajiv.

In a very real sense, the above examples demonstrate how difficult it is to create a secular state and culture of tolerance, even when the dual processes of secularization and differentiation lead to separating the sacred from the secular. Religious groups inevitably aspire to gain as much control as possible even though the state does not officially endorse any particular religion. Nowhere is this better demonstrated than with the rise of the Bharatiya Janata Party (BJP) that advocates adherence to the traditional caste system as embodying the mainstream of India's culture and historic character.

The rioters who destroyed the centuries-old mosque at Ayodhya were members of the BJP. BJP is a part of the Hindutva movement, which is a Hindu umbrella for right-wing nationalist groups. BJP is Hinduism's conservative political voice. It includes a diverse mixture of Hindus who range from common citizens to scholars. For BJP members, the secular state has gone too far and too fast in marginalizing traditional Hindu values and culture. From the Party's viewpoint, Hinduism embodies the essence of India's historic heritage without which the nation would cease to have its unique identity. BJP members view the separation of the sacred from the secular, also called secularism, as an ideology that leaders like Gandhi and Nehru imported from the West. Many BJP supporters accept the view that the government should mirror the country's Hindu heritage.

In effect, this means reinforcing the traditional caste system. Clearly this goes contrary to the very concept of a modern society where mobility patterns are fluid across social class boundaries and where men and women have equal access to both domestic and nondomestic roles. For traditional Hindus, social mobility across caste boundaries is unthinkable. Caste status is ascribed at birth and determined by karma accumulated in a previous life cycle. One's caste status at birth determines his or her entire destiny during any given lifetime and is released only upon death.[6] Given that Hinduism in India is not only a religion but also a social system, the conservative reaction to menacing social transformations is understandable. The emergence of the Hindutva movement and national political groups like the BJP are right wing reactions to changes that the creation of the secular state produced.

Modern India contains all of the tensions that the separation of the sacred from the secular creates. It is simultaneously one of the most politically secular and religiously diverse nations in the world. Virtually all of the major religions of the world can be found in India. After nearly 60 years of political independence, India contains all the religious, political, and cultural forces that can either sustain peaceful coexistence, as it does in the main, or give way to outbursts of violence, which always simmer below the surface. It is a nation where the ideal of democratic egalitarianism that the Constitution lawfully embodies challenges traditional Hindu inequalities associated with caste, sex, sexuality, and gender.

For good or ill, India is a bellwether nation for making cultural pluralism work in a constitutional state that contains all of the internal dynamics that emerge from separating the sacred from the secular. India is a real life laboratory for determining whether the world religions will bring greater peace and justice into the global village of the twenty-first century or more hatred and hostility.

Hindu migration outside India has led to the creation of Hindu minorities in over eighty nations. In states that permit the free exercise of religion, Hinduism can quite easily become transplanted under conditions of minimal social stress with surrounding populations. In major cities in the United States, throughout Europe, and in numerous other nations around the world, Hindus have established new communities and created many local temples for the worship of their multiple deities.

Once outside India, the record shows that Hinduism can readily take its place alongside other religions in cultures with traditions of religious pluralism and where popular support for the caste system does not exist. No doubt, Hindu tolerance based on the view that there are many paths to the One Truth contributes to its adaptation and acceptance. This does not mean that majority group discrimination against nonmainstream religious minorities disappears altogether. It would be naïve to assume that it would. At the same time, in social and political environments that separate the sacred from the secular, religions like Hinduism can find a home next to religions whose adherents hold very different worldviews.

Buddhism

Unlike Hinduism, Buddhism does not give philosophical support to any social system. Its worldview is disengaged from all of them and can function freely in any one of them where laws that protect the public expression of religion exist. Its goal is personal enlightenment and liberation from worldly attachment. At the same time, in nations that are predominantly Buddhist, political and other social structures embody Buddhist ideals and are led by Buddhists whose beliefs influence their behavior and who uphold traditional Buddhist culture. In addition, within the past 50 years, Buddhism has turned its face outward to engagement with issues of social justice.

More than any other ancient Indian King, Asoka demonstrated the relevance of Buddhism to the conduct of daily life during his reign in the third century BCE. Upon the successful completion of his military campaigns that expanded his empire, Asoka became overwhelmed with remorse over the realization that he had brought death to so many innocent people. After his conversion to Buddhism, he renounced his formerly violent ways. In an effort to create a broader sense of social duty, he spread Buddhism by placing rocks and pillars engraved with the teachings of Buddha throughout his kingdom. Also, the Mahayana doctrine of the compassionate bodhisattva took the monks out of secluded monastic settings and into the world where they integrated into the life of the laity.

As Buddhism spread throughout Southeast Asia and migrated north to China, Korea, and Japan, it blended with local traditions such as Tibet's shaman-centered religions of *bon*. In some areas it grew to a position of dominance as in Thailand, Burma (now called Myanmar), Laos, Cambodia, and Sri Lanka. In 1782, King Rama I declared Buddhism the official religion of Thailand, where today over 90 percent of the population still remain Buddhist. Thailand is unique among all Buddhist nations, because it has never been conquered by outside invaders. In 1932, it became a secular constitutional monarchy that includes an elected parliament and prime minister. Like European nations such as Spain and England, the monarchy of Thailand no longer has political control over the country. It serves mainly as a symbol of the nation's culture and continuity with the past.

At this point, it is instructive to compare the status of Hinduism in India with Buddhism in Thailand in regard to separating the sacred from the secular. While both contain a dominant religion, India has been and continues to be far more religiously pluralistic than Thailand. In addition, Hindus view the historic caste system of India as sacred. By contrast, for Buddhists no social structure is inherently sacred. Modern Hindu leaders struggle to preserve Hinduism's historic dominance as evidenced by the rise of the conservative Hindutva movement and the BJP. In the process, sporadic violence threatens the religious freedoms that India's secular state guarantees.

In Thailand greater cultural homogeneity and Buddhist hegemony have spared the nation from the heinous killings that religious hatred has inflicted on India. This does not mean that Thailand is free of civil disturbance. Quite the contrary is true. Violent eruptions have occurred on numerous occasions during the past 70 years. However, these usually result from military intervention into the political process due to allegations of corruption and disagreements over governance and the status of democracy and not from religious hostilities.

In addition, the Thai state supports Buddhism through the Religious Affairs Council that a secular staff manages. Despite the separation of the sacred from the secular, the Council provides resources for temple maintenance and Buddhist instruction in the schools. It makes appointments to religious posts and intervenes in religious disputes. Thus, Buddhism reaches into the highest levels of civil government without being established as an official state religion. Despite the pervasive presence of Buddhism, Thailand is not a religious state in the same way that King Abdullah views Saudi Arabia as an Islamic State governed by the sacred book of the *Qur'an*. Even though both India and Thailand have secular governments, in Thailand Buddhism enjoys a higher level of government support than does Hinduism in India. Sadly, in neighboring Sri Lanka, the clash between these two ancient traditions has led to civil war in which the Tamil Hindus struggle to overthrow the controlling Sinhalese Buddhists.[7]

As these few examples demonstrate, the relationship between the sacred and the secular is inherently laden with tensions that never disappear. Although the process of secularization leads to separating the private realm of the spirit from the public domain of the state, there is no guarantee of peaceful coexistence. Religious leaders continue to seek influence at the highest levels of government, and civic officials must respond to the stresses that exist between the nation's legal structure and religious culture. In Thailand, this has led to relative harmony. In India, intermittent outbursts of violence have threatened the state's capacity to maintain its secular neutrality. In Sri Lanka, ongoing violence has broken the tension, as Buddhists battle Hindus over control of the state.

In secular societies where Buddhism is not the dominant religion, Buddhism has adjusted readily to secularization and the separation of the sacred from the secular. Like Hindus, Buddhists have established religious communities in over eighty nations around the world, including China where the Communist Party allows Buddhism to exist as one of its official religions. No doubt, the historic Buddhist emphasis on cultivating the spirit meshes comfortably with secularization. Theravada began as a sacred movement separated from the secular world. Even the empathetic bodhisattvas of the Mahayana Branch directed their compassion toward the spiritual liberation of the laity and not toward altering political, economic, and other social structures.

Modern engaged Buddhism has broadened traditional doctrines to include greater emphasis on social responsibility. In this sense, it parallels the efforts of the ancient King Asoka to spread Buddhist teachings throughout his Kingdom in South Asia during the third century BCE. Today's Engaged Buddhism emerged during the Vietnam War in the 1960s through the writings of the Vietnam Buddhist Thich Nhat Hanh. According to Thich Nhat Hanh, cultivating the spirit serves not only the purpose of personal liberation but also as preparation for the nonviolent transformation of society. Social responsibility starts by finding internal tranquility that leads to external peace.[8] During the past 40 years, numerous Engaged Buddhist groups have been created around the world in nations or regions as diverse as Australia, German-speaking Europe, and South Africa.[9] The exiled and popular Dalai Lama who received the Nobel Peace Prize in 1989 for his nonviolent efforts to free Tibet from Chinese control epitomizes modern Engaged Buddhism.

Engaged Buddhists have created activist programs for improving the environment, prison and health care systems, race relations, gender equality, and numerous educational programs. In short, outside of Buddhist-dominated societies of Southeast Asia such as Thailand, Sri Lanka, etc., secularization and the separation of the sacred from the secular have served Buddhism well. Like Hinduism, it has allowed Buddhist leaders to spread their faith throughout multiple regions of the world. It has also led Engaged Buddhists to create nonviolent social programs that will contribute to increasing peace and justice in the emerging global village of the twenty first century.

Jainism

Jainism is the smallest of the Asian religions—numbering only a few million members. Prior to 1970 no Jain monk had ever left India. According to Jain cosmology, the universe is undergoing a cycle of decline that will last for 21,000 years before another period of ascendancy begins. Although no date has been set for the next upturn, nonetheless, the Jain view of the cyclical nature of time has served for centuries as a disincentive for missionary expansion. When monk Shree Chitrabhanu spoke at a Swiss religious conference in 1970, he took the first step in expanding Jainism into the emerging global village. For the past 35 years, Jain monks established religious centers in the United States, Brazil, Canada, Kenya, and the United Kingdom. Like all religions, Jainism is stretching beyond its historic boundaries and into the wider world.[10]

Because of its limited numbers, Jainism has never been the dominant religion in any society. Currently, it is found in only five countries. There is an advantage to this. Unlike Hindus who fear the loss of their dominant status because of India's secular state, the separation of the sacred from the secular enables smaller religious groups like Jainism to prosper. One cannot fear the loss of what one never had. At the same time, because of social reformers like Mahatma Gandhi and Martin Luther King, Jr., who integrated the Jain doctrine of noninjury or ahimsa into their highly successful nonviolent political strategies, this small religion has had an impact way beyond its size. The power of Jainism derives from how its deep ethical commitment to the sacredness of all life has inspired and continues to inspire some of the world's most prominent leaders. In secular societies that foster a robust pluralism, all three of the Asian religions of Hinduism, Buddhism, and Jainism find a place.

MIDDLE EASTERN RELIGIONS

Zoroastrianism

The once dominant religion of the vast ancient Persian Kingdom has about 150,000 remaining practitioners. Like Jainism, it is not the numerical strength of Zoroastrianism that is the source of its long-standing influence. Rather it is its theological imagery that the universe consists of a cosmic battle between the forces of good and evil, which parallels in one form or another the other Middle Eastern religions. Since Zoroastrianism is not the major religion of any modern state, its adherents do not have to struggle to retain a position of dominance as Hindus do in India.

Currently, Zoroastrian communities are located in less than a dozen countries around the world. The largest group is concentrated in India where religious tolerance has allowed practitioners to express their faith freely. No longer the warlike religion that it was during the height of the Persian Empire (and having survived centuries of persecution), the Zoroastrian emphasis on cultivating the virtuous life of good thoughts, words, and deeds helps create a moral climate conducive to increasing peace and justice in the global village.

Judaism

The Jewish relationship to the separation of the sacred from the secular begins with the Diaspora that occurred after the Romans defeated the Jewish rebellion in 70 CE along with the rise of the nineteenth century Zionist movement that spearheaded the creation of modern Israel in 1948. For nearly two millennia, existing as a minority religion in many different societies proved to be a mixed blessing for Judaism. The cyclical pattern of persecution in Europe and Russia led Theodor Herzl and other Zionists to conclude that the Jews needed a nation of their own.

As a religion, Judaism is so intricately enmeshed in the present operations and future of Israel that it is virtually impossible to think of one without the other. While some writers view Zionism as a political movement inspired by nonreligious secular Jews and Judaism as a nonpolitical religion, it is not possible to understand modern Israel apart from the legacy of the promised land. After all, the "Zion" part of "Zionism" is another name for Jerusalem.

Followers of all three Abrahamic Faiths regard the Holy Land as sacred space. For Christians it is the place of Jesus' birth; for Muslims it is the location of Muhammad's Night Journey; for religious Jews it is the land that God gave to them forever. Even though Israel came into existence through the secular politics of the United Nations, Judaism is to Israel what Hinduism is to India and Buddhism is to Thailand. One cannot think of the society without the religion. While officially secular, all three nations involve widespread interweaving of religion and politics. In all three, the sacred and the secular are separated but inseparable.

This means that sacred-secular tensions are a daily reality in the lives of Israelis. While Zionists created Israel as a secular state where Jews from all over the world could live in freedom, Israel has come to symbolize the preservation of Jewishness as a distinct religious, ethnic, and cultural identity. Not only must the state of Israel protect itself from surrounding enemies who want to destroy it, but it must also contend with internal tension among

Jews who hold different views of the relationship between Judaism and the state. While Israel is not a constitutionally Jewish state, Jewish identity in all its myriad interpretations is its civil religion.

At the same time, Israel differs from nations such as India in one important respect. Conservatives like the BJP and other right-wing political groups are struggling to preserve Hinduism as India's historic and cultural identity that they perceive the secular state and other religions threaten. In Israel, the secular state exists to provide Jews with a homeland, even as diverse Jewish groups differ over policies related to directing Israel's future. "Just as the sacred may undergo secularization, so may the secular undergo sacralization."[11] For Jews, it is not a matter of whether they will survive in Israel. Rather, it is a question of how Judaism relates to the secular state that protects it.

In addition, serious disputes exist among Jewish groups over the future of the occupied territories that Israel conquered during the 1967 war. Despite the government's recent removal of Jewish settlements from both the Gaza Strip and parts of the West Bank, Jews are far from unanimous in their view that this strategic venture will contribute to Israel's long-term security or survival. The recent loss of Ariel Sharon's leadership due to a stroke has aggravated this uncertainty.

In the past, disagreements on this issue have led to tragic consequences. In 1995, a right-wing Jewish extremist assassinated Prime Minister Yitzhak Rabin because he feared that Rabin would trade away too much sacred territory in a land for peace swap with the Palestinians. Israel's ongoing construction of the separation barrier (the Wall) between Israel and the West Bank is another sign of the government's continuing struggle to protect itself from jihad-terrorist groups like the Hamas party that won the majority of votes in the recent Palestinian election and that seeks to destroy the nation of Israel in order to create an Islamic state.

In short, for more than two millennia, Judaism has demonstrated a capacity to survive in the Diaspora under rabbinical leadership despite cycles of persecution. At times and in many places, religious pluralism has served the needs of both Judaism and society well. Jews have made enormous contributions to the advancement of knowledge, science, the arts, and other social areas. At other times, pluralism has not been Judaism's friend. For fed up, secular Zionists, the creation of the modern state of Israel in 1948 following the horrors of the Nazi Holocaust held out the promise that Jews would have a secure homeland of their own—free from ghetto confinement and cruel treatment. However, what many religious Jews pictured as a return to the Biblical promised land, Palestinians and other Muslims saw as an invasion and occupation. The result has been perpetual war.

Just how far peace and justice can be advanced in the global village of the twenty-first century will depend in part on whether adherents of world religions, especially within the three Abrahamic faiths of Judaism,

Christianity, and Islam can find nonviolent ways to resolve Israeli-Palestinian hostilities.

Christianity

Prior to the rise of modernism, the Christian worldview encompassed every aspect of the societies it helped create. Like the other world religions that emerged in other parts of the planet, the Christian worldview in the West supplied the sacred canopy under which its adherents defined their place in the cosmos. No area of personal or social life remained untouched by ecclesiastical control. It was simply taken for granted that the Christian worldview defined reality and that clerics held the right to define the truth for believers and nonbelievers alike. Even during the Reformation when Catholics battled Protestants, it was assumed that the winner held the high ground for determining the prevailing form of Christianity. For decades, disagreeing Christians killed each other, sometimes massively, over the right to control the process of defining reality.

The European Renaissance and Enlightenment ushered in the secularization process that led to differentiating the sacred from the secular. With the rise of colonialism and the creation of the democratic-secular state throughout the nations of Europe, parts of Asia and Africa, Latin America, and in the United States, Christianity became constitutionally disestablished. This does not mean that Christianity ceased to exercise influence any more than Hinduism in India or Judaism in Israel. The contrary is true. Many scholars of Religion have shown that secularization has given rise to alternative ways in which Christianity and the state interact.[12]

Numerous typologies have been developed to describe the alternative ways in which religions interact with society and politics. These range from state-sponsored religions to ostracized cults that exist outside the mainstream of a society's sacred beliefs. In countries with strict nonestablishment laws, the influence of the sacred over the secular varies according to the size of any particular religion in relationship to others. In a pattern of pluralism where one religion dominates all others, as in the cases of India, Thailand, and Israel, the advocates of that religion exert, or seek to exert, disproportionate influence over the nation. As a general rule, a dominant religion in a culturally homogeneous society can outcompete minority religions in influencing the secular state. In pluralistic societies where the size of diverse religious groups is more even, the tendency of any one group to dominate is diminished.

Since Christianity is currently the world's largest religion, no one pattern prevails in all the 200 or so societies where it is located around the globe. One of the main effects of the Renaissance and Enlightenment is that Christianity has become well adapted to the secularization process that has led to separating the sacred from the secular. This means that in those secular societies where Christianity remains or has become the dominant religion, its influence is greater than in those societies where it is in the minority.

For example, throughout the countries of Central and South America, Roman Catholicism exercises more influence over private lives and public policies than any other form of Christianity. The historical origin of this pattern is, of course, the Spanish and Portuguese conquest and conversion of native populations during the sixteenth and seventeenth centuries. The principal competition to Catholic dominance comes from Pentecostal Protestants whose emphasis on spiritual renewal through charismatic enthusiasm is challenging the staid formality of Catholicism. Liberation theologians, who call for greater social justice in the distribution of wealth, also confront the overidentification of clerics with powerful and often corrupt political and economic leaders.

Contrast the ubiquitous presence of Roman Catholicism throughout Latin America with the marginal influence of Christianity in Japan, where the combination of Buddhism and Shintoism tower above all other forms of religious expression. The post-World War II disestablishment of all religions from the secular state in Japan fostered a robust pluralism that includes Christianity as a minority religion whose influence is not nearly as significant as it is in the nations of Central and South America. The Japanese pattern parallels India's, where Christianity exists as a minority religion with limited influence amidst a dominant Hindu culture.

Like other areas of the world, religious pluralism is growing in Europe and the United States. The separation of the sacred from the secular has led to changes in the pattern of religious participation between Americans and Europeans. Research shows consistently that more Americans than Europeans participate in organized religious activities such as church membership, worship attendance, prayer, and so on. At the same time, Europe has not abandoned its historic identification with its Christian origins.

For example, Turkey's desire for membership in the European Union has met stiff opposition from many Europeans, leaders and laity alike, who view "Muslim Turkey" as culturally incompatible with "Christian Europe." There is irony here because modern Turkey is one of the most secular of all states where Islam is the dominant religion. Like all the governments of Europe, Turkey maintains strict separation between religion and politics. This, however, is not the issue. Turkey is 97 percent Muslim, and this is the source of Europe's anxiety despite European secularization and diminished Christian influence.

As more Muslims migrate to Europe, confrontations between Muslims and Europeans grow. The recent terrorist train bombings in Madrid and London at the hands of radical Muslims and the secular French government's confrontation with Muslims over wearing headscarves in the public schools are two cases in point. This does not mean that all European Muslims are violent extremists or are incapable of adjusting to secular laws. It means simply that the growth of religious pluralism has introduced stresses that did not heretofore exist within the secular nations of Europe.

Despite much protest and resistance from Christian groups in the past, one of the major effects of the Enlightenment on Christianity is that it has become a religion compatible with secularization and the privatization of the sacred. Christianity has made its peace with modernism. While some Christians still aspire to a return of the "good old days" when the Church dominated society, and some want to impose on everyone their sectarian views through control of public policy,[13] most do not.

At the same time, this does not mean that Christians have ceased trying to influence the larger society any more than Hindus, Buddhists, Jews, or other religious groups. Nor does it eliminate completely the resort to violence as in the case of extremist antiabortion Christians who murder doctors. It means only that by and large Christianity has accepted the Enlightenment norms of liberty, equality, democracy, and individual rights that include the freedom of religion, and as some have held—even helped shape them. In the world of religious pluralism, Christians have learned that the privatization (and protection) of faith (or faiths) offers ample democratic and nonviolent opportunities to influence public norms and policies.

Islam

When discussing Islam, it is essential to avoid simplistic stereotypes based on the disproportionate amount of negative publicity that the media gives to the acts of terrorism that radical Muslim extremists justify in the name of Allah. It is especially necessary to steer clear of defining Islam as an inherently violent religion while viewing all others as peaceful religions. All religions have blood on their hands. The only issues are when they got it, how they got it, and why they got it. At heart, all religions advocate peace despite their historic violation of this most sacred of all norms.

Islam, like all spiritual traditions, exists in a world where the process of secularization has led to privatizing religion. Some religions are able to accept a constitutional disconnection of religion from the state more than others. For many Muslims, especially conservatives, it is unacceptable even to consider the possibility that the sacred could be separated from the secular. Islam is an entire way of life. Nothing is excluded—from personal beliefs to social, political, and economic behavior.

Islamic scholar Mir Zohair Husain writes that Islam is an organic religion, which means that the religion cannot be separated from society. It possesses a comprehensive code of conduct and legal structure for regulating every aspect of a Muslim's life. For Islamic adherents who reject the modern world's distinction between the sacred and the secular, the entire Muslim community, or umma, must be governed by the totality of Islamic law and morality that is contained in the *Shariah*. "Drawn from the *Quran* and the

Sunnah (Prophet Muhammad's words and deeds), the *Shariah* has something to say about every aspect of life: manners and hygiene, marriage and divorce, crime and punishment, economics and politics, war and peace, and so forth. By strictly regulating a devout Muslim's life, the *Shariah* binds the temporal to the eternal."[14] King Abdullah of Saudi Arabia reflected the Wahhabist organic view of Islam when he proclaimed at his recent inauguration that he was adopting the *Qur'an* as the country's constitution and Islam as its course.

This does not mean that all nations where Islam is the dominant religion have adopted the *Qur'an* or the *Sharia* as their constitution or that they are identical in the way in which they understand the relationship between the sacred and secular. As already indicated, wide variations exist in the Muslim world on this issue. Starting with the idea that Islam is an organic religion, Muslims have made four types of responses to the secular world and the privatization of religion that secularization has caused. They are Fundamentalism, Traditionalism, Modernism, and Pragmatism.

Fundamentalists are intensely devout and austere. They have been educated almost exclusively in Muslim schools and environments. Their thinking includes only minor influences from non-Muslim sources. They look to the classic and medieval eras of Islam's history for current inspiration. They are extremely opposed to modern secular ideas and institutional practices, especially Western or Socialist. They often launch jihads or violent resistance movements to stop the momentum of secularization. They oppose democracy and the ideas of popular sovereignty. They advocate the establishment of an Islamic State governed by the Sharia as interpreted by dedicated and knowledgeable Fundamentalist clerics or public officials. They stand in opposition to both non-Muslim religions and Muslims who do not share their view of Islam. They are purists who believe in the revolutionary restoration of Islam based on scriptural literalism. They are extreme exclusivists. Despite their religiopolitical differences, the leaders of Saudi Arabia, Iran, the Muslim Brotherhood, and Al-Qaeda are Fundamentalists.

Traditionalists share many of the same characteristics as Fundamentalists, especially in their opposition to the secularization process that they see as stemming from the corruptions of Western civilization. Most are not politically active and filter Islam's glorious past through nostalgic eyes. They promote policies and programs that are compatible with the spirit and letter of the Sharia while tolerating local customs that do not contradict their traditional viewpoint. They are not as inclined as Fundamentalists to resort to violence to stop secularization from encroaching on Islam. Rather they often assume fatalistically or passively that Allah will determine the course of history. Most are Islamic scholars who are disengaged from politics.

Modernists are also devout Muslims but flexible and innovative, especially with regard to interpreting the Islamic Scripture. They are not as rigid or puritanical as are Fundamentalists or Traditionalists. They are broadly educated and have been influenced by many Western ideas and practices. The majority are not clerics. They are eclectic Muslim thinkers who combine their own traditions with ideas from secular Western capitalist and socialist countries providing they are consistent with core Islamic beliefs. In this regard, they must walk a fine line. Contrary to Fundamentalists and Traditionalists, Modernists accept the notion that popular sovereignty is consistent with the assertion that Allah is the Ultimate Sovereign who rules through democratic processes that promote political agreements within the Muslim community or umma. Writers like Sayyid Ahmad Khan and Muhammad Iqbal, who helped found modern Pakistan, are two well-known Islamic Modernists.

Pragmatists are nonpracticing Muslims who remain ostensibly religious. They never originate from the ranks of the clergy. Pragmatists accept and promote the reality of secularization. They possess moderate knowledge of Islam but look to many non-Muslim sources that even some Modernists would oppose provided they serve the purpose of socioeconomic development. They prefer not to implement the Sharia as the basis for creating a Muslim state. They prefer organizing the state according to a secular constitution and make concessions to conservative Muslims only as political expediency. As dynamic reformers, Pragmatists might or might not use democracy and often resort to violence to gain or maintain political power. They are the most intellectually liberal of all Muslim politicians, such as Iraq's unseated Saddam Hussein, Egypt's Anwar al-Sadat, and Pakistan's Zulfikar Ali Bhutto.[15]

Islam's adaptation to secularization and modernism has been uneven. Some predominantly Muslim countries have assimilated Western ideas, while others have rejected them. Some modern Muslim countries have been able to adjust to rapid modernization more than others. Many saw Westernization and secularization as a means to the end of modern Islamic revitalization, but in many locations throughout the Muslim world this proved to be ineffective for several reasons.

Modernization created an identity crisis for many Muslims who saw their historic identity being eroded. Rulers who adopted Western ways were not viewed as legitimate by the masses because their ideas differed so radically from those of conventional Islam. Modern secular ideas never really penetrated very deeply into the core of Muslim culture down to the grass roots level. From the perspective of justice, the wealth gap widened as secular leaders became richer while the masses of Muslims became poorer. The governing elites who embraced the Western emphasis on separating the sacred from the secular ignored the public's desire to participate in the political process.[16]

In combination, these several factors fueled Arab anger. In addition, virtually the entire Muslim world viewed the creation of modern Israel by the United Nations in 1948, as led by the United States, was one of the

last vestiges of Western colonial domination of Arab lands. It activated jihad resistance against further Western expansion. With the collapse of the
Soviet Union, many Muslims feared that the only remaining superpower,
the United States, would weaken indigenous cultures by spreading Western ideas around the world. Stationing U.S. troops in Islam's holiest land
of Saudi Arabia was the last straw for Fundamentalists who resorted to
terrorism as the only effective method of defending the Muslim world, the
dar-al-Islam, against encroachments by the evil West, the dar-al-Harb.

The 9/11 destruction of New York's World Trade towers, the Madrid
and London bombings, and numerous other terrorist attacks around the
world have created the impression that all Muslims are engaged in a clash of
civilizations with the West, as described by Samuel Huntington. No doubt,
some are. However, most are not. This applies to nations where Muslims
are a majority of the population as well as in nations where they are in the
minority. The vast majority of Muslims live peacefully with non-Muslim
neighbors. The Islamic response to secularization is not uniform throughout
the Muslim world any more than in the other world religions. While the
historic view of Islam as an organic religion clashes with the separation
of the sacred from the secular, like all the religions of the world, Islam is
undergoing adjustment to the reality of secularization.

Islam's future relationship to other religions will depend on whether the
majority of Muslims will continue to live peacefully within the religiously
pluralistic global village. This applies, of course, to the followers of all the
world religions as well. At the same time, for many radical Muslims the
only acceptable alternative is the creation of an Islamic planet based on
the *Qur'an* and the Sharia. Because they hold the view that Islam is an
organic religion that covers every aspect of society, they reject out of hand
all sacred-secular distinctions.

While Islamic Fundamentalists and Traditionalists long for the reestablishment of a glorious past and reject most of the secular changes that have
occurred during the past four centuries, most Muslims do not. Instead, they
are caught up in the struggle to find the right balance between the historic
view of Islam as an organic religion and the process of secularization that
has led to creating the modern secular state that disestablishes religion but
at the same time allows for its free exercise. Some observers refer to this as
a twenty-first century struggle between moderate and conservative Muslims
for the soul of Islam.

SEPARATING THE SACRED FROM THE
SECULAR—THREAT OR OPPORTUNITY

Some religions more than others are better suited to accept the separation
of the sacred from the secular. Religions that define any given social structure
as divine or their legal and moral codes as embodying the perfect will of

God for all time will struggle more with secularization than other religions. The separation of the sacred from the secular will appear as a threat to Hindus who spiritualize the caste system, to Jews who assert God gave them the promised land of Israel, to Christians who define the Church as God's earthy repository of revealed Truth or the *Bible* as God's inerrant Word for everybody, and to Muslims who view the Sharia as Allah's perfect legal and moral code for structuring the totality of society.

This does not mean that uniformity of belief exists among all of the followers of any given faith. It means merely that the tendency to resist separating religion from the larger society is greater in some religions more than others because of assumptions that are inherent in their worldviews. By definition, privatizing the sacred is a greater challenge in exclusivist religions that strive to encompass all aspects of human life from personal beliefs, to gender roles, to economic and political structures.

Irrespective of where they line up along the sacred-secular continuum that ranges from total integration to complete separation, all the world religions confront the same worldwide reality of secularization and religious pluralism. Due to historical circumstances, some religions have had more time to adjust to secularization than others. Because secularization arose during the European Enlightenment, the European religions of Judaism and Christianity were the first to feel its impact. By and large, despite initial and at times painful resistance by Christians, both Catholics and Protestants, the followers of both Judaism and Christianity have adjusted to living peacefully within the secular states that have disestablished religion and allowed for its free exercise.

Because of the British influence over Gandhi, in 1947 modern India became a secular state. This gave India's diverse religious populations the right to freely express and practice their beliefs, although it has also threatened many conservative Hindus who fear the loss of their country's historic and cultural identity. Many are still learning to live comfortably with secularization. Some never will.

As Islam continues its worldwide resurgence in the post-Colonial era, Muslims who migrate to non-Muslim countries are encountering the same secularization forces that adherents of other religions experienced earlier in history. While most Muslims live peacefully within a pluralistic secular state, others do not. Many feel threatened that secularization will weaken their faith. Because of their organic view of religion and society, conservative Muslims in particular reject the privatizing of Islam as one religion among many.

From a historical perspective, a revivalist Islam is the last of the great world religions to confront the powerful forces that modernity has unleashed into the world. While the acceptance of the secular state, religious pluralism, and democracy has become and is continuing to become more widespread among the adherents of all religions, this process has advanced more rapidly for some than for others. It remains to be seen whether later arriving Muslims who are presently grappling with secularization will follow the same path as the majority of the devoted followers of other religions or whether they will pursue a different course.

Despite where the adherents of all the world religions currently stand on accepting or rejecting the separation of the sacred from the secular, their future status in the world will depend on how they answer to the following question. Do secular states that constitutionally separate religion from politics have any advantage over those that do not? Leonard Swidler, founder of the Center for Global Ethics, puts this issue in simple terms. "Union of religion and state? Separation of religion and state? These are two clear positions, each claiming to be the best for the creative welfare of humankind?"[17] Which is the right answer? Separating religion from the state is the preferred choice. Societies that unite religion with power politics are destined to fall behind societies that separate these two spheres from each other as comparative studies of earlier Egyptian, Greek, and Roman civilizations demonstrate. In addition, other societies as Medieval Christendom; the more recent Islamic, Indian, and Chinese empires; and the USSR and Eastern Europe followed this pattern. In all cases, these once mighty cultures rose to power and then declined because societies that coupled religion and politics stagnated into rigid societies.

All civilizations sooner or later confront new problems that arise from changing circumstances. In order to survive, they must respond with new sources of problem-solving creativity. If not, they will degenerate and die. Although humans possess enough innate intelligence and imagination to overcome most new obstacles, the fall of both ancient and modern civilizations demonstrates that their leaders lacked the capacity to do so. No civilization is exempt from this historical reality: fusing religion with politics is a deadly combination because religiopolitical elites will try to keep "things as they are" or "return to what they were." History shows that this is not possible in the long run. Those societies that respond to challenging social change in new and creative ways stand the best chance of long-term survival.

In order to remain a viable actor on the world stage of the twenty-first century, every society must develop and update itself constantly. For better or worse, every society must respond to the challenges of modernity and secularization with its focus on human rights and religious pluralism. Society functions best when religion (the sacred) is separated from politics (the secular). The "separation of religion and state is *essential* to the true full functioning of both religion and state, and to human progress ... Said in other words: The separation of religion and the state is a necessary, though not sufficient, cause of the unending creative development of humanity."[18]

The modern pattern of separating the sacred from the secular does not automatically result in moral deterioration. Every society needs a cohesive ethic to survive. The separation of religion from the state frees each to respond fully in their respective spheres of responsibility. The state promotes the common good of all, which includes protecting the right to the free exercise of religion; and religion provides the sacred canopy that brings ultimate meaning to life. Religion creates the moral visions that inform the political leaders' perceptions of the common good.

Thus, separating the sacred from the secular lowers the risk of social stagnation, whereas merging the two increases it. Rather than choking off the wellspring of creativity that results when religiopolitical elites impose uniformity of belief on everyone, through violence if necessary, keeping religion constitutionally apart from politics opens the door to grass roots creativity. Separating the sacred from the secular does not threaten the long-term viability of a society. Instead it enhances the opportunity to both morally and imaginatively confront and resolve threatening trends and social challenges.

CHAPTER 12

Three Global Village Scenarios: Peace, Justice, and the World Religions

This final chapter develops three scenarios on how the world religions will affect the future. Before describing these alternatives, it is necessary to discuss how modern futurists think systematically about the future. This will set the background for envisioning the three possibilities. The time frame for the scenarios will extend to midcentury—to the year 2050. The chapter will conclude by defining the most preferred future as well as which of the three possible futures will most probably become the actual future of how the world religions will affect the future of peace and justice in the global village of the twenty-first century.

HOW TO THINK ABOUT THE FUTURE

The popular understanding of predicting the future carries a "crystal ball" connotation. Futurists should be able to foresee the future with complete accuracy. Or what's a futurist for? However, at best, crystal ball gazing is a precarious business. As modern futurists know well, most predictions about the future do not come to pass. Simply stated, the physical, social, and personal factors that comprise earth-existence are so complex that no individual or group can possibly see all the contingencies and connections. Imagine those who lived in the year 1900 and predicted the events that would take place during the next 100 years. No one foresaw two World Wars, the rise of Fascism and Communism, nuclear weapons and a Cold War, and the rise of religion-based terrorism at the end of the century.

While any attempt to predict the future conjures up visions of ancient star gazing clairvoyants, modern futurists try to avoid such images by applying scientific methods to thinking about the future. Even though it sounds paradoxical and counterintuitive, most modern futurists do not try to predict the future at all. Instead, they envision alternative futures that are embedded in the present and assume that the future is developmentally open. The present contains many potential futures any one of which might become the actual future.

First and foremost, anyone who thinks systematically about the future must possess the ability to be both analytical and synthetic. In order to envision alternative futures, it is necessary to "break down," so to speak the multiple factors that comprise the present and that will drive the future. Above all, futurists identify trends and their potential cross-impacts in order to anticipate possible outcomes. They consult experts for insight. They use computers to make complex calculations. At the same time, human choice and chance play a major role in determining which of the many possible futures will become the actual future. Some factors like technology and demographics, which will influence the short-term future, can be known in advance. However, others cannot, especially for the long-term future that involves human choice.

Because the future does not yet exist, envisioning it requires expressing the imagination at the highest level. Creating alternative futures as mental pictures involves combining or "bending" in imaginative ways and in different directions the many factors or trends that comprise the present. Anticipating "out of the blue" or totally unexpected events that alter the course of the future is any futurist's greatest challenge. Future visions are always subject to change as human choice and chance intervene to alter the direction that the present appears to be taking. In other words, the future seldom unfolds as a linear extension of present trends. Because of life's complexity, uncertainty, and constant change, the human capacity to foretell the direction of the future with pinpoint precision is significantly limited.[1]

In short, no equation exists for eliminating the ambiguities that surround predicting the future. At the same time, this need not foreclose the possibility of thinking systematically about the future. It merely requires abandoning naïve beliefs about the power of human foresight to predict with a high degree of accuracy. A more constructive approach involves the development of different scenarios that can be tracked and altered as the future unfolds. In particular, it entails thinking about alternative futures in four specific ways—as possible, plausible, probable, and preferred.

The first two of these four "p" words belong together for the following reason. In any given set of circumstances, multiple futures can be envisioned. However, not all of them carry equal credibility. Some may be so far off the radar screen of reality that they simply are not believable. For example, Science Fiction is a form of thinking about the future. While it can be vastly entertaining, like beaming Captain Kirk from some distant planet to a nearby circling spaceship, such a vision of the future is not scientifically credible at this point in time.

Instead, any possible future must be a plausible extension of the present and based on the known facts of any specific situation, as best they can be discerned. This does not mean that unanticipated or wild card factors will not appear and lead to altering any image of the future. In many cases, they do; and when they do, it becomes necessary to modify the future vision that they affect. In this way, futurists visualize alternative scenarios that are both possible and plausible and that could evolve into becoming the actual future.

Not all possible (and plausible) visions of the future are equally likely to occur. Some possible futures are more probable than others at any moment in time. As the future unfurls, the probability of occurrence of any anticipated future may change depending on shifts in trends and how they interact, human choices, chance, or unforeseen events. The probabilities associated with all possible futures may rise or fall depending on what is happening in the present. It is the futurist's task to keep scanning the environment for the appearance of new forces that may steer the future in new or unanticipated directions.

The fourth way to think about the future is to identify a preferred future. The preferred future may or may not be one of the current possible futures. On the one hand, this might entail a new way of imagining how to organize society, which at the moment possesses a low to zero probability of occurring in the foreseeable future but which might increase over time. On the other hand, it might involve preferring one of the futures that exist among present possibilities.

Because human choice is central to the process of creating the future, identifying a preferred future enables a person or group to act in such a way as to make an idea a reality. In this way, envisioning a preferred future leads humans to make choices that result in increasing the probability of occurrence of any possible future. Over time, making a preferred, possible, and plausible future more probable drives it in the direction of becoming the actual future. Since preferred futures are based on values and values are an integral part of any religious worldview, the world religions will have a direct affect on the shape of the future. Simply stated, all religions have a vision of a preferred future, and their adherents act in ways that will turn it into becoming the actual future.

The three futures developed in this chapter are based on envisioning what the world might be like by the year 2050. Extending the time frame to midcentury provides a broad span of time for observing how the future will emerge and in which direction. The three alternatives provide yardsticks for measuring the trajectory of future social change, which in turn will lead to modifying the scenarios, if necessary, or confirming that the actual future is going in the direction that one of some combination that the three scenarios depict.

Why three scenarios? In truth, selecting any number is arbitrary. In developing visions of alternative futures, two extremes should be avoided. The first involves too few and the second too many. Developing less than three restricts the imagination. Envisioning only one future increases the probability of inaccuracy in the vast majority of cases because the present always contains various futures. Taking a dual approach by envisioning the future as only "either–or" possibilities leads to oversimplifying inherently complex relationships that in combination create multiple alternatives.

On the opposite end, envisioning four or more can easily blur the lines of distinction that provide sharp images of alternatives. Trying to fine-tune all the many factors that will shape the future and envisage the endless gradations of possibilities result in an inability to foresee divergent possibilities. The main purpose for creating scenarios is to provide future visions that are dissimilar with minimal blurring of the boundaries that separate them. Since the future does not yet exist, envisioning alternatives takes place in the imagination. The best way to develop multiple futures is to express the imagination through mental pictures that are clear and distinct. In order to achieve this goal, experience shows that three works best.[2]

With this brief background on how to think about the future as possible, plausible, probable, and preferred, the next step involves laying out three different scenarios on whether the world religions will be a force for good or ill in the twenty-first century global village. Will they bring more peace and justice or hatred and hostility?

ALTERNATIVE FUTURES OF THE IMPACT OF THE WORLD RELIGIONS ON THE GLOBAL VILLAGE

The following three scenarios envision alternative effects that the world religions will have in bringing greater peace and justice or hatred and hostility into the global village. The "voice" in each scenario narrative is that of someone who is living in the year 2050. This hypothetical person is reflecting on the state of the global village along with crucial changes that have occurred around the world during the first half of the twenty-first century. All three of these scenarios are both possible and plausible.

Scenario 1: I'm Right and You're Wrong

It is the year 2050 CE. Many changes have occurred since the start of the new millennium half a century ago as economic, cultural, and religious interpenetration has continued to expand throughout the global village with the speed of a galloping horse. Sadly, most of these changes have taken a turn for the worse. Intergroup hatreds are now more widespread than ever. Hostile and violent confrontations erupt somewhere on the planet with appalling predictability. The vision of universal peace that found the world hopeful at the turn of the century has faded into a far distant memory. The earth is caught in a downward spiral that is sliding into a Hobbesian war of all against all—a dreaded and terrifying clash of civilizations. The global village is disintegrating into the uncompromising chaos of "I'm right and you're wrong." When it might turn around and head in the opposite direction is anyone's guess.

Much of the blame for this sad twist of fate falls at the feet of religion. The world's two largest spiritual traditions, Christianity and Islam, have turned their backs on the quest to find the common ground that would transcend their differences. Other faiths have followed in their footsteps. The bright future of cooperation that emerged on the horizon of the twenty-first century has disappeared into the darkness of uncompromising conflict. Leaders and laity alike stand behind an inflexible wall of intolerance. Steeped in their sacred stories and scriptures, they stubbornly refuse to stretch beyond the boundaries of their exclusive worldviews.

Not only do harsh antagonisms pit the proponents of the world religions against each other, but rivalries within each religion fragment the faithful followers into competing camps as well. Hostilities exist at both the in-terfaith and intrafaith levels, as conservatives and liberals alike reject each other's interpretations of the same faith. Each side claims exclusive posses-sion of the Truth. Protestants and Catholics tussle for the hearts and minds of Christians. Islamic Sunnis and Shi'ites remain mired in historic hatreds. Conservative Hindus struggle to preserve the ancient caste system against modernists who seek to abolish it.

Despite the existence of a universal core of ethics that the world religions share, they remain divided along the lines of their worldview differences. Instead of embracing common moral standards, they emphasize the unique-ness and superiority of their individual worldviews over those of their spir-itual competitors. Many leaders fear that the loss of their distinctiveness will create a crisis of identity among the laity, which will leave them feeling adrift in a purposeless universe. The thought that they might be wrong and others right is not even an option. Being faithful means shunning alterna-tive worldviews and not yielding to doubts of any kind. The deep anxieties that permeate all the world religions create high walls of separation that block cooperation on ethical issues. It is a time of digging in and protecting worldview turf.

Inter- and intrareligious hostilities do not remain within the boundaries of the world's sacred traditions. They spill over into virtually every other area of society—from politics to personal relationships. The social change momentum that reduced the inequalities among men and women during the last half of the twentieth century has been reversed. As the first half of the twenty-first century unfolded, the fear of losing control drove men to retreat into centuries-old patterns of male domination. Regardless of worldview differences, male leaders within all the world religions began quoting their scriptures and traditions to justify maintaining control over women.

Despite diverse monotheistic, pantheistic, and atheistic worldviews, men became united in the belief that the Creator or creation intends for men to exercise authority over women. By mid-twenty-first century, the notion that males and females complement each other in sexual behavior and gender role socialization has devolved in the direction of female subordination. Women's options both inside and outside the home have diminished as men have reasserted their authority in all areas of society. The long-term prospect of combining complementary sexual relationships with gender role equality has proven to be unworkable. In short, the fragility of the "complementary sexuality/gender equality" combination in the area of male-female relationships has given way to greater sexual and gender inequality.

Male bullying of women is on the rise. Religious conservatives everywhere maneuver women out of the public sphere and into the domestic domain. They point to every imaginable sacred book as justification for how the divine powers of the universe expect women to look and behave. Catholics continue to resist female ordination. Some Protestants discontinue the practice of educating women for the clergy. Conservative Muslims insist that women be covered from head to foot while in public. Hindus point to their sacred traditions as the sources of authority for relegating women to subservient caste roles. The feminist movement that gained momentum during the last half of the twentieth century is weakening as patriarchal pressures resurface. The drive for greater justice in the global village grows fainter as male discrimination against females grows.

The prospect of peace also fades as historic hatreds and terrorism expand. The sad coupling of widespread anxiety among the followers of the world's diverse religions and reassertion of patriarchal dominance has kindled the flame of violence as a way to settle disputes. When women refuse to return to past patterns, male outlaw groups resort to Taliban-like tactics that lead to killing nonconforming females. Suicide bombers look for soft targets as they seek to spread fear among officials and civilians alike. True believers riot against nonbelievers who disagree with them. Compromising is seen as weakness.

Nowhere is this more evident than in the political realm where the leaders of the world religions seek to abolish secularization and the corresponding separation of the sacred from the secular. Conflicts over control of public policy lead to outbursts of interreligious violence. The idea that society ought to function as an organic whole under the control of religion gains currency among diverse religious leaders and their political allies. Support for the secular state decreases as democracy becomes merely the means by which various religious groups compete to gain control and then eliminate opposition.

Patriarchal-exclusivists of every kind push their followers to grab power wherever they can get it for the purpose of imposing their views on society. Tolerance gives way to belligerence as religious leaders seek to advance their partisan interests through political hegemony that they justify according to their worldviews. When they gain control, they drive out opponents and insist on reorganizing society along the lines of their religious beliefs and ancient moral and legal codes. To reinforce their brand of orthodoxy, they punish nonconformists and silence dissenting voices.

By midcentury, the fragmenting global village leads to a widening of "gaps" across a broad spectrum of social arenas. In addition to the growing disparities among men and women, powerful male elites use their positions of privilege to leverage lopsided amounts of wealth. Income gaps widen as rich politicoreligious leaders become even richer at the expense of the poor. As unemployment grows, so do feelings of helplessness among the poor classes. Crime rates and violence increase as the desperate poor struggle to survive. Corruption expands among top leaders who have few scruples about using police power to maintain political control and protect privileges.

The media routinely refer to this half-century megatrend as "creeping theocracy." In clear language, enthusiasm for the secular state has lost ground to support for the theocratic state among exclusivist Christians, Muslims, Hindus, Buddhist, and conservative religious leaders of every stripe. The centuries-old momentum toward separating the sacred from the secular is slowly being reversed. The global village is drifting away from growing integration and toward greater fragmentation. Despite the potential of the worldwide communications web to break down barriers, the opposite effect has occurred. Awareness of pluralism has caused religious leaders and laity to retreat into the security of their worldviews rather than into an open space of new possibilities for cooperation.

While the trend toward theocracy has offset the feelings of insecurity that the threat of religious pluralism created for large numbers of devout followers of the world religions, it has also produced a dramatic downside: isolation and stagnation. By 2050, the gap between secular democracies and theocracies was widening. While many factors contributed to the growing disparity, one in particular stands out above the rest: the role of women. Simply stated, patriarchy bottled up half of the theocratic state's source of creativity. Male control cut off the expression of female initiatives and talents. The threat and use of violence created a climate of fear that inhibited a problem-solving approach to social change.

Control of political power by religious elites who sought to impose their traditional worldviews proved to be a two-edged sword. While it resulted in a high level of internal conformity, it came at the cost of remaining closed to new ideas. As the rest of the world moved forward, governing politicoreligious elites fell behind even as they got richer. As secular states adapted to new trends and opportunities, religious leaders and their political allies sought to suppress them be sitting on the status quo as defined by their traditional worldviews. Women suffered; nonconformists suffered; the gap between the rich and the poor widened; and world tensions increased. Clearly, by midcentury, the world religions had brought more hatred and hostility into the global village than peace and justice.

Scenario 2: Despite Our Differences, We Can Live Together

It is the year 2050 CE. Many changes have occurred since the start of the new millennium half a century ago as economic and political interpenetration has continued to expand. By midcentury it had become clear to even the most nostalgia-minded religious exclusivists that there would be no return to the earlier days of religious and cultural isolation. The globalization momentum that began picking up speed during the latter decades of the twentieth century has not slowed down. The sprawling electronic communications web now encircles the entire planet. As missionaries from the world religions continue their migration to foreign lands beyond their native soil, by midcentury many homogeneous regions have become increasingly heterogeneous. The long-term global trend toward growing worldwide religious pluralism continues unabated.

As pluralism spreads, the number of states or regions that are controlled by exclusivist religious elites steadily shrinks. Ever so slowly but surely, intergroup hostilities ebb as the inhabitants of the global village learn how to live with diversity. The third millennium vision of peace that inspired a hopeful generation at the start of the twenty-first century has begun to unfold. Just as the collapse of the Cold War removed the threat of violent superpower confrontation at the end of the twentieth century, the growing acceptance of pluralism by the middle of the twenty-first century has reduced the fear of a deadly clash of civilizations. For nearly 50 years, the vast majority of citizens in the global village have started to say, "Despite our differences, we can live together." By midcentury, the planet had become a more peaceful place than it was at the end of the second millennium.

Much of the credit for this trend toward greater peace can be attributed to religion. This did not occur because all the differences among the leaders and laity of the world religions disappeared. As in the past, many inter- and intrafaith disagreements continued to exist throughout the first half of the twenty-first century. The religions of the world brought greater peace into the global village because of how their devout followers chose to deal with their differences. By 2050, the growing spirit of cooperation that appeared on the horizon of the twenty-first century had progressed far beyond everyone's expectation. Religious leaders and laity alike broke down the walls of intolerance that separated them and began searching for creative responses to the challenge of pluralism.

Competing camps of traditionalists and modernists still exist but the acrimony between them has faded at both the inter- and intrareligious levels. The vast majority of followers of the world religions have matured in their ability to live with the tension caused by deep devotion to their own beliefs and respectful appreciation of the views of others. By midcentury an amazing change of attitude had taken on a life of its own. As a consequence of experiencing the day-to-day reality of global pluralism, followers of all the world faiths began to soften the exclusivist claim that they alone possessed the Truth. This was no easy transition, but despite the persistence of deep differences, the trend toward accepting others as spiritual equals grew in strength.

The citizens of the global village were learning to live productively rather than destructively with religious pluralism. Every day and everywhere on the planet for 50 years, the worldwide web of mass communications and transportation reinforced millions of encounters among persons of diverse faiths. Slowly but surely the world's inhabitants began to accept the fact that while a single Truth may exist, human beings can only experience it as many truths. As a result, widespread tolerance toward worldview variations increased along with an expansion of worldwide dialogue in addressing global issues.

Ever so gradually the world's religious leaders adopted an alternative attitude toward their scriptures. They began to realize at a deeper level that exclusivist claims to Truth rest on narrow perceptions of sacred texts. Stated differently, sacred stories about the divine reinforce exclusivism. They began to accept more readily that sacred accounts of spiritual truths are historically conditioned and that no human being sees all of reality from the point of view of Ultimate Reality. At the most profound level, for the first time in the evolution of humankind, leaders and laity alike came to understand collectively that all of their sacred narratives contain some of the truth but not all of it. More importantly, they embraced the belief that their combined truths were greater than the single truth that each of them possessed.

The growing tolerance of diversity eased the defensiveness that so often in the past accompanied exclusive claims to Truth. Instead of concentrating on their disagreements, leaders of the world religions searched for the common ground that would unite them. Growing interreligious tolerance gave rise to another major twenty-first century trend. By midcentury, the citizens of the global village were spending more time and energy searching for ethical similarities than accentuating worldview differences. In turn, this opened the door to numerous new possibilities for interfaith cooperation.

Monotheists, pantheists, and atheists around the world increasingly began to see the futility of continuing to bless patriarchal patterns with divine support. They began stressing their scriptures' egalitarian themes rather than the male hierarchical ones. By mid-twenty-first century two trends had become particularly noticeable. The first one involves combining complementary sexual relations with gender equality. The earlier anxiety over successfully coupling these two possibilities receded during the first half of the century. The long-term prospect of this combination proved to be entirely workable.

The second trend entails stretching the standards of acceptable sexual relationships beyond traditional heterosexual norms to also include other forms of sexual expression. The growing worldwide shift toward accepting religious pluralism as a positive trend spilled over into greater receptivity toward diversity of beliefs and behaviors in other areas as well. During the first 50 years of the new millennium, greater tolerance of difference in general emerged as one of the major megatrends of the global village.

Opportunities for the just treatment of women in all spheres of life, both inside and outside the home, expanded steadily during the first half of the twenty-first century. The feminist critique of patriarchy that emerged during the twentieth century gained momentum in the twenty-first century around the planet. More women advanced into the ranks of the ordained clergy than ever before. The demand for greater male-female equality across the board in all areas has kept the pressure on traditionalists who have remained steadfast in resisting greater gender equality because of their beliefs about the "divine nature of things." In the midst of a growing acceptance of gender role equality and justice, pockets of patriarchal control persist, even though they are shrinking in size.

The prospect of peace expands as historic hatreds and hostilities fade. By midcentury, the total number of terrorist attacks has dropped dramatically and is increasingly limited to confined geographical regions. The growing acceptance of pluralism enabled outspoken and courageous middle-of-the-road believers of all the world religions to isolate violent extremists. Learning to live with pluralism in the global village has come to mean being tolerant of differences. The search for peace has become more than just a hopeful vision that sits at the center of all the world religions. Leaders and laity alike have joined together in the common search for nonviolent solutions to world problems.

At the same time, religious extremists continue their terrorist ways in areas where enduring hatreds make compromise impossible. Although not as widespread as in the past, many of the historic dissensions between Jews, Christians, Muslims, Hindus, Buddhists, and others continue to fester. The fear of a worldwide clash of civilizations has devolved into limited intergroup conflicts. Diehard adherents refuse to give ground, especially in increasingly restricted regions where disputes over land or nationalist aspirations appear irresolvable. Seemingly intractable religious subcultures of violence persevere for one purpose: to eliminate the "enemy" or die trying. While the trend toward "nibbling away" at violence has shown visible results in promoting peace throughout a growing number of regions in the global village, the worldwide push for peaceful solutions to conflict in violence-prone regions has met with limited success.

The movement away from employing violence as a way to settle disagreements is closely connected to another global megatrend: the growing acceptance of secularization. By midcentury, it has become clear to more and more people around the earth that there exists a close correlation between violence and the organic view of the relationship of religion to society. Whereas separating the sacred from the secular fosters interreligious tolerance while it simultaneously enables diverse religions to prosper, the organic view stresses that only one religion ought to determine the beliefs and behaviors of everyone. By definition, the existence of religious diversity threatens anyone who adheres to the organic point of view, which in turn increases the tendency to resort to violence as a way to exert religion's control over society.

In sum, as acceptance of secularization and religious pluralism increase, the number of devoted followers of the organic view of religion and society decrease. More people begin to realize that separating the sacred from the secular does not threaten the status of religion. Rather, it enhances it by guaranteeing the freedom of expression. Leaders, laity, men, and women across the spectrum of diverse beliefs unite to a greater extent than ever to find ways of bringing greater peace and justice into the global village. The gaps between advantaged and disadvantaged members of society begin to narrow in many areas. Democratic power sharing becomes more widespread at the highest political levels. The issue of the economic welfare of all persons moves to the center of public policy concerns.

By 2050, a growing number of world citizens begin to realize that secularization and religious pluralism do not undermine the values foundation that every society needs in order to operate at the highest ethical level. They are the precondition for fostering values. As worldview defensiveness shifts toward finding common ethical ground, the followers of the world religions increasingly emphasize the values that unite them rather than the philosophical or theological ideas that divide them. Accepting pluralism means respecting differences. This leads to creating the legal structures that will protect diversity and the right of religious freedom.

Nations in which the followers of the various world religions learn to live together more harmoniously and seek creative ways to solve emergent problems gain advantage over those that sit on the status quo or seek to turn the hands of the clock back to a nostalgic golden age. Despite the continuing tensions that persist in the global village as a result of ongoing exclusivist claims, slowly but surely, by midcentury the world religions had brought more peace and justice into the global village than hatred and hostility. This in turn has opened the door to new possibilities for cooperation in the latter half of the twenty-first century.

Scenario 3: Look At Us! We're Becoming One Family

It is the year 2050 CE. Many changes have occurred since the start of the new millennium half a century ago as economic, cultural, and religious interpenetration has continued to expand throughout the global village. The speed at which globalization has been spreading around the planet has increased beyond anyone's wildest imagination. In the short span of just 50 years, the hopeful vision of universal peace that seemed like a distant mirage at the start of the twenty-first century has become a reality. The once-dreaded fear of clashing civilizations has all but disappeared except for a few increasingly isolated and ineffective exclusivists who are still intent on forcing their will on everyone. Everywhere at points near and far, citizens of the global village seem to be saying, "Look at us! We're becoming one family."

Much of the credit for the rapid pace at which the entire planet has progressed toward living in worldwide harmony goes to the remarkable turnaround that the leaders and laity of the world religions made in seeking to overcome their differences. While some settled in at the level of learning to live with pluralism, others found this to be too limiting. It simply did not go far enough. They wanted more than peaceful coexistence among diverse groups, because they feared that tolerance could easily give way to intolerance. Pluralism could backslide toward exclusivism and the hatreds that it always creates. As a result, they pushed the faithful to think beyond pluralism and to aspire to an inclusivist religious vision that would unite the global village.

Many traditionalists and modernists began moving beyond the bottleneck of their theological and philosophical differences. Like pluralists, they recognized that they stood on common ethical ground in their collective commitment to the values of compassion, mercy, love, kindness, and justice, among others; but they wanted more. They searched for ways to stretch the boundaries of inclusivism beyond ethics and into the domain of divergent worldviews. This was not an easy task but in the end it began to show visible results.

They started with the assumptions that they all possessed a piece of the larger Truth but that no one spiritual tradition could claim all of it. Nobody viewed collaboration as a pretext to proselytize. They sought to weave together their many truths into an integrated worldview tapestry of greater truth. They shared the common belief that the Truth has not been given once and for all. Early in the twenty-first century, they became convinced that the search for truth is an open ended and emergent process that is never finished. They were adamant in their commitment not to freeze their combined vision into a final version of the truth, but instead to see it merely as a platform to the continuing discovery of even greater truths.

Realists laughed; but the inclusivists made steady progress in creating a growing consensus among the followers of the world's diverse religions.

Slowly but surely they began to inspire confidence in doubters that non-cooperating leaders of the world religions could transcend their worldview disputes and produce a broader and more inclusive vision of the truth that they all could share. Despite their monotheistic, pantheistic, and atheistic differences, they searched their diverse scriptures in order to find common theological and philosophical footprints.

If the world religions contain shared values, might not they also embody similar worldview insights that squabbling over differences for centuries obscured? This was the most difficult task of all; but by midcentury the widening circle of inclusivists had become resolute in their conviction that historical disagreements would no longer divide them. They had become world citizens in every sense of the word. They lived by the belief that the global village required not only a global ethic but a global worldview as well.

The historic patterns of patriarchy receded as the momentum toward inclusivism accelerated. By definition, inclusivism embraces both men and women as equal partners in the pursuit of truth and in sharing gender roles. The norm of complementary sexuality was giving way to sexual equality. Many inclusivists concluded that despite the advances that pluralists made in tolerating each other's differences, many patterns of male-female inequality continued to exist within the world's religious communities. Being tolerant implied that the leaders and laity of the world religions had to exercise restraint in criticizing each other's internal moral standards, including patriarchal ones. Inclusivists concluded that pluralism, which also went by the name multiculturalism, could become a sophisticated rationale for preserving patriarchal and other privileges. By 2050, inclusivists had broken through this constraint.

For 50 years, the trend toward greater male-female equality expanded into a broad range of social arenas. Education and employment levels of women around the world increased. The growing income gaps of the early twenty-first century had begun to level off and in some areas even decreased. In larger numbers, men began sharing in domestic duties including the day-to-day tasks related to raising their children. More women sought political leadership throughout various regions of the global village. Nations where the trend toward male-female equality in all areas took hold began to surpass those where male dominance persisted. By midcentury the reason had become clear: Patriarchal structures stultify the initiative of half their citizens who because of birth happen to be females. Egalitarianism fosters the full expression of every citizen's aspirations.

With the emergence of greater justice in every social arena, by midcentury the global village has become a more peaceful place than at any time in the past. Worldwide commitment to separating the sacred from the secular had begun to weaken the influence of exclusivist religious leaders over the development of public policy. The global trend toward the establishment of the democratic secular state has made it possible for the followers of all the world religions to have a voice in the political process without fear of persecution.

Throughout the global village, the movement toward inclusivism helped to create an expanding moral consensus that was weakening the hatreds, hostilities, and resort to violence that characterized the first quarter of the twenty-first century. Political hotspots slowly cooled down throughout the Middle East, India, Northern Ireland, and elsewhere. With the creation of the Palestinian state at the end of the first decade, the amount of politically motivated killing dropped dramatically throughout the Israeli-Palestinian region. The United States backed away from its policy of unilateral intervention into the affairs of other nations and began seeking multilateral solutions to seemingly irresolvable global dilemmas. This action alone eased many of the world's most entrenched tensions.

By the year 2050, the trend toward inclusivism had created good and visible results. At the most fundamental level, inclusivists were leaving a legacy of cooperation in ways that few people imagined at the start of the third millennium. They became the global village's visionaries who pointed beyond exclusivists' logjams and pluralists' limited possibilities. They had become the world's big picture thinkers and worldwide activists. Not only had the leaders and laity of the world religions sown the seeds of this twenty-first century trend, they continued to nurture the vision of an everexpanding, peaceful, and just global village.

PEACE AND JUSTICE IN THE GLOBAL VILLAGE: MOST PREFERRED AND PROBABLE FUTURE

Which of the above three scenarios is the most preferred? Which one or combination is the most probable? Identifying the preferred future involves stating a normative preference that reveals any author's value preferences including those of this writer. Modern futurists understand that there exists a strong tendency to convert a preferred future into the most probable future. From a psychological perspective, the forecaster projects his or her subjective desires and visions onto the future. While identifying a preferred future might motivate a person to work hard to make it the actual future, there is no guarantee that this will occur.

Thus, to the extent that it is possible, forecasting the most probable future requires more than wishful thinking. It calls for the ability to think analytically, and as objectively as possible, about multiple trends and their cross-impacts, emergent trends, possible future choices, and chance events that could affect the actual course of the future. Identifying a preferred future and acting to make it happen is but one factor among many factors that must be considered when projecting the most probable future. The actual future will emerge out of a combination of both subjective and objective driving forces. In truth, many of these forces are currently visible. At the same time, many other forces, and probably most, are not.

From the perspective of the impact of the world religions on the global village of the twenty-first century, what is the preferred future? What is the most probable future? What is the relationship between the two?

The Preferred Future

The most preferred future of the impact of the world religions on the global village of the twenty-first century is inclusivism. Exclusivism is the least preferred because of the hatred and hostility that it inevitably produces. While a good case can be made for pluralism as the most preferred future, the inclusivist position contains fewer limitations. The strength of the pluralist option is that it envisions a world where tolerance toward diversity becomes normative. Under early twenty-first century conditions where so much hatred, hostility, and violence continue unabated, the world as a whole would take a major step toward greater peace and justice if the trend toward tolerance between the world religions were to increase.

As we have seen in Scenario 2, when diverse groups learn to live together creatively despite their differences, death and destruction decrease. Religious leaders and laity of all the world religions begin cooperating in the search for solutions to seemingly incorrigible problems. They set aside the desire to defend their diverse worldviews and focus on the shared ethical foundation that promotes collaboration. They actively look for ways to get beyond the impasse that past antagonisms have converted into concrete. The tolerance that pluralism promotes opens up the future to new possibilities for intra- and interreligious cooperation that those who perpetuate intolerance do not even see. In short, this is the strength of the pluralist position, which far surpasses the exclusivist alternative in bringing greater peace and justice into the global village.

Nonetheless, the pluralist option has two major limitations. The first restricts the adherents of one religion from criticizing the practices of other religions. In the name of tolerance, members of the world religions learn to live positively with each other's worldview dissimilarities. However, this closes off the possibility of criticizing practices that perpetuate historical injustices against oppressed groups that live beyond the boundaries of any given religious group. Tolerance of diversity can become a cover to perpetuate oppression. The inclusivist scenario transcends this limitation by envisioning that the global ethic that all the religions already incorporate ought to be applied universally across the boundaries of all worldviews. Tolerance toward continuing injustice is unacceptable no matter where it occurs.

The second limitation of pluralism is its fragility. The potential for drifting toward exclusivism remains a constant threat. The norm of tolerance remains viable only in so far as the followers of the world religions are able to live creatively in the tension of commitment to their personal beliefs and openness toward the beliefs of others. Stated differently, pluralism's strength lies in learning to live with alternative perceptions of truth. At the same time, pluralism's weakness is that it stalls at this level and is incapable of moving to higher conceptual ground.

For example, on the upside the pluralism scenario assumes that the followers of the diverse religions accept that Truth is greater that the truths that each religion contains. On the downside this scenario assumes that it is not possible to go beyond currently existing diverse perceptions of Truth. With pluralism, the different theistic, pantheistic, and atheistic assumptions that different religions make about Ultimate Reality create an absolute barrier that cannot be transcended conceptually. The best humankind can do is to accept, tolerate, and live harmoniously with worldview diversity.

The inclusivist scenario moves beyond this limitation. It starts from the perspective that while developing a common worldview might not be possible at this stage of human evolution, the future is not forever closed to this possibility. At some unknown future time, the adherents of the world religions will transcend their differences and articulate a common worldview that coincides with their shared commitment to values such as justice, kindness, compassion, mercy, love, and so on.

Thus, the least preferred future is exclusivism because the adherents of the world religions cannot get beyond their worldview differences to the level of ethical cooperation. Pluralism is the second most preferred future because it fosters cooperation at the moral level while tolerating worldview differences that cannot be transcended at the conceptual level. Inclusivism is the preferred future because it envisions that the adherents of the diverse world religions will evolve toward sharing a common view of both Ultimate Reality and morality. It presumes that at some future date the global village will have not only a global ethic but also a global worldview. The other two scenarios fall short of this comprehensive and integrated vision.

The Most Probable Future

Is the preferred inclusivist future that embraces both a global worldview and ethic likely to become the most probable future by 2050? The answer is no. The reason is clear and simple. Even the most casual observer of current world events will conclude that humankind is not ready for this possibility. This means that the future will move in the direction of greater exclusivism, greater pluralism, or a combination of the two. From this writer's perspective, the most probable future is one that will trend toward more exclusivism followed by greater pluralism. These two will not grow in equal amounts by the year 2050, because quite simply this is not mathematically possible. If one expands, then the other has to contract either absolutely or relatively.

It is possible that the global balance between exclusivist and pluralist trends could remain unaltered, but this is not likely to occur.

What is the most probable future to mid-twenty-first century? From now until 2025, exclusivism will increase. Between 2025 and 2050, pluralism will replace it. This projection should not be viewed as a prediction. It is merely a snapshot forecast at this point in time regarding what is likely to happen up to a specific future point in time. There is nothing special about the date 2050. It is merely a useful "easy-for-the-mind-to-grasp" number for making plausible projections. At the same time, the forecast of "first more exclusivism and then more pluralism" is not being made superficially. Rather, it is a reasoned projection based upon combining several of the driving forces that have been described throughout this book.

First, globalization is a relatively recent human phenomenon made possible by the expanding worldwide web of global communications and mass transportation. According to Mittleman's three-stage process, accelerated globalization (the third and most recent stage) began in the early 1970s and has picked up speed since then. One of the major consequences of this process is that adherents of the world religions are encountering each other around the planet to a far greater extent than at any time during the past. With the end of the Cold War, the world religions vigorously reemerged. This does not mean that interreligious contact did not exist prior to the past 30 years. It means merely that the amount and scope of interpenetration has accelerated very rapidly during the past three decades.

Second, the Era of Europe's political-colonial domination of the world is over, although debate continues regarding the extent to which there are lingering effects such as the Israeli-Palestinian conflict. Third, the growth of religious pluralism has become one of the world's major megatrends as the followers of all the world religions migrate to new regions beyond their homelands. There are more worldwide face-to-face interreligious encounters at the start of the third millennium than in any previous century. Historically homogeneous societies are becoming more heterogeneous.

While religious diversity offers opportunities for more interreligious dialogue, the opposite possibility also exists. Encountering the "other" for the first time can produce as much threat as comfort, especially when the followers of the world's diverse religions differ dramatically in their Truth claims. It is the author's contention that exclusivism will increase in the next two decades because interreligious defensiveness appears to be associated with the current stage of globalization.

In addition, a sad correlate of the post-Cold War/post-Colonial Era globalization process is the spread of worldwide terrorism and the resort to violence as a means to settle rekindled interreligious hatreds that date back hundreds of years. Based on present international conflicts, it is reasonable to forecast that during the next two decades, or maybe more, the world will pass through a period of growing exclusivism. In short, as worldwide religious pluralism continues to grow in the post-1970s period of accelerated globalization, exclusivism will grow and conflict will increase.

By the end of the first quarter of the twenty-first century, the number of exclusivists who insist on imposing their views on everyone will decline and the number of pluralists who are learning to live peacefully amidst diversity will increase. By then, the global village will be trending toward greater interreligious tolerance. Terrorism and violence will gradually decline as a way to settle political and other disputes. The reason: the world will become fed up with the carnage that religious extremists create. This will occur not only across the boundaries of the world religions, but it will also occur within them. Moderation and tolerance will replace extremism and intolerance as the dominant attitude toward persons of different faiths as well as within faiths.

After several decades of terrorism, followers of all the world religions will gradually come to recognize that killing only begets more killing and that the terrorists' only future is the desire to perpetuate more terrorism. In short, terrorism does not have a long-term future. By midcentury, the momentum toward more peace will begin to prevail in the global village. Over time, the more the followers of the world religions interact through face-to-face contact, the more they will discover that dealing with disagreements through violence is increasingly counterproductive. This does not mean that disputes will disappear. Rather, it means that contending factions will progressively seek nonviolent ways to resolve them.

While the shift toward pluralism will become more pronounced by midcentury, it would be naïve to anticipate that religiously motivated killing will disappear entirely. It will continue but in increasingly isolated areas and with diminished impact. As the total sum of cooperative endeavors widens by 2050, centuries-old interreligious distrust will weaken and a greater spirit of cooperation among the followers of the world religions will emerge. Declining defensiveness will open the door more widely to further collaboration by followers of the world's diverse faiths as they search for solutions to seemingly intractable world problems.

By midcentury, the growing trend toward seeking peaceful ways of dispute resolution will help promote greater justice in the global village. While patriarchal structures and their religious defenders will continue to exist, the norm of male-female equality will increase its momentum by 2050. The secularization trend will not diminish. Rather, it will expand for the following reason. As globalization brings greater religious pluralism into the global village, the followers of the world faiths will realize that separating the sacred from the secular does not undermine religion or the values foundation of a society. Secularization promotes religion, which in turn fosters moral development and character formation.

Some nations will continue defending theocracy based on their organic view of the relationship of religion to society, but most will not. Support for the secular state will grow along with legal rights that protect the free exercise of all religions. The gap between the secular states that emphasize democracy, equality, and religious pluralism and the theocracies and auto-cracies that support male-dominated hierarchies will widen as the former taps into the talents of all its citizens and not merely half of them. In short, as the second half of the twenty-first century begins to unfold, the mega-trend away from exclusivism and toward pluralism will open unforeseen possibilities for bringing greater peace and justice into the global village.

One issue remains. Is there a time in the future when inclusivism might emerge as a major world-altering trend? If so, what would this entail? At one level, inclusivism parallels many of the limitations of exclusivism but on a global scale. Would everyone in the global village be expected to accept the same beliefs? Or could a globally inclusive worldview incorporate diverse interpretations? These questions cannot be answered at this juncture of human evolution, because humankind has never encountered this possibility. The long-term integrated global village is still in the early stages of formation. While plausible, the inclusivist scenario remains the least probable future at this point in time.

In addition, from the perspective of the seemingly irresolvable early twenty-first century conflicts that currently exist on the earth, it might appear impossible that humankind will ever evolve beyond some combination of exclusivism and pluralism. Perhaps the future generations who will inhabit the global village will be forever destined to swing back and forth between these two scenarios depending on the religious, cultural, social, political, and other differences that exist at any given moment. Then again, it is in the nature of the future to bring forth surprises beyond anyone's wildest expectation.

As trivial as it might sound, the only recourse in knowing what potential future will become the actual future is that time will tell. In the meantime, it is reasonable to forecast that in the short run exclusivism will prevail over pluralism as followers of the world religions encounter each other for the first time in the emerging global village. As they continue to live alongside each other over the next several decades, pluralism will gradually replace exclusivism. Tolerance will replace intolerance. Trust will replace suspicion. By midcentury, the leaders and laity of the world religions will join together in increasing numbers to bring greater peace and justice into the global village. They will gradually unite in overcoming many of the hatreds and hostilities that prevailed early in the century.

The future beyond 2050 is more open-ended. If pluralism continues to spread, peace and justice will expand along with it. There is, of course, no guarantee that this will occur. The trend toward exclusivism may become stronger by midcentury. In addition, even if pluralism gradually replaces exclusivism by then, the trend toward exclusivism can always reemerge. At the same time, it is reasonable to project that sooner or later persons living amidst religious pluralism over a long period of time will search for ways to live in peace and justice with their neighbors. Assuming that religious pluralism will continue to spread in the emerging global village of the twenty-first century, then the norm of learning to live with differences will gradually become more universal. Then, who knows? This might set the stage for the next level of human evolution—the eventual development of an inclusive worldview that builds on an already existing global ethic.

NOTES

CHAPTER 1: GLOBALIZATION AND WORLD TRANSFORMATION IN THE NEW MILLENNIUM

1. Marshall McLuhan, *Understanding Media: The Extensions of Man*, New York: McGraw-Hill, 1964.

2. John Rawls, *A Theory of Justice*, Cambridge, MA: Harvard University Press, The Belknap Press, 1971.

3. Manuel Velasquez, *Business Ethics: Concepts and Cases*, 5th ed., Upper Saddle River, NJ: Prentice-Hall, 2002, pp. 107–122.

4. Karen T. Muraoka, "A Survey of Globalization Theories," Oxford Conference Press Release, p. 2, at http://www.toda.org/grad/oxford/muraoka.htm. Accessed: October 15, 2002.

5. Malcolm Waters, *Globalization*, London, UK: Routledge, 1955, p. 3.

6. James H. Mittelman, "The Dynamics of Globalization," in *Globalization: Critical Reflections*, edited by James H. Mittelman, Boulder, CO: Lynne Rienner Publishers, Inc., p. 3.

7. Thomas L. Friedman, *The Lexus and the Olive Tree*, New York: Anchor Books, 2000, p. 9. Also see Friedman's most recent book in which he elaborates in greater detail his view of globalization: *The World Is Flat: A Brief History of the Twenty-First Century*, New York: Farrar, Straus and Giroux, 2005.

8. See Immanuel Wallerstein, "The Modern World System," in *Social Theory: The Multicultural and Classic Readings,* edited by Charles Lemert, Boulder, CO: Westview Press, 1976, pp. 391–397.

9. James H. Mittelman, *The Globalization Syndrome: Transformation and Resistance*, Princeton, NJ: Princeton University Press, 2000, p. 19.

10. Mittelman, *The Globalization Syndrome*, p. 19.

11. Frances Cairncross, *The Death of Distance: How the Communications Revolution Will Change Our Lives*, Boston, MA: Harvard Business School Press, 1997, pp. 4–14.

12. Walter Truett Anderson, *All Connected Now: Life in the First Global Civilization*, Boulder, CO: 2001, p. 52.

13. Gary Gereffi, "The Elusive Last Lap in the Quest for Developed-Country Status," in *Globalization: Critical Reflections*, edited by James H. Mittelman, Boulder, CO: Lynne Riener Publisher, 1997, p. 53.

14. Robert J. Samuelson, "The Spirit of Capitalism," *Foreign Affairs* (January/February 2001), p. 205.

15. James H. Mittleman, "How Does Globalization Really Work?" in *Globalization: Critical Reflections*, edited by James H. Mittelman, Boulder, CO: Lynne Riener Publisher, 1997, p. 238.

16. See especially Francis Fukuyama, *The End of History and the Last Man*, New York: Avon Books, 1992 for an analysis, indeed, a celebration, of the triumph of liberal democracy and the market place system over autocratic forms of government and central command economic structures.

17. Mittelman, *The Globalization Syndrome*, p. 42.

18. Samuel P. Huntington, *The Clash of Civilizations and the Remaking of World Order*, New York: Simon & Schuster, 1996, p. 40.

19. Leonard Swidler, "The Intimate Intertwining of Business, Religion, and Dialogue," *Envisioning a Global Ethics*, Global Dialogue Institute Anthology (September 19, 2002), p. 1.

20. Rodney Stark, *The Rise of Christianity*, New York: HarperCollins, 1997, p. 7.

21. See McDougal Littell, *World History*, Evanston, IL: McDougal Littell Inc., 1999, pp. 238–249, 440–459, and 697–700.

22. Huntington, *The Clash of Civilizations and the Remaking of World Order*, p. 51.

23. Philip Jenkins, *The Next Christendom: The Coming of Global Christianity*, New York: Oxford University Press, 2002, p. 4.

24. Todd M. Johnson, "Religions, Statistical Project of," in *Encyclopedia of the Future*, vol. 2, edited by George Thomas Kurian and Graham T. T. Molitor, New York: Simon & Schuster Macmillan, 1996, pp. 797–799.

25. See the map 1.2 in Huntington, *The Clash of Civilizations and the Remaking of World Order*, pp. 24–25.

CHAPTER 2: RELIGIOUS PLURALISM IN A GLOBAL CONTEXT

1. James C. Livingston, *Anatomy of the Sacred: An Introduction to Religion*, 5th ed., Upper Saddle River, NJ: Pearson Prentice Hall, 2005, pp. 4–12.

2. Paul Tillich, *The Dynamics of Faith*, New York: Harper, 1957, p. 1.

3. Marvin Citron and Owen Davies, *Cheating Death: The Promise and the Future Impact of Trying to Live Forever*, New York: St. Martin's Press, 1998.

4. See William A. Young, *The World's Religions: World Views and Contemporary Issues*, 2nd ed., Upper Saddle River, NJ: Pearson Prentice Hall, 2005, pp. 387–390. N.J. Demerath III, in *Crossing the Gods: World Religions and Worldly Politics*, New Brunswick, NJ: Rutgers University Press, 2001, p. 9, writes: "religious labels are dangerous to apply, especially the often misleading shibboleth of fundamentalism. In some settings, the most extreme religionists are pursuing new visions rather than returning to older litanies. And just as the great majority of religionists in every faith are not extreme, so are significant minorities within the extremist camps

not primarily religious as they pursue essentially secular agendas by using religion strategically."

5. Marilyn Ferguson, *The Aquarian Conspiracy*, Los Angeles, CA: J. P. Tarcher, Inc., 1980, p. 29. Also see Barbara Marx Hubbard, *Conscious Evolution*, Novato, CA: New World Library, 1998, for a five-stage plan for human evolution toward inclusivism.

6. Aldous Huxley, *The Perennial Philosophy*, New York: Harper & Row, 1945.

7. Young, *The World's Religions*, 2nd ed., 2005, p. 387.

8. Harold Coward, *Pluralism: Challenge to World Religions*, Maryknoll, NY: Orbis Books, 1985, p. vii.

9. For an excellent analysis of twentieth century tyranny based on Aryan and Marxist ideologies, see Daniel Chirot, *Modern Tyrants: The Power and Prevalence of Evil in Our Age*, New York: The Free Press, 1994.

10. Saudi Arabia is an example.

11. Peter Berger, *The Sacred Canopy: Elements of a Sociology of Religion*, New York: Anchor Books, 1990.

CHAPTER 3: ASIAN RELIGIONS

1. "That Is You," in *Scriptures of the World's Religions*, 2nd ed., edited by James Fieser and John Powers, New York: McGraw-Hill, 2004, pp. 24–25.

2. The third and smaller expression of Buddhism is called Vajrayana or Diamond Vehicle. It is also called Tantra or Tantric Buddhism and is found mainly in Tibet. In truth, it is really one of many diverse forms of the Mahayana branch. Christopher S. Queen, for example, quotes Buddhist historian John Dunne when he writes in his "Introduction: A New Buddhism," in *Engaged Buddhism in the West*, edited by Christopher S. Queen, Boston, MA: Wisdom Press, 2000, p. 22, "It is important to note that for both the Indian systematizers and Tibetan scholars, the Vajrayana is part of the Mahayana ... anyone who practices tantra necessarily has Mahayana vows ... The upshot is that the tantric practitioner is just a special kind of Mahayanist, and the Vajrayana is just a special branch of the Mahayana." The author assumes that the two major branches of Buddhism are Hinayana and Mahayana and that Vajrayana is a part of Mahayana.

CHAPTER 4: MIDDLE EASTERN RELIGIONS

1. Maurice Richter, *Technology and Social Complexity*, Albany, NY: State University of New York Press, 1981.

2. Jenkins, Philip, *The Next Christendom: The Coming of Global Christianity*, Oxford, UK: Oxford University Press, 2003.

CHAPTER 5: WORLDVIEW COMPARISONS: SEARCH FOR COMMON GROUND

1. Karl Rahner, "Christianity and the Non-Christian Religions," in *Christianity and Other Religions*, edited by John Hick and Brian Hebblethwaite, Glasgow, Scotland: Fount Publishing, 1980, pp. 63–78.

2. Steven T. Katz, "Language, Epistemology, and Mysticism," in *Philosophy of Religion: A Global Approach*, edited by Stephen H. Phillips, Forth Worth, TX: Harcourt Brace & Company, 1996, p. 204, writes, "It is my view based on what evidence there is, that the Hindu experience of Brahman and the Christian experience of God are not the same."

3. H. Richard Niebuhr, *Radical Monotheism and Western Culture*, New York: Harper, 1960.

4. Immanuel Kant, *Critique of Pure Reason*, translated into English by F. Max Muller, New York: Anchor Books, Doubleday & Company, 1966.

CHAPTER 6: ASIAN RELIGIONS

1. From "*The Laws of Manu*," chapters 4, 8, and 9, in *Scriptures of the World's Religions*, edited by James Fieser and John Powers, 2nd ed., New York: McGraw Hill, 2004, pp. 44–51. All references to "*The Laws of Manu*" come from this collection.

2. *The Bhagavad-Gita*, translated from the Sanskrit with an Introduction by Juan Mascaro, Baltimore, MD: Penguin Books, 1966, chapter 1, verses 28–30. All references to the *Gita* come from this publication.

3. Arnold Hunt, Marie T. Crotty, and Robert B. Crotty, *Ethics of World Religions*, Revised ed., San Diego, CA: Greenhaven Press, Inc., 1991, pp. 111–112.

4. Hunt, Crotty, and Crotty, *Ethics of World Religions*, p. 141.

5. William A. Young, *The World's Religions: Worldviews and Contemporary Issues*, 1st ed., Englewood Cliffs, NJ: Prentice Hall, 1995, p. 214.

6. Sallie B. King, "Panel #3 Presentation," in *The United Nations and the World's Religions: Prospects for a Global Ethic*, edited by Boston Research Center for the 21st Century, Cambridge, MA: Boston Research Center for the 21st Century, 1995, pp. 75–82.

7. King, "Panel #3 Presentation," pp. 78–79.

8. Young, *The World's Religions*, 2nd ed., 2005, p. 102.

9. Young, *The World's Religions*, 2nd ed., 2005, pp. 99–100.

CHAPTER 7: MIDDLE EASTERN RELIGIONS

1. "Virtues and Obligations," in *Scriptures of the World's Religions*, 2nd ed., edited by James Fieser and John Powers, New York: McGraw-Hill, 2004, pp. 251–252.

2. Thomas Aquinas, "Summa Theologica," in *Basic Writings of Saint Thomas Aquinas*, edited by Anton C. Pegis, New York: Random House, 1945.

CHAPTER 8: ETHICAL COMPARISONS: SEARCH
FOR COMMON GROUND

1. See Harold Coward, *Pluralism: Challenge to World Religions*. Maryknoll, New York: Orbis Books, 1985, for a helpful discussion of the diverse circumstances from which the world's largest and most influential religions arose.

2. For a detailed discussion of the Christian view of justice, see Thomas R. McFaul, *Transformation Ethics: Developing the Christian Moral Imagination*, Lanham, MD: University Press of America, Inc., 2003, Chapter 6 "Justice and Liberation."

3. Wendell Bell, *Foundations of Futures Studies: Human Science for a New Era*, Vol. 2, *Values, Objectivity, and the Good Society*, New Brunswick, NJ: Transaction Publishers, 1997, p. 175.

4. Bell, *Foundations of Futures Studies*, Vol. 2, p. 174.

5. Rushworth M. Kidder, *How Good People Make Tough Choices: Resolving the Dilemmas of Ethical Living*, New York: A Fireside Book, 1996, pp. 91–92. In his earlier book, *Shared Values for a Troubled World*, Hoboken, NJ: John Wiley & Sons, 1994, Kidder describes the research that resulted in developing the list of universal values.

6. Leonard Swidler, "Toward a Universal Declaration of a Global Ethic," published by the Center for Global Ethics, last revised date, September 16, 2001, p. 9.

7. Swidler, "Toward a Universal Declaration of a Global Ethic," pp. 9–10.

8. Leonard Swidler, "Toward a Universal Declaration of a Global Ethics," p. 2.

9. Swidler's Middle Principles in "Toward a Universal Declaration of a Global Ethics," pp. 3–5.

10. Richard Falk, "Panel #1 Presentation," in *The United Nations and the World's Religions: Prospects for a Global Ethics*, edited by Boston Research Center for the 21st Century, Cambridge, MA: Boston Research Center for the 21st Century, 1995, p. 20.

11. "Toward a Universal Declaration of a Global Ethic," in *The United Nations and the World's Religions*, pp. 124–125.

CHAPTER 9: VIOLENCE AND THE WORLD RELIGIONS

1. For an extensive historical analysis of religious perspectives on war and peace, see J. William Frost, *A History of Christian, Jewish, Hindu, Buddhist, and Muslim Perspectives on War and Peace*, Vol. I—*The Bible to 1914*, and Vol. II—*A Century of Wars*, Lewiston, NY: The Edwin Mellen Press, 2004. Also see John Ferguson, *War and Peace in the World's Religions*, New York: Oxford University Press, 1978.

2. Frost, Vol. I, p. 146.

3. *The Mahabharata: An English Version Based on Selected Verses*, translated and edited by Chakravarthi V. Narasimham, New York: Columbia University Press, 1965, pp. 101–102.

4. Ferguson, *War and Peace in the World's Religions*, p. 52.

5. Ferguson, p. 52.

6. Frost, Vol. I, p. 158.

7. Ferguson, pp. 33–34.

8. Ferguson, p. 21.

9. See the Books of Joshua and Judges for accounts of Israel's conquest of Canaan.

10. Frost, Vol. II, p. 656.

11. Frost, Vol. I, p. 75.

12. For a thorough discussion of the variety of pacifist positions that arose during nearly 2,000 years of Christian history, see John Howard Yoder, *Nevertheless: Varieties of Religious Pacifism*, Scottsdale, PA: Herald Press, 1992. Also see Roland Bainton, *Christian Attitudes toward War and Peace*, London, UK: Hodder and Stoughton, 1960.

13. See Michael St. Clair, *Millenarian Movements in Historical Context*, New York: Garland Publishers, 1992.

14. J. Philip Wogaman, *Christian Ethics: A Historical Introduction*, Louisville, KY: Westminster/John Knox Press, 1993, p. 33.

15. Thomas R. McFaul, *Transformation Ethics: Developing the Christian Moral Imagination*, Lanham, MD: University Press of America, 2003, p. 75.

16. Ferguson, p. 122.

17. See David R. Smock, *Perspectives on Pacifism: Christian, Jewish, and Muslim Views on Nonviolence and International Conflict*, Washington, DC: United States Institute of Peace Press, 1995, pp. 29–35.

18. Ferguson, pp. 130ff; Frost, Vol. I, pp. 193–225.

19. Frost, Vol. II, p. 779.

CHAPTER 10: SEX, SEXUALITY, AND GENDER AND THE WORLD RELIGIONS

1. A small number of persons called hermaphrodites are born with both male and female reproductive organs. This Chapter will restrict the discussion to non-hermaphrodite males and females.

2. For example, see Courtney W. Howland, ed., *Religious Fundamentalisms and the Human Rights of Women*, New York: St Martin's Press, 1999; David W. Machacek and Melissa M. Wilcox, eds., *Sexuality and the World's Religions*, Santa Barbara, CA: ABC-CLIO, Inc., 2003; and Arvind Sharma and Katherine K. Young, eds., *Feminism and World Religions*, Albany, NY: State University of New York Press, 1999.

3. Jeffrey S. Lidke, "A Union of Fire and Water: Sexuality and Spirituality in Hinduism," in Machacek and Wilcox, eds., *Sexuality and the World's Religions*, p. 111.

4. *The Illustrated Kama Sutra, Ananga-Ranga, Perfumed Garden: The Classic Eastern Love Texts*, translated by Sir Richard Burton and F.F. Arbuthnot, edited by Charles Fowkes, Rochester, VT: Park Street Press, 1987.

5. Quoted in Moojan Momen, *The Phenomenon of Religion: A Thematic Approach*, Boston, MA: Oneworld Publications, 1999, p. 437.

6. Lidke, p. 125

7. Liz Wilson, "Buddhist Views on Gender and Desire," in Machacek and Wilcox, eds., *Sexuality and the World's Religions*, p. 146

8. Peter Harvey, "Sexual Equality" in *An Introduction to Buddhist Ethics*, Cambridge, UK: Cambridge University Press, 2000, p. 361.

9. Rita M. Gross, "Strategies for a Feminist Revalorization of Buddhism," in Sharma and Young, eds., *Feminism and World Religions*, pp. 85–95.

10. Mary Pat Fisher, *Living Religions*, 6th ed., Upper Saddle River, NJ: Prentice-Hall, 2005, p 126.

11. Fisher, p. 225.

12. William A. Young, *The World's Religions: Worldviews and Contemporary Issues*, 2nd ed., Upper Saddle River, NJ: Pearson Education, Inc., 2005, p. 360.

13. Rebecca Alpert, "Sex in Jewish Law and Culture," in Machacek and Wilcox, eds., *Sexuality and the World's Religions*, pp. 183–184.

14. Judith Plaskow, "Jewish Memory From a Feminist Perspective," in Judith Plaskow and Carol Christ, eds., *Weaving the Visions: New Patterns in Feminist Spirituality*, San Francisco, CA: HarperSanFrancisco, 1989, p. 49.

15. James C. Cavendish, "The Vatican and the Laity: Diverging Paths in Catholic Understanding of Sexuality," in Machacek and Wilcox, eds., *Sexuality and the World's Religions*, pp. 213–225.

16. Amy DeRogatis, "Varieties of Interpretations: Protestantism and Sexuality," in Machacek and Wilcox, eds., *Sexuality and the World's Religions*, p. 236.

17. Rosemary Radford Ruether, "Feminism in World Christianity," in Sharma and Young, eds., *Feminism and World Religions*, p. 240.

18. Riffat Hassan, "Feminism in Islam," in Sharma and Young, eds., *Feminism and World Religions*, p. 268.

19. Aysha Hidayatullah, "Islamic Conceptions of Sexuality," in Sharma and Young, eds., p. 262.

20. Hidayatullah, pp. 262–263.

CHAPTER 11: THE SACRED AND THE SECULAR AND THE WORLD RELIGIONS

1. Adam Smith, *An Inquiry into the Nature and Causes of the Wealth of Nations*, edited by Edwin Cannan, 5th ed., London, UK: Methuen and Co., Ltd., 1904.

2. John Locke, *Second Treatise on Civil Government*, Oxford, NY: Clarendon, 1690.

3. Jean-Jacques Rousseau, *The Social Contract and Discourses*, translated by G. D. H. Cole, London, UK: J. M. Dent, Ltd., 1947.

4. N. J. Demerath III, *Crossing the Gods: World Religions and Worldly Politics*, New Brunswick, NJ: Rutgers University Press, 2001, pp. 107–125.

5. Salah Nasrawi, "Saudis Vow To 'Hear, Obey' Newly Invested King Abdullah," in *Chicago Tribune*, section 1, August 4, 2005, p. 8.

6. For a scathing critique of the ongoing negative effect of the caste system within modern India, see Arthur Bonner et al. eds., *Democracy in India: A Hollow Shell*, Washington, DC: The American University Press, 1994.

7. Demerath III, *Crossing the Gods*, pp. 132–137.

8. Patricia Hunt-Perry and Lyn Fine, "All Buddhism Is Engaged: Thich Nhat Hanh and the Order of Interbeing," in Christopher S. Queen, ed., *Engaged Buddhism in the West*, Boston, MA: Wisdom Publications, 2000, pp. 35–66.

9. Queen, ed., *Engaged Buddhism in the West*, pp. 423–481.

10. Mary Pat Fisher, *Living Religions*, 6th ed., Upper Saddle River, NJ: 2005, p. 125.

11. Demerath III, *Crossing the Gods*, p. 107.

12. See James C. Livingston, *Anatomy of the Sacred: An Introduction to Religion*, 5th ed., Upper Saddle River, NJ: Pearson Education, Inc., pp. 135–160; H. Richard Niebuhr, *Christ and Culture*, New York: Harper & Row, 1951, and *The Social Sources of Denominationalism*, New York: New American Library, 1975; Ernst Troeltsch, *The Social Teaching of the Christian Churches*, vols. I and II, New York: Harper Torchbooks, 1960; Bryan Wilson, *Religion in Sociological Perspective*, Oxford, UK: Oxford University Press, 1982.

13. See Michael Corbett and Julia Mitchell Corbett, *Politics and Religion in the United States*, New York: Garland Publishing, Inc., 1999, p. 404. The goal of the Chalcedon Foundation, a Christian Reconstructionist group, is to remake every aspect of society according to the Bible, especially the individual, family, church, and the state. "They advocate a thoroughly 'Christian civilization.'"

14. Mir Zohair Husain, *Global Islamic Politics*, New York: HarperCollins College Publishers, 1995, p. 31 (Italics included in author's writing).

15. Husain, chapters 2–6, pp. 27–157.

16. Husain, pp. 162–177.

17. Leonard Swidler, "The Intimate Intertwining of Business, Religion, and Dialogue," *Envisioning a Global Ethic*, Global Dialogue Institute Anthology, September 19, 2002, p. 2.

18. Swidler, p. 9.

CHAPTER 12: THREE GLOBAL VILLAGE SCENARIOS: PEACE, JUSTICE, AND THE WORLD

1. See Nicholas Rescher, *Predicting the Future: An Introduction to the Theory of Forecasting*, Albany, NY: State University of New York Press, 1998; John L. Petersen, *Out of the Blue: Wild Cards and Other Big Future Surprises*, Arlington, VA: A Danielle LaPorte Book, 2000; Edward Cornish, *Futuring: The Exploration of the Future*, Bethesda, MD: World Future Society, 2004; and Bertrand de Jouvenel, *The Art of Conjecture*, New York: Basic Books, 1967.

2. Peter Swartz, *The Art of the Long View: Planning for the Future In An Uncertain World*, New York: Doubleday/Currency, 1991.

BIBLIOGRAPHY

Anderson, Walter Truett. *All Connected Now: Life in the First Global Civilization.* Boulder, CO: Westview Press, 2001.

Aquinas, Thomas. "Summa Theologica." In *Writings of Saint Thomas Aquinas.* Edited by Anton C. Pegis. New York: Random House, 1945.

Arab Human Development Report. New York: UN Development Programme and the Arab Fund for Economic and Social Development, May 2005.

Armstrong, Karn. *Islam: A Short History.* New York: Modern Library, 2002.

Bainton, Roland. *Christian Attitudes toward War and Peace.* London, UK: Hodder and Stoughton, 1960.

Bandstra, Barry L. *Reading the Old Testament: An Introduction to the Hebrew Bible.* 2nd ed. Belmont, CA: Wadsworth Publishing Company, 1999.

Barber, Benjamin R. *Jihad vs. McWorld: Terrorism's Challenge to Democracy.* New York: Ballantine Books, 1995.

Beech, Waldo, Ed. *Christian Ethics: Sources of the Living Tradition.* New York: The Ronald Press, 1955.

Bell, Wendell. *Foundations of Futures Studies: Human Science for a New Era.* Vols. 1, 2. New Brunswick, NJ: Transaction Publishers, 1997.

Berger, Alan. *Judaism in the Modern World.* New York: New York University Press, 1994.

Berger, Peter. *The Sacred Canopy: Elements of a Sociology of Religion.* New York: Anchor Books, 1990.

The Bhagavad-Gita. Translated from the Sanskrit with an Introduction by Juan Mascaro. Baltimore, MD: Penguin Books, 1996.

Bonner, Arthur Ed. *Democracy in India: A Hollow Shell.* Washington, DC: The American University Press, 1994.

Borman, William. *Gandhi and Non-Violence.* Albany, NY: State University of New York Press, 1986.

Boulding, Kenneth E. *The Meaning of the Twentieth Century: The Great Transition.* New York: Harper and Row, 1964.

Cairncross, Frances. *The Death of Distance: How the Communications Revolution will Change our Lives.* Boston, MA: Harvard Business School Press, 1997.

Chirot, Daniel. *Modern Tyrants: The Power and Prevalence of Evil in Our Age.* New York: The Free Press, 1994.

Citron, Marvin and Owen Davies. *Cheating Death: The Promise and Future Impact of Trying to Live Forever.* New York: St. Martin's Press, 1998.

Corbett, Michael and Julia Corbett. *Politics and Religion in the United States.* New York: Garland Publishing, Inc., 1999.

Cornish, Edward. *Futuring: The Exploration of the Future.* Bethesda, MD: World Future Society, 2004.

Coward, Harold. *Pluralism: Challenge to World Religions.* Maryknoll, NY: Orbis Books, 1985.

Dawson, Christopher. *The Dynamics of World History.* LaSalle, IL: Sherwood Sugden Co., 1978.

Dean, Thomas, Ed. *Religious Pluralism and Truth: Essays on Cross-Cultural Philosophy of Religion.* Albany, NY: State University of New York Press, 1995.

de Jouvenel, Bertrand. *The Art of Conjecture.* New York: Basic Books, 1967.

Demerath III, N. J. *Crossing the Gods: World Religions and Worldly Politics.* New Brunswick, NJ: Rutgers University Press, 2001.

Dunne, John. "Introduction: A New Buddhism." In *Engaged Buddhism in the West.* Edited by Christopher S. Queen. Boston, MA: Wisdom Press, 2000.

El Fadl, Khaled Abou. *The Place of Tolerance in Islam.* Boston, MA: Beacon Press, 2002.

Esposito, John L. *What Everyone Needs to Know about Islam.* New York: Oxford University Press, 2002.

Ferguson, John. *War and Peace in the World's Religions.* New York: Oxford University Press, 1978.

Ferguson, Marilyn. *The Aquarian Conspiracy.* Los Angeles, CA: J. P. Tarcher, Inc., 1980.

Fieser, James and John Powers, Eds. *Scriptures of the World's Religions.* 2nd ed. New York: McGraw-Hill, 2004.

Fisher, Mary Pat. *Living Religion.* 6th ed. Upper Saddle River, NJ: Prentice-Hall, 2005.

Friedman, Thomas L. *The Lexus and the Olive Tree.* New York: Anchor Books, 2000.

———. *The World Is Flat: A Brief History of the Twenty-First Century.* New York: Farrar, Straus and Giroux, 2005.

Frost, J. William. *A History of Christian, Jewish, Hindu, Buddhist, and Muslim Perspectives on War and Peace.* Vols. I and II. Lewiston, New York: The Edwin Mellen Press, 2004.

Fukuyama, Francis. *The End of History and the Last Man.* New York: Avon Books, 1992.

Gereffi, Gary. "The Elusive Last Lap in the Quest for Developed-Country Status." In *Globalization: Critical Reflections.* Edited by James H. Mittelman. Boulder, CO: Lynne Riener Publisher, 1997.

Harvey, Peter. *An Introduction to Buddhist Ethics: Foundations, Values and Issues.* Cambridge, UK: Cambridge University Press, 2000.

Howland, Courtney W., Ed. *Religious Fundamentalisms and the Human Rights of Women.* New York: St. Martin's Press, 1999.

Hubbard, Barbara Marx. *Conscious Evolution.* Novato, CA: New World Library. 1998.

Hunt, Arnold, Marie T. Crotty, and Robert B. Crotty. *Ethics of the World Religions.* Rev. ed. San Diego, CA: Greenhaven Press, Inc., 1991.

Huntington, Samuel P. *The Clash of Civilizations and the Remaking of World Order.* New York: Simon Schuster, 1996.

Husain, Mir Zohair. *Global Islamic Politics.* New York: HarperCollins College Publishers, 1995.

Huxley, Aldous. *The Perennial Philosophy.* New York: Harper Row, 1945.

The Illustrated Kama Sutra, Ananga-Ranga, Perfumed Garden: The Classic Eastern Love Texts. Translated by Sir Richard Burton and F. F. Arbuthnot and edited by Charles Fowkes. Rochester, VT: Park Street Press, 1987.

Jenkins, Philip. *The Next Christendom: The Coming of Global Christianity.* New York: Oxford University Press, 2002.

Johnson, Todd M. "Religions, Statistical Project of." In *Encyclopedia of the Future,* Vol. 2. Edited by George Thomas Kurian and Graham T. T. Molitor. New York: Simon Schuster Macmillan, 1996.

Kant, Immanuel. *Critique of Pure Reason.* Translated by F. Max Muller. New York: Anchor Books, Doubleday, 1966.

Katz, Steven T. "Language, Epistemology, and Mysticism." In *Philosophy of Religion: A Global Approach.* Edited by Stephen H. Phillips. Fort Worth, TX: Harcourt Brace Company, 1996

Kidder, Rushworth M. *How Good People Make Tough Choices: Resolving the Dilemmas of Ethical Living.* New York: A Fireside Book, 1996.

———. *Shared Values for a Troubled World.* Hoboken, NJ: John Wiley Sons, 1994.

Lapidus, Ira. *A History of Islamic Societies.* 2nd ed. Cambridge, UK: Cambridge University Press, 2002.

Larson, Gerald James. *India's Agony over Religion.* Delhi, India: Oxford University Press, 1997.

Littell, McDougal. *World History.* Evanston, IL: McDougal Littell Inc., 1999.

Livingston, James C. *Anatomy of the Sacred: An Introduction to Religion.* 5th ed. Upper Saddle River, NJ: Pearson Prentice Hall, 2005.

Locke, John. *Second Treatise on Civil Government.* Oxford, UK: Clarendon, 1690.

Machacek, David W. and Melissa M. Wilcox, Eds. *Sexuality and the World's Religions.* Santa Barbara, CA: ABC-CLIO, Inc., 2003.

The Mahabharata: An English Version Based on Selected Verses. Translated and edited by Chakravarthi V. Narasimham. New York: Columbia University Press, 1965.

McFaul, Thomas. *Transformation Ethics: Developing the Christian Moral Imagination.* Lanham, MD: University Press of America, Inc., 2003.

McGrath, Allister E. *The Future of Christianity.* London, UK: Blackwell, 2002.

McLuhan, Marshall. *Understanding Media: The Extensions of Man*. New York: McGraw-Hill, 1964.

Mittelman, James H. *Globalization: Critical Reflections*. Edited by James H. Mittelman. Boulder, CO: Lynne Rienner Publishers, 1997.

———. *The Globalization Syndrome: Transformation and Resistance*. Princeton, NJ: Princeton University Press, 2000.

Momen, Moojan. *The Phenomenon of Religion: A Thematic Approach*. Boston, MA: Oneworld Publications, 1999.

Muraoka, Karen T. "A Survey of Globalization Theories." In Oxford Conference Press Release, at http://www.toda.org/grad/oxford/muraoka.htm.

Nasr, Seyyed Hossein. *The Heart of Islam: Enduring Values for Humanity*. San Francisco, CA: HarperSanFrancisco, 2002.

The New Encyclopedia of Islam. Revised edition by Cyril Glasse and Huston Smith. Walnut Creek, CA: AltaMira Press, 2003.

Niebuhr, H. Richard. *Christ and Culture*. New York: Harper Row, 1951.

———. *Radical Monotheism and Western Culture*. New York: Harper, 1960.

———. *The Social Sources of Denominatinalism*. New York.: New American Library, 1975.

Panikkar, Raimundo. *The Intrareligious Dialogue*. New York: Paulist Press, 1978.

Petersen, John L. *Out of the Blue: Wild Cards and Other Big Future Surprises*. Arlington, VA: A Danielle LaPorte Book, 2000.

Plaskow, Judith and Carol Christ, Eds. *Weaving the Visions: New Patterns in Feminist Spirituality*. San Francisco, CA: HarperSanFrancisco, 1989.

Polak, Fred L. *The Image of the Future*. Translated by Elise Boulding. New York: Elsevier, 1973.

Queen, Christopher S., Ed. *Engaged Buddhism in the West*. Boston, MA: Wisdom Publications, 2000.

Rahner, Karl. "Christianity and the Non-Christian Religions." In *Christianity and Other Religions*. Edited by John Hick and Brian Hebblethwaite. Glasgow, Scotland: Fount Publishing, 1980.

Ram-Prasad, D. "Multiplism: A Jaina Ethics of Toleration for a Complex World." In *Ethics in the World Religions*. Edited by Joseph Runzo and Nancy M. Martin. New York: Oneworld Publications, 2001.

Rawls, John. *A Theory of Justice*, Cambridge, MA: Harvard University Press, the Belknap Press, 1971.

Rescher, Nicholas. *Predicting the Future: An Introduction to the Theory of Forecasting*. Albany, NY: State University of New York Press, 1998.

Richter, Maurice. *Technology and Social Complexity*. Albany, NY: State University of New York Press, 1981.

Rouner, Leroy S., Ed. *Religious Pluralism*. Notre Dame, IN: University of Notre Dame Press, 1984.

Rousseau, Jean-Jacques. *The Social Contract and Discourses*. Translated by C. D. H. Cole. London, UK: J. M. Dent, Ltd., 1947.

Samuelson, Robert J. "The Spirit of Capitalism." *Foreign Affairs* (January/February, 2001), 205–211.

Sharma, Arvind and Katherine K. Young, Eds. *Feminist and the World Religion*. Albany, New York: State University of New York Press, 1999.

Smith, Adam. *An Inquiry into the Nature and Causes of the Wealth of Nations*, 5th ed. Edited by Edwin Cannan. London, UK: Methuen and Co., Ltd., 1904.

Smock, David R. *Perspectives on Pacifism: Christian, Jewish, and Muslim Views on Nonviolence and Internatinal Conflict*. Washington, DC: United States Institute of Peace Press, 1995.

St. Clair, Michael. *Millenarian Movements in Historical Context*. New York: Garland Publishers, 1992.

Stark, Rodney. *The Rise of Christianity*. New York: HarperCollins, 1997.

Strong, John S. *The Experience of Buddhism: Sources and Interpretations*. Belmont, CA: Wadsworth, 1995.

Swartz, Peter. *The Art of the Long View: Planning for the Future In An Uncertain World*. New York: Doubleday, 1991.

Swidler, Leonard. "The Intimate Intertwining of Business, Religion, and Dialogue." In *Envisioning a Global Ethics*. Global Dialogue Institute Anthology, September 19, 2002.

———. "Toward a Universal Declaration of a Global Ethic." Published by the Center for Global Ethics. Last revised date, September 16, 2001.

Tillich, Paul. *The Dynamics of Faith*. New York: Harper, 1957.

Toffler, Alvin and Heidi Toffler. *War and Anti-War: Survival at the Dawn of the 21st Century*. Boston, MA: Little, Brown, 1993.

Troeltsch, Ernst. *The Social Teaching of the Christian Churches*. Vols I and II. New York: Harper Torchbooks, 1960.

The United Nations and the World's Religions: Prospects for a Global Ethic. Edited by Boston Research Center for the 21st Century. Cambridge, MA: Boston Research Center for the 21st Century, 1995.

Velasquez, Manuel. *Business Ethics: Concepts and Cases*. 5th ed, Upper Saddle River, NJ: Prentice-Hall, 2002.

Wallerstein, Immanuel. "The Modern World System." In *Social Theory: The Multicultural and Classic Readings*. Edited by Charles Lemert. Boulder, CO: Westview Press, 1976.

Waters, Malcolm. *Globalization*. London, UK: Routledge, 1955.

Wilson, Bryan. *Religion in Sociological Perspective*. Oxford, UK: Oxford University Press, 1982.

Wogaman, J. Philip. *Christian Ethics: A Historical Introduction*. Louisville, KY: Westminster/John Knox Press, 1993.

Yoder, John Howard. *Nevertheless: Varieties of Religious Pacifism*. Scottsdale, PA: Herald Press, 1992.

Young, William A. *The World's Religions: World Views and Contemporary Issues*. 2nd ed. Upper Saddle River, NJ: Pearson Prentice Hall, 2005.

INDEX

About the Author

THOMAS R. MCFAUL is Professor of Ethics and Religious Studies Emeritus at North Central College in Naperville, Illinois. He is the author of *Transformation Ethics: Developing the Christian Moral Imagination* and many other articles and books.